THE SHAPE OF Q

Signal Essays
on the Sayings Gospel

Edited and Introduced by
John S. Kloppenborg

Fortress Press

Minneapolis

For

Wendy Cotter
and
Ron Cameron

amicis certissimis

THE SHAPE OF Q
Signal Essays on the Sayings Gospel

Cover design: Spangler Design Team

Library of Congress Cataloging-in-Publication Data

The shape of Q : signal essays on the Sayings Gospel / edited and
   introduced by John S. Kloppenborg.
    p. cm.
  Includes bibliographical references and indexes.
  ISBN 0-8006-2600-1 (alk. paper) :
  1. Q hypothesis (Synoptics criticism) I. Kloppenborg, John S.,
1951– .
BS2555.2.S45 1994
226'.066—dc20   93-28256
                                                          CIP

Manufactured in the U.S.A.   AF 1-2600
98   97   96   95   94   1   2   3   4   5   6   7   8   9   10

Contents

Acknowledgments

The editor gratefully acknowledges the kind permission to excerpt or reprint materials from the following sources:

Chapter 2 is excerpted from Helmut Koester, "One Jesus and Four Primitive Gospels." *Harvard Theological Review* 61 (1968) 203–47; repr. as pp. 158–204 in James M. Robinson and Helmut Koester, *Trajectories through Early Christianity*. © 1971 Fortress Press. Used with permission.

Chapter 3 is excerpted from James M. Robinson, "LOGOI SOPHON: On the Gattung of Q." Pp. 103–13 in James M. Robinson and Helmut Koester, *Trajectories through Early Christianity*. © 1971 Fortress Press. Used with permission.

Chapter 4: Dieter Lührmann, "Q in der Geschichte des Urchristentums." Pp. 84–104 in *Die Redaktion der Logienquelle*, Wissenschaftliche Monographien zum Alten und Neuen Testament, vol. 33. © 1969 Neukirchener Verlag des Erziehungsvereins GmbH. Used with permission.

Chapter 5: Heinz Schürmann, "Beobachtungen zum Menschensohn-Titel in der Redequelle." Pp. 124–47 in R. Pesch and R. Schnackenburg, *et al.*, eds., *Jesus und der Menschensohn: Für Anton Vögtle*. © 1975 Verlag Herder KG; repr. as pp. 153–82 in *Gottes Reich—Jesu Geschick: Jesu ureigener Tod im Licht seiner Basileia-Verkündigung* © Verlag Herder KG. Used with permission.

Chapter 6: Arland D. Jacobson, "The Literary Unity of Q." *Journal of Biblical Literature* 101 (1982) 365–89. © 1982 The Society of Biblical Literature. Used with permission.

Chapter 7: Dieter Zeller, "Redaktionsprozesse und wechselnder 'Sitz im Leben' beim Q-Material." Pp. 395–409 in Joël Delobel, ed., *Logia: Les Paroles de Jésus—The Sayings of Jesus: Memorial Joseph Coppens*, Bibliotheca ephemeridum theologicarum lovaniensium, vol. 59. © 1982 Uitgeverij Peeters. Used with permission.

Chapter 8: Ronald A. Piper, "Matthew 7,7-11 par. Lk 11,9-13: Evidence of Design and Argument in the Collection of Jesus' Sayings." Pp. 411–18 in Joël Delobel, ed., *Logia: Les Paroles de Jésus—The Sayings of Jesus: Mémorial Joseph Coppens*, Bibliotheca ephemeridum theologicarum lovaniensium, vol. 59. © 1982 Uitgeverij Peeters. Used with permission.

Chapter 9: John S. Kloppenborg, "The Formation of Q and Antique Instructional Genres." *Journal of Biblical Literature* 105 (1986) 443–62. © 1986 The Society of Biblical Literature. Used with permission.

Chapter 10: Migaku Sato, "Die Gestalt der Q-Quelle." Pp. 16–47, 62–65 in *Q und Prophetie: Studien zur Gattungs- und Traditionsgeschichte der Quelle Q*, Wissenschaftliche Untersuchungen zum Neuen Testament, 2d series, vol. 29. © 1988 J. C. B. Mohr (Paul Siebeck). Used with permission.

Preface

The organizing focus for the essays in this volume is the literary criticism of the Sayings Gospel Q, the methods that have been developed for its analysis, and the major results of its study. The essays have been selected because each marks a significant advance in the study of Q or because a key methodological point is at stake. Taken together, they trace a particular aspect of the history of the study of Q from the early part of this century to the present.

This anthology had its origins in the need for accessible and representative readings for senior undergraduate and graduate students pursuing interests in the Sayings Gospel Q. Many of the key articles reprinted here were virtually inaccessible to students, either because they were published in obscure journals or hard-to-find *Festschriften*, or because many students lack sufficient facility in German, which was the dominant language of Q studies up to the mid-1980s.

Mr. Neil Parker provided a preliminary draft of the translation of Heinz Schürmann's article on the Son of Man. All the other translations and the final version of the Schürmann article are my responsibility. Professors Lührmann, Zeller, Schürmann, and Sato kindly reviewed drafts of the translations and provided helpful suggestions, saving me from various infelicities. Professor Schürmann graciously updated his article, accommodating some of the terminology to that of his more recent publications, and he has rewritten one of the sections entirely. I am grateful to all the authors represented in this collection for their generous permission to reprint the essays.

I would also like to thank Heinz Guenther and Gordon Jensen, from whose critical eyes I have benefited. My dean, Michael A. Fahey, made available funds for proofreading and has been a source of constant encouragement. I am especially pleased to be able to work with Michael West and

Marshall Johnson of Fortress Press, who have encouraged this project from the beginning and whose commitment to excellence in publication and research renders a profound service to the academy and the church.

In all but Bultmann's essay, the references to Q have been converted to the "Q" format, developed by the Society of Biblical Literature's Q Seminar. Texts from the Sayings Gospel Q are cited by *Lukan* versification preceded by "Q." Thus, Q 6:20b represents that Q text found at Matt 5:3 // Luke 6:20b. This form of citation implies no judgment regarding the question of whether the wording of Q is more faithfully represented by Matthew or Luke. In the case of Matthaean special material that may be credited to Q, the siglum Q/Matt is used (e.g., Q/Matt 5:41).

The pagination of the original articles is indicated within the text as bold numerals enclosed in brackets (e.g., [155]). All of the bibliographical references have been converted to a social-science format. Full bibliographical data may be found in the consolidated bibliography at the end of the volume.

—*John S. Kloppenborg*

Introduction

JOHN S. KLOPPENBORG

Since the late 1950s New Testament scholarship has come to regard the evangelists not merely as collectors of traditions but as authors in their own right, selecting, arranging, and editing materials in accordance with a particular style and overall literary conception, in order to fit a theological vision that might address a particular community. Evidence of literary design, both at the micro-level of the individual pericope and at the macro-level of the Gospel as a whole, serves as one of the means of ascertaining the theological intentions of the evangelist. Thus, for example, Mark's strategic use of christological disclosures and confessions and his careful uses of the secrecy commands and of the motif of incomprehension underscore Christology as the key issue for the Gospel and, presumably, for the community Mark addressed. Luke's arrangement of his materials in parallel sequences not only reflects historiographic conventions current in the Graeco-Roman world but also has the key apologetic function of reinforcing commonalities and continuities between the Baptist and Jesus, Jesus and the post-Easter church, Paul and Jesus (Talbert 1975).

The successes of redaction criticism on the canonical Gospels encouraged its application to other documents, including one of the sources of Matthew and Luke, the so-called Q source, now called the Sayings Gospel Q.[1] The change in nomenclature, indeed, is indicative of a shift in focus, for it implies that Q is of interest not merely because it offers a solution to the source-critical problems of other (later) documents (Matthew and

1. The term *Sayings Gospel* has, of course, no special claim to authenticity as the original title of Q, which is lost. German authors normally refer to Q as "die Spruchquelle," "die Logienquelle" or "die Rede(n)quelle," while French authors tend to use simply "Q" or "la source Q." English and North American authors use "Q," "the Q source," or "the Synoptic

1

Luke), but because it is of intrinsic interest as one of the earliest expressions—perhaps *the* earliest expression—of Christianity in Palestine. Application of redaction criticism to the Sayings Gospel helped expose the distinctiveness of its theology, which lacks a narrativized understanding of the passion and resurrection of Jesus but which is able by other means to depict Jesus as the definitive mediator between the divine and human worlds (see Kloppenborg 1990b). Redaction or composition criticism threw Q's theology into sharp relief, distinguishing it not only from that of Matthew and Luke, who quarried it for sayings, but also from much earlier expressions of Christian theology—Mark, Paul, and the sources of John. The Sayings Gospel was as different from these as they were from each other.

Evidence of design and deliberate structure serves not only to expose the distinctive theology of Q; it turns out to be relevant to a yet more basic issue, that of the very existence of the document. It is well-known that Q is an inference of the two-document hypothesis and that it must be reconstructed from Matthew and Luke. Several other solutions to the Synoptic problem do not require the positing of Q, the solutions of Johann Jacob Griesbach (1789-90) and Austin Farrer (1957), for example. But the presence of deliberate structuring devices within the double-tradition (Q) material—devices noticeably different from those used to organize Matthew and Luke—would afford important corroboration of the existence of Q (see Jacobson 1982b; repr. here, chap. 6). For it is exceedingly unlikely that a subset of materials mechanically abstracted from two Gospels would display an inherent genre and structure unless in fact that subset substantially represented a discrete and independent document. It is precisely the lack of identifiable structure and the absence of stylistic or theological unity in the so-called M materials that make it virtually impossible to conclude that these materials were ever embraced in a discrete pre-Matthaean document.

For the majority of the essays in this volume, and indeed for most Q studies in general, the two-document hypothesis is assumed without argument and, with a few notable exceptions, the outcomes of the literary investigation of Q have not been used to corroborate this solution to the Synoptic problem. Dieter Lührmann's conclusions—reinforced by the subsequent studies of Jacobson (1978) and Kloppenborg (1987)—have significance in this regard, first, because, as he has shown, the announcement of judgment and the polemic against "this generation" are used to organize and frame the collection; and, second, because neither of these motifs is a

---

Sayings Source." The SBL Q Seminar has introduced "Sayings Gospel," in part to avoid the term *source*, which inevitably obscures Q as a document of intrinsic interest in its own right (much like calling the second Gospel "the Markan source"). And in part, this designation is intended to convey the notion that Q represents a "gospel" as much as do the narrative Gospels.

key organizational motif for Matthew or Luke. Although Lührmann does not make much of this point as far as the Synoptic problem is concerned, he has identified precisely the features that lend credence to the conclusion that the double tradition is not simply an abstraction of Synoptic criticism but represents a discrete document with deliberate organization and intention.

Evidence of deliberate composition and design is key not only to the establishing of the theological intentions of those who framed the Sayings Gospel but also to the determination of literary genre. In raising the question of genre, Q scholarship mirrored developments in other areas of the study of early Christian literature. The recent investigations of the genre of the Gospels (Talbert 1977; Aune 1987), Acts (Pervo 1987), and even the rhetorical genres of Pauline letters (Betz 1979) are not pursued merely in the interests of achieving a tidy literary taxonomy. On the contrary, what is at stake here is the conviction that genre provides a clue to the type of communication intended by the author and a key to the way in which the audience would construe the document. In turn, considerations of the literary design, genre, and the argumentative or rhetorical style of ancient Christian documents may be utilized in understanding the social level and catchment of the intended audience (see Robbins 1991; Kloppenborg 1991).

This discussion, too, has an impact upon the debate about the Synoptic problem. It has occasionally been argued that the lack of literary analogies for the double-tradition material amounts to an argument against the existence of Q (Farrer 1957; Goulder 1989:51). But such a conclusion betrays either an ignorance of the sizable number of instructions, gnomologia, and chriae collections that were extant (see Kloppenborg 1987; Küchler 1979), or the application of theological criteria designed to make all comparison impossible. For example, Werner Kümmel attempted to mitigate the similarities between Q and collections such as the *Gospel of Thomas* merely by observing that the latter presupposes "gnostic theology" (1975:76)—as if relatively minor differences in content could obscure major similarities in form. It should be obvious that ad hoc strategies of this sort, if applied generally, would immobilize all meaningful comparison. One must acknowledge that the existence of generic analogies for Q is not by itself a compelling indication of its existence (see Dungan 1970:79-80). But the fact that the double tradition, once disembedded from Matthew and Luke, displays the generic characteristics of other antique sayings collections serves as an important corroboration of the existence of Q, especially since the double-tradition materials have not been abstracted from Matthew and Luke in such a way as deliberately to create that structure or genre.

The essays in this volume represent part of the endeavor to place the Sayings Gospel and the Q-people in the context of early Christianity. They have been selected to illustrate both the points of consensus and of disagreement in three key areas of literary investigation: first, the method appropriate to the analysis of sayings or sentence literature; second, the models appropriate for understanding the formation of Q; and, finally, the theological perspective and literary conception of the framer(s) of the Sayings Gospel.

As the essays show, significant points of consensus have been achieved, both on methodological issues and in matters of substance. It is now clear that the tradition-historical method used in Siegfried Schulz's monumental study of Q (1972), while valuable for some purposes, tells little about the formation of Q as a document. The mainstream of Q scholarship has adopted a more strictly literary-critical method, first articulated by Lührmann (1969:11–23) and used in various forms and with minor adjustments by Jacobson (1978, 1987), Kloppenborg (1984, 1986 [repr. here, chap. 9], 1987, 1990c), Zeller (1982 [repr. here, chap. 7]), Schürmann (1975 [repr. here, chap. 5]), Sato (1988 [repr. here, chap. 10]), Kosch (1989), Vaage (1991), März (1991), and others. This type of analysis begins not with the questions of authenticity, tradition-historical provenance, or form but with the concrete arrangement of sayings in the final form of Q, using this arrangement as a clue to the redactional intentions of its framers. Naturally, this analysis presupposes the pioneering work of Streeter (1911) and, in particular, V. Taylor (1953, 1959) on the order of Q, and the efforts to reconstruct the text of Q.[2]

It is also clear that the Sayings Gospel is far from a random collection of sayings; on the contrary, it reflects various topical emphases. There is now a broad consensus that the polemic against "this generation" and the announcement of its imminent judgment are key redactional themes, as well as agreement that both sapiential forms and the figure of heavenly Sophia play important roles in the composition of Q. The combination of sapiential, prophetic, and apocalyptic elements and the uneasy juxtaposition of hortatory with polemical materials have served as some of the occasions for the refinements of literary method and for the development of models for understanding the composition of Q.

Naturally, there are disagreements, many of which have to do with the compositional model adopted. For example, Sato disputes the notion of the "final redaction" of Q assumed by Lührmann, Jacobson, and Zeller and is reluctant to draw a line between Q and the pre-Matthaean and pre-Lukan expansions of Q, Q^{Mt}, and Q^{Lk}. While all agree that the composition of Q involved several stages, no single model of composition has won the day. Did a single redaction compass disparate and originally independent tradi-

---

2. After the pioneering reconstruction of Q by Harnack (1907, ET 1908) and B. Weiss (1908), the most thorough reconstruction was offered by Schulz (1972). Polag's 1979 reconstruction is valuable but lacks a detailed apparatus. A thoroughly documented, collaborative reconstruction is now being published by the International Q Project (1990, 1991). For synopses designed for the study of Q, see Neirynck (1988) and Kloppenborg (1988).

tional units (Lührmann)? Or does Q have several layers (Jacobson, Kloppenborg) or several subdocuments (Sato)? Or was the process one of gradual aggregation of materials into large blocks or discourse, which were assembled as a document only at the end (Schürmann)? Related to the problem of compositional model is that of the genre of Q: whether it is closer to wisdom literature (Koester, Robinson, Kloppenborg, Piper) or to prophetic collections (Kelber, Boring, Sato).

Rudolf Bultmann's little-known essay of 1913 represents a landmark in the study of the Sayings Gospel, not only because it is one of his earliest essays on the Synoptics and his only essay on Q but because it signaled an important step beyond Jülicher and Harnack. At least in the early editions of his *Introduction to the New Testament* (Jülicher 1900, ET 1904), Jülicher adopted the view that Q had been composed "without conscious art" and that its purpose was to hand on sayings of Jesus "in an authentic form" (1904:356, 358). Harnack believed Q to be free of "any discernible bias" and thus presented Jesus' sayings in a virtually unadulterated form (1908:171). These judgments, however, had been cast into doubt by Wellhausen's argument that Q was secondary to and often dependent on Markan formulations (Wellhausen 1905:73–89; 1911:64–79), and that Q had *intentionally* omitted narrative materials (1911:160). It was not Harnack's work (which Bultmann never cites) but Wellhausen's that had the decisive influence on Bultmann. Even though there is no indication that Bultmann accepted Wellhausen's view of the relation of Q to Mark, he saw clearly that Q rendered direct evidence not of the Jesus of history but rather of the community that transmitted the document.

The design of Q was not Bultmann's interest. Nevertheless, he notes in passing several features to which subsequent critics would also draw attention: the way in which apocalyptic notions frame the collection (Q 3:7-9, 16-17; 17:23-37; 22:28-30), the importance of the polemic against "this generation," and in particular the uneasy relationship between apocalyptic sayings and those "that have the character of a completely non-eschatological, thoroughly secular proverbial wisdom" (see p. 28). But his observations on Q's general lack of interest in the Torah (p. 29) and the way in which Q 16:17 seems to be a deliberate mitigation of an antinomian reading of Q 16:16 have only recently been developed by Kosch (1989) and Kloppenborg (1990c), working independently, into a critique of earlier views of Q as representing a Torah-observant Judaism (Schulz 1972:169, 172-73; Wild 1985).

One of the ironies of Bultmann's essay on Q, which so perceptively treated the document as evidence of conflicting and competing theological streams within the early church, is that with the flowering of the approach pioneered for Q in 1913 into the form-critical method, Q as a document was increasingly ignored. What was of interest was the oral material lying behind Q and the Synoptic Gospels. Written documents were thought to be mere sedimentations of oral tradition, without intrinsic interest as documents.

A notable exception to this tendency was the 1924 essay of B. W. Bacon, in which he sought to discover an organizing point of reference within the Q-material. This point he found in Matt 12:18-21 (= Isa 42:1-4), which he ascribed to Q on the grounds that it did not, in his view, accord especially well with the redactional intention of Matthew. Viewed through the optic of Isaiah 42, Q was transformed from a "mere agglutination of sayings" into a true Gospel "in which Jesus was set forth as the redeeming 'Wisdom' of God, the Suffering Servant of Isaian prophecy, humbled in obedience unto rejection and death, and, therefore, also 'highly exalted'" (1923-24:688).

Bacon's suggestion received little attention in subsequent discussions of Q, probably because it was founded on a rather dubious ascription of Matthaean material to Q, and because he was not able to relate the themes of Isaiah 42 convincingly to more than a handful of Q sayings (mostly from Q 7:18-35; 11:14-26). More influential, but also more modest in scope, were T. W. Manson's comments on the structure of Q (1949). Like Bultmann, Manson noted the eschatological tone of both the beginning and ending of the document and argued that this was a deliberate part of Q's architecture (1949:16). Viewing Q as a catechetical supplement to the Easter kerygma, Manson contended that it represented a "very early attempt at a systematic account of the teaching of Jesus" arranged in four sections (1949:147):

1. Jesus and the Baptist	Q 3:7—7:35
2. Jesus and the Disciples	Q 9:57—11:13
3. Jesus and Opponents	Q 11:14—12:34
4. The Future	Q 12:35—17:37

In Manson's view, the first section of this structure was designed to show the relationship—indeed, the contrast—between Jesus and the last representative of the prophetic order, John, whose activity remained firmly anchored within the "old covenant." John represented prophecy and the expectation of a royal messiah and fiery judge, while Q's Jesus offered the kingdom and the merciful love of God as the ground of human hope. Hence John's announcement of the Coming One in Q 3:7-9 was both "fulfilled and falsified" by Jesus (1949:71). Manson's second and third sections turn their attention to Jesus' followers, the promises and benefits they will receive, and the persecution and opposition they should expect. The final section announces destruction upon the "existing world-order"—the economic and political structures that are antithetic to the values enunciated in Jesus' own vision of the kingdom.

Manson proposed a relatively simple model for understanding the organization of Q. He discerned a loose topical organization appropriate, he supposed, to the catechetical purposes that Q served. He made no attempt to demonstrate any logic to the construction and arrangement of sayings within each of these large sections, nor did he examine the composition of the smaller clusters of sayings. But while his topical outline proved useful in some later analyses of Q,[3] the assumption that Q functioned as a catechetical document was soon to be abandoned.

Three key developments inaugurated the current phase of the study of Q, each occurring within the Bultmannian school and each challenging the axioms of the earlier era. First, it was recognized that Q offered a kerygma in its own right. Second, and deriving partially from the first development, renewed attention was paid to the overall structure and framing of the document (i.e., its literary genre). Finally, with the discovery of various compositional and rhetorical patterns in smaller units of Q-material and recognition of the way in which these patterns fit into larger compositional strategies, a full composition history and redactional analysis of the document could be written. None of these developments could have occurred under the older regime of form criticism, with its assumption that nothing in principle distinguished the oral from the written phases of early Christian tradition: written documents were merely sedimentations of oral tradition and reflected the same "laws" that had governed oral tradition (Bultmann 1968:6). Under such an assumption, the question of the *literary* character of Q could scarcely even arise. And as long as the Easter kerygma was considered to be the sine qua non of Christian preaching (Bultmann 1962:64), it was hardly possible for Q to be anything but a catechetical supplement.

Q AS KERYGMA

The first and third of these developments can be associated with Bultmann's student, Günther Bornkamm, himself one of the pioneers of redaction criticism (e.g., Bornkamm, Held, and Barth 1963). At Heidelberg, Bornkamm's student Heinz Eduard Tödt completed a doctoral dissertation (1956), later published as *Der Menschensohn in der synoptischen Überlieferung* (1959, ET 1965), in which he made a strong case for supposing that Q did not represent, as Kümmel (1975), Streeter (1924), or Manson (1949) had thought, a paraenetic supplement to the Easter kerygma. In fact, many Q-pericopae displayed no paraenetic interest at all. Instead, Q presented a "kerygma" organized along its own distinctive lines: Son of Man Christology. The Q-group's recognition that Jesus was the coming

3. Crossan (1983:155–56, 342–45) accepts the general outlines of Manson but modifies the third and fourth divisions: (3) Jesus and Opponents, Q 11:14–52; (4) Jesus and Apocalypse, Q 12:2—22:30. The first three of these divisions correspond to those of Jacobson (1978:24, 227, 256), who, however, arrived at this division independently of Manson. But Jacobson expresses doubts over Crossan's fourth division, since the material in it does not display much obvious unity (1987:287–88).

Son of Man and that as such he also possessed ἐξουσία ("authority") on earth functioned as the hermeneutical equivalent of the "Easter faith," impelling the Q-people to collect and re-present Jesus' sayings afresh:

> The community which preserved the Q material for us, concentrating its attention almost exclusively on Jesus' preaching, was convinced that Jesus' pointing to the coming of God's reign had not lost its meaning in the post-Easter situation, but must be proclaimed anew. The group of the disciples was regarded as authorized to resume this teaching (Luke 10.16). The meaning of the hortatory sections, too, was not understood separately but in connexion with "the most essential subject of our Lord's preaching, namely, that the kingdom of God is at hand." The nature of these sections is thus not determined by the passion but by the imminence of God's reign. (Tödt 1965:249; quoting Dibelius 1953:98).

Tödt's thesis that Q represented a distinct sphere of Christian thinking was soon echoed by Bornkamm (1958:759), while his conclusion that Q could not be regarded as a catechetical supplement was confirmed in England, apparently independently, by W. D. Davies (1966:366–86), who made no reference to Tödt. But the consequences of this development were perhaps grasped most clearly by another of Bultmann's students, Helmut Koester of Harvard University. Rather than positing the theological normativity of a ubiquitous passion kerygma, Koester described the variety of early Christian *kerygmata*, first by geographical region, analyzing the various forms and theological tendencies in evidence in Syria and western Palestine, Edessa, and the countries around the Aegean (1965, repr. 1971a), and then in a later essay, by literary form (1968, repr. 1971b).

In the 1968 essay, "One Jesus and Four Primitive Gospels," part of which is here reproduced as chapter 2, Koester advanced the hypothesis that (a) underlying the canonical Gospels are several primitive gospel forms, none of which is organized on the pattern of the passion kerygma, and that (b) the primary theological tendencies of these gospel forms are often most clearly visible not in the canonical Gospels but in the apocryphal gospels (1971b:166). Alongside the genres of aretalogy (collections of miracles) and revelation discourse, Koester sketched the contents and theological tendencies of the "sayings gospel" (187), which he had already described as "the most original gattung of the Jesus tradition" (1971a:135). In accord with the second part of his hypothesis, Koester's treatment of the "sayings gospel" takes the *Gospel of Thomas* as its starting point and focus. It is in *Thomas* that he discerns the primary internal principle of the genre:

> the authority of the word of wisdom as such, which rests in the assumption that the teacher is present in the word which he has spoken. If there is any "Easter experience" to provide a Christology congenial to this concept of the *logoi*, it is here the belief in "Jesus, the Living One" (incipit of the *Gospel of Thomas*). (1971a:138–39)

Tödt's modest conclusion was thus clarified and legitimated within the framework of a comprehensive theory of Gospel origins. When he came to Q, Koester viewed it through the optic of the *Gospel of Thomas* and the Sayings Gospel genre. From this vantage, Son of Man apocalypticism, notably lacking in *Thomas*, seemed anomalous. In his 1965 essay Koester suggested, almost en passant, that this feature might represent a "domestication" of the genre and hence an attenuation of its gnosticizing proclivity (1965:301; 1971a:138). In a later essay, he worked out this suggestion more fully:

> If the genre of the wisdom book was the catalyst for the composition of sayings of Jesus into a "gospel," and if the christological concept of Jesus as the teacher of wisdom and as the presence of heavenly Wisdom dominated its creation, the apocalyptic orientation of the *Synoptic Sayings Source* with its christology of the coming Son of man is due to a secondary redaction of an older wisdom book. (1980:113)

Not only did the *Gospel of Thomas* evidence the same genre as Q; it was in important respects a *better* example of the genre of a "wisdom gospel" than the Sayings Gospel, for the latter had already undergone an apocalypticizing redaction that moved it closer to Mark in content, if not in genre. That wisdom theology represented an early development in the history of primitive Christianity was indicated, Koester argued, by the fact that the influence of sapiential theologies could be detected not only in the canonical Gospels of Matthew and John but a generation earlier, at Corinth in the mid-first century.

Thus Koester returned to the problem of the tension between apocalyptic and wisdom that Bultmann had earlier observed (see below, 27–28). His suggestion that the apocalypticism expressed in Q's Son of Man sayings represented a secondary development within the Sayings Gospel was not really proved in his essay, since it required the dual assumptions that the *Gospel of Thomas* represents the genre of "wisdom gospel" better than Q and that from a compositional point of view purer expressions of a genre are both logically and chronologically prior to mixed genres. Koester's suggestion did, however, provide one of the essential clues used in later compositional analyses of Q.

The hypothesis that Q was most fundamentally a sapiential composition received indirect support both from Dieter Zeller, whose study of sapiential admonitions in the Synoptics concluded that Q emerged from the kernel of six clusters of sapiential admonitions (1977b:191–92), and from the essay (1982, repr. here, chap. 7) and monograph (1989) of Ronald A. Piper, who demonstrated the thoroughgoing sapiential character of several key compositions in Q. Koester's suggestion provided one of the explicit starting points of John S. Kloppenborg's *Formation of Q: Trajectories in Ancient Wisdom Collections*, which proposed a stratigraphic model for the composition of Q, consisting of a formative level of topically organized sapiential instructions; a layer of secondarily inserted materials organized around the motifs of the announcement of judgment, condemnation of "this generation," and the Deuteronomistic view of history; and finally, a handful of later nomocentric glosses (1987; cf. also 1986 [repr. here, chap. 9], 1990c).

WISDOM GENRES AND THE SAYINGS GOSPEL

Once interpretation of the Sayings Gospel had been freed from the passion kerygma, and its autonomy as an expression of primitive Christian faith recognized, other issues could emerge. A second major development, almost simultaneous with the work of Koester, occurred in the work of Koester's collaborator and fellow Bultmannian, James M. Robinson. Already in his review of recent German scholarship (1962:82–88), Robinson had seen that Q represented a discrete and autonomous sphere of theologizing, independent of the passion kerygma. The density of language relating to heavenly Wisdom (Sophia) and the Spirit suggested a reading of Q that placed it on a theological trajectory stretching from the personification of Sophia in *1 Enoch* 42:2, through the wisdom Christology of the Corinthian pneumatics, and ending in the Sophia speculations of the *Hypostasis of the Archons* from Nag Hammadi Codex II (1962:82–83). For Robinson, in effect, Q was a kind of Σοφίας Πραξεῖς ("Acts of Sophia").

What Robinson described *in nuce* in 1962 was worked out in much greater detail in his influential contribution to the 1964 Bultmann *Festschrift*, ΛΟΓΟΙ ΣΟΦΩΝ: Zur Gattung der Spruchquelle Q" (1964, ET 1971b [excerpted in this volume, chap. 3]). Robinson's interest lay in the process of collection of Jesus' sayings and the hermeneutical significance of such collections. He began by tracing the development of the sayings genres in gnostic circles, from sayings collections such as the *Gospel of Thomas* to their eventual replacement by the genre of the dialogue with the Resurrected One (*Thomas the Contender, Pistis Sophia*). That sayings genres were not restricted to gnostic circles became clear, however, in Robinson's analysis of the use of the term λόγοι in the Synoptic Gospels and early patristic literature, where he was able to demonstrate the existence of small collections underlying, for example, Mark 4 and *1 Clem.* 13.2; 46.7-8.

Robinson connected the genre of collected sayings, christened λόγοι σοφῶν, "sayings of sages," with OT and Near Eastern sapiential collections, many of which also referred to themselves as λόγοι or its equivalent in other languages. Although the tendency immanent in the genre was not gnosticizing as such,[4] the genre exerted a significant influence on the interpretation of the sayings. The tendency of the genre was to present the

---

4. In another essay, Robinson takes a slightly stronger position: "Indeed the very gattung of 'Sayings of the Sages' of which Q is an instance seems to have been moving through a trajectory that led from wisdom literature to Gnosticism" (1971a:43).

speaker of the sayings as a sage, and hence the inclusion of sayings of Jesus in such collections had an important christological consequence. Because sapiential collections also tended to associate the sage with a heavenly source of wisdom, Sophia, a full-blown Sophia Christology could emerge in this genre.[5] Once the generic tendencies of "sayings of the sages" are coordinated with the late antique development of the Jewish Sophia into the gnostic redeemer, the continuities between Q, the *Gospel of Thomas*, and the *Pistis Sophia* become evident. Robinson conjectures that the gnosticizing associations disinclined the "orthodox" church from continuing the use of the genre.

Robinson's essay can itself be located on a major scholarly trajectory in the assessment of Q or, to be more precise, at the point at which two distinct trajectories diverge, one characterizing Q as prophecy and the other as wisdom. On the one hand, Robinson associated the genre of collected λόγοι with the oral transmission of Jesus' sayings, and in that sense it was a transitional genre. As oral transmission was replaced by scribal transmission, sayings collections were replaced by narrative (canonical) Gospels and gnostic dialogues:

> With the final discontinuation of the oral transmission of Jesus' sayings, the *Sitz im Leben* of the gattung was gone; hence orthodoxy contented itself with the canonical gospels, while Gnosticism devoted itself all the more to imaginary dialogues of the Resurrected with his disciples. (Robinson 1971b:102-3).

Although Robinson himself did not speak of Q as prophetic, he had raised the question of how a collection of sayings, modeled on wisdom genres, could have acquired a gnosticizing character. The answer for Werner Kelber came when Robinson's supposition was coupled with Koester's suggestion that the soteriology operative in sayings collections such as the *Gospel of Thomas* is that the kingdom and indeed the "Living One" himself is uniquely present in his own words. With this suggestion the groundwork was laid for understanding Q as an oral, contemporizing (rather than historicizing) re-presentation of Jesus' sayings.

In his landmark reassessment of the nature of oral tradition, Kelber advanced the thesis that sayings collections such as *Thomas* and Q had a contemporizing, oral hermeneutic, betraying a "prophetic self-consciousness" (1983:200-201). Of course, Kelber was not the first to associate Q with prophecy; half a century earlier Streeter had compared Q with Jeremiah, noting that a collection of sayings prefaced by an account of Jesus' baptism and temptation resembled a book of prophetic oracles prefaced by a prophetic call story (1924:291; cf. Gilbert 1911-12). Kelber's

---

5. This association is discussed briefly in Robinson's essay but worked out in much greater detail by Kloppenborg (1987:274-76, 284-87, 319-22).

basis for designating Q as prophetic, however, had less to do with the structure of the collection than with its "linguistic ontology." Q's direct and contemporizing mode of presentation of Jesus' sayings became feasible through prophetic performances in which the "Living Jesus" became present in his words. This point allowed Kelber to explain why the resurrection, conceived as a temporal event, played no role in Q: "In the oral, prophetic mode of Q the power of speech united the earthly and the future Son of man into the present efficacious one" (1983:203). It also allowed him to explain why Q displayed no interest in the death of Jesus: a collection devoted to the presentation of Jesus, living in his speech, has no interest in what put an end to his speech.

Almost simultaneously, M. Eugene Boring published his major study of early Christian prophecy in which he too regarded Q as fundamentally prophetic in nature, since, by his estimation, twenty-two Q-sayings were the product of Christian prophets and a further twenty had been reformulated by them (1982:137–39, 180). Although Boring focused less on the psycholinguistic dynamics of oral performance as such, his conclusions paralleled those of Kelber. While parts of Q understood Jesus to be an envoy of heavenly Wisdom, prophetic self-understanding permeated the collection, so that the focus had shifted to the exalted or "living" Jesus whose sayings were actualized in the speech of Christian prophets (1982:182). This understanding of Q, as it turned out, helped make sense of the paucity of sayings of Jesus in Mark and Mark's polemic against *Christian* pseudo-prophets. Mark was suspicious of the mode of Christian prophecy represented by Q and hence presented the "message of the living Lord in a narrative form," allowing no post-resurrectional sayings at all (1982:202; see now Boring 1991:191–234).

The most thorough defense of the prophetic genre of Q was mounted by Migaku Sato in Q *und Prophetie* (1988). Sato, who rejected as inadequate Robinson's designation of Q as λόγοι σοφῶν, began by comparing Q with the prophetic books of the Hebrew Bible on the level of gross forms. The claim to a divine origin for the prophet's words conveyed by the OT messenger formula appears in Q in at least one of its earliest constituent collections (10:16—Redaction "B"),[6] in the main redaction (11:49-51), and in the later interpolations (10:22), although Q goes considerably beyond prophetic books in its claims to an exclusive mediation of the knowledge of divine will. Sato sees in the baptismal account (Luke 3:21-22), which he ascribes to Q, an analogy to the prophetic call story that legitimated the prophet and his words. Q and prophetic books are also similar in what they lack: parables and similitudes are generally missing; and since Sato excludes the parabolic materials in Luke 14–15, 19 from Q, he is left with only 7:31-32; 12:39, 42-46; and 13:18-21, which for him do not function as teaching devices but are deployed instead in the polemic against Israel. Like

6. On Sato's compositional analysis of Q, see below, chap. 10.

prophetic books, Q shows no interest in miracle stories as such but transforms both 7:1-10 and 11:14-15 into apophthegms. Finally, the lack of a passion story is explained by appealing to the fact that no prophetic book contains an account of the death of the prophet. The configuration of *Mikrogattungen* typical of prophetic books—visionary accounts (3:21-22; Q/Luke 10:18), prophetic announcements, oracles of salvation and doom, invectives, woes, admonitions, beatitudes, and "eschatological correlatives" (more accurately termed "prophetic correlatives")—is reflected in Q and at each of Sato's compositional levels.

The principal development of Robinson's thesis took a rather different form. His contention that Q belonged to the realm of sapiential discourse met with relatively swift approval, notwithstanding a reluctance to accept his suggestion that this characterization placed Q on a gnosticizing trajectory (see, e.g., Kümmel 1975:72–73, 74–75; Schenke 1978:361; Küchler 1979:562–63). Robinson, however, had not worked out the details of his hypothesis by showing, for example, how the compositional characteristics of Q resembled other sapiential collections or by specifying which of the several subtypes of wisdom literature Q most resembled. Detailed studies followed almost immediately and the result, more than twenty-five years later, has been an impressive confirmation of his thesis along with several important qualifications.

Without referring explicitly to Robinson, Ernst Bammel proposed that Q should be thought of as a testament, comparable to the *Testaments of the Twelve Patriarchs*, and containing both paraenetic material and apocalyptic previews (Bammel 1970). This proposal cannot be said to have been especially successful, probably because it was predicated on a reconstruction of Q 22:28-30 that required elements normally ascribed to Luke's editing, and because Q otherwise lacks the standard features of a testament.[7] In a brief survey of recent scholarship on Q, Ulrich Luz noted the twofold consensus that Q represented a theological and social configuration independent of, but parallel to, pre-Pauline, pre-Johannine, and other pre-Synoptic configurations, and that Q seems to have arisen from a milieu characterized by wisdom-oriented apocalyptic (1973:528). His own proposal was to associate Q—as a document displaying both sapiential and apocalyptic elements—with *1 Enoch*, which also represented a group that formed around a human figure (in this case, from primeval history) who had been exalted to the stature of the Son of Man and whose teaching consisted in paraenetic materials (1973:533).

Robinson's hypothesis was taken up in Max Küchler's detailed survey of early Jewish wisdom traditions (Küchler 1979). While Küchler's main interest did not lie with Q, he borrowed Robinson's term λόγοι σοφῶν to

---

7. Bammel's argument was based on the contention that Q 22:28-30 should be reconstructed (with Luke), depicting Jesus as conferring benefits on his successors (i.e., those who share in his "testings").

designate a large set of Near Eastern, biblical, and postbiblical wisdom collections: for example, Ahikar, Proverbs, Qohelet (Ecclesiastes), Sirach, Philo *Hypothetica* 7.1-9; Josephus *Contra Apionem* 2.190-219; *m. 'Abot*, *'Abot de Rabbi Nathan*, *Pseudo-Phocylides*, *Pseudo-Menander*, and Syriac Ahikar. Early Christian sayings collections such as Q, the *Gospel of Thomas*, and the *Sentences of Sextus* belonged to this genre but were not, he insisted, the sole heir to the older Israelite λόγοι σοφῶν; on the contrary, "in early Judaism there existed all the way up to the classical rabbinic period an unbroken tradition of sapiential collections, which provided the context for the Christian activity of collection" (1979:173). Rather than positing an exclusively gnosticizing tendency for the genre, Küchler observed that a variety of usages and theologies were also possible, in particular the presentation of norms, instruction, and admonition (1979:564).

Building on Küchler's work, John S. Kloppenborg attempted to work out a typology of Near Eastern and circum-Mediterranean forms of sententious wisdom, to indicate the internal dynamisms of wisdom genres and to trace some of the lines of generic transformation (1987:263-316). The three principal genres were the instruction,[8] characterized principally by second-person plural imperatives and maxims; the gnomologium;[9] and the chriae collection.[10] Analysis of almost one hundred collections showed that apart from the almost unanimous tendency to ascribe the sayings to named sages, there were few other uniform features and no discernible "immanent tendencies" common to all. Instead, each genre had several possible transformations and a few typical internal dynamics. For example, there is no single type of internal organization but instead a range of structuring strategies, from completely random ordering, to the use of catchwords or numerical patterns, to topical groupings. Especially clear in the instructional genre is the tendency to associate the speaker, explicitly or implicitly, with some transcendent source of wisdom. This option is also evidenced among gnomologia but only rarely seen in chriae collections. Nonetheless, all three genres could develop in the direction of a *bios*, often by the addition of a narrative preface, sometimes taking the form of a testing or ordeal story. The content of the collection itself could take the form of imperatives or maxims expecting compliance, enigmatic or seemingly contradictory sayings requiring a form of sapiential "research," or witticisms that disclose the ethos or character of the speaker and that characterize a particular way of life.

When placed in the context of ancient sayings collections, the Sayings Gospel Q may be seen to exhibit some of the transformations typical of those genres: the strong preference for second-person imperatives and maxims; topical grouping of the materials; the association of the speaker (Jesus)

---

8. On instructions, see Brunner 1970; Kitchen 1979; Lichtheim 1983.

9. Barns 1950, 1951; Horna and von Fritz 1935.

10. On chriae in general, see Hock and O'Neil 1986; Butts 1986, 1987; Mack 1989.

with heavenly Wisdom; the presence of an ordeal story; and the use of chriae, which establish both the character of the speaker and that of the persons addressed or described by the speaker.

What emerged from the discussion of the genre of Q was more than literary taxonomy. Q could no longer naively be compared with the narrative Gospels—which through their canonization achieved a normativity and self-evident "appropriateness," and alongside which the Sayings Gospel would inevitably appear deficient. It would now have to be seen with its own characteristic literary and generic integrity and typicalities. This is true whether Q is seen as exhibiting the features of a prophetic book (Boring, Kelber, Sato) or as organized along the lines of an instruction, gnomologium or chriae collection (Robinson, Küchler, Kloppenborg). This development is of a piece with the first, since the recognition of Q as exhibiting *generic* features that are distinguishable from those of the canonical Gospels also implies that Q would have distinctive *theological* features, because genre inevitably exerts influence on the contents of a work and, conversely, the choice of a particular genre reflects certain preunderstandings of the nature of those contents.

THE SHAPE OF Q

The third important transition in the scholarship on the Sayings Gospel came in 1969 with the publication of Dieter Lührmann's *Die Redaktion der Logienquelle*. From one point of view, Lührmann merely extended to Q the method of redaction criticism that his teacher at Heidelberg had so successfully applied to Matthew. But Lührmann also confirmed Tödt's basic insight that Q could not be understood as paraenetic supplement to the Easter kerygma, even if he also disagreed with Tödt's high valuation of the role of Son of Man Christology in Q (1969:96–97 [repr. here, chap. 4]; see also Schürmann 1975, 1983 [repr. here, chap. 5]). The key discovery of Lührmann was two interrelated redactional themes, the polemic against "this generation" and its coming judgment by God. Lührmann demonstrated that a significant set of Q-pericopae had been organized and edited with these two overarching themes in view,[11] and that other units, notably the opening "sermon" (Q 6:20b–49), were probably pre-redactional units incorporated into Q by the major framing redaction.

Whereas Harnack and many others held, partly on the strength of Papias's statements about Aramaic *logia* compiled by Matthew (Eusebius, *Hist. eccl.* 3.39.15–16), that Q represented Aramaic-speaking Christianity, Lührmann argued that the redaction of the Sayings Gospel was in a Greek-speaking community, that the Gentile mission was already in full swing.

---

11. Lührmann detects Q's redactional interests in the organization of Q 3:7-9, 16-17; 7:18-35; 11:14-23, 24-26, 29-32; 11:39-44, 46-52 (1969:24–48); Q 12:2-9 (1969:49–52); Q 9:57-60; 10:2-16, 21-22 (1969:58–68); and Q 12:39-40, 42-45; 17:24, 26-30, 34-35, 37; 19:12-27 (1969:69–75). Q 6:20-49 represents a pre-redactional formation (1969:53–56).

From the point of view of method, this conclusion has an important ramification. If Lührmann is right, there are theological differences to be observed not only between Aramaic-speaking and Greek-speaking Christianities but also *among* Greek-speaking Christianities. While the passion kerygma was the theological starting point for Paul, it was not so for either Q or the Johannine signs source or even for Mark.

Lührmann's contribution was not only to isolate one discrete stage in the composition of Q but also to articulate a method for determining compositional patterns in Q. Since Q did not contain "seams" and "summary statements" that could be used as clues to redactional intention, Lührmann based his conclusion on three observations: first, the compositional effect created by the juxtaposition of originally independent units of tradition; second, a comparison with Mark in the cases of traditions that both Mark and Q share; and third, the isolation and analysis of materials that were arguably formed near the time of the redaction of Q (1969:20–22). In varying forms, these principles have informed most of the subsequent analyses of Q.

The application of Lührmann's insights, both methodological and material, led to more sophisticated stratigraphical and compositional analyses.[12] While Lührmann had identified one redactional moment, subsequent studies would focus their attention on both the stages prior to the polemical stage and those following it, thereby producing more complex models of the composition of Q. While there is broad acceptance of Lührmann's discovery, there is more debate regarding the materials that do not fit easily into the category of "polemic against this generation," principally sapiential materials. Two somewhat divergent approaches have been developed, one that treats some of these other materials as pre-redactional and others as secondary additions, and a second that considers the bulk of the sapiential materials to belong to earlier subcollections or even an earlier document.

Lührmann's basic insights were carried forward by Arland D. Jacobson in his dissertation (1978) and in several subsequent articles (1982a, 1982b [repr. here, chap. 6], 1987, 1992). Although Jacobson posited a relatively complex (three-stage) literary development for Q, he was in basic agreement with Lührmann that at the formative or "compositional" stage, Q's sayings were edited to stress the Deuteronomistic motif of Israel's impenitence and coming judgment provoked by that impenitence (1978). Jacobson was also ready, like Lührmann, to acknowledge that larger pre-redactional units were used in the compositional process. The "inaugural sermon" was one such a pre-redactional unity, consisting of 6:20b-23b, 27-35, 36-38,

---

12. The analyses of Q by Schulz (1972), Hoffmann (1972), and Polag (1977), though published after Lührmann's work, did not use Lührmann's essentially literary-critical method of analysis. Hoffmann, while acknowledging diversity within the Q-materials, minimized the differences between tradition and redaction, and Schulz employed thoroughly tradition-historical criteria to isolate two strata of Q. Polag's analysis also used non-literary-critical criteria. See further Kloppenborg 1984.

40-41, 42b-45, 46-49 and divided into two sections: the first, a call to imitate God (6:20b-23b, 27-38); and the second, a call to imitate the teacher (6:40-41, 42b-49). Insertions at the compositional stage include 6:23c, reflecting the Deuteronomistic motif of Israel's persecution of the prophets,[13] and 6:39, 42a, which introduce a sharp polemical tone into the later part of the sermon.[14] Jacobson's main compositional phase, which brought together existing clusters and individual sayings, includes three blocks:

1. Q 3:(1-6), 7-9, 16abd, 17; 6:20b-23ab, 27-49; 7:1-10, 24-27; 16:16; 7:31-35;
2. Q 9:57-60; 10:2-16;
3. Q 11:14-20, 23, 29-32, 24-26, 27-28 (?), 33-36, 46, 42, 43 (?), 39-41, 44, 47-51, 52 (?).

Of these, Q 3:8b; 6:23c, 39, 42a; 7:1-10; 16:16; 7:31-35; 10:12; and perhaps 11:51b were due to the activity of the compiler of this stage (Jacobson 1987:288-89).

Where Jacobson moved substantially beyond Lührmann was in positing a second redactional phase, characterized by the motifs of secret revelation (Q 10:21-22; 11:2-4, 9-13) and enthusiasm (Q 11:2-4, 9-13; 17:5-6), the tendency to subordinate John to Jesus (Q 3:16c; 7:18-23, 28), and an interest in the miraculous (Q 7:18-23; 17:5-6). Jacobson also included Q 12:2-12, 22-34 in this redaction (1987:289; 1978:94, 218-20, 221-22). Since the temptation story seemed to reject the enthusiasm and thaumaturgy of this second stratum, Jacobson suggested that it represented a final, correcting redaction.[15]

Like Jacobson, Migaku Sato located a major compositional moment in the assembling of materials with the announcement of judgment and a polemic against "this generation" in view (Sato 1988:45; see below, p. 176). But he departed from both Lührmann and Jacobson in positing two preredactional compositions, Redaction "A," consisting of Q 3:(2-4?), 7-9, 16-17, (21-22?); 6:20b-49 (excluding 6:39-40, 43-45); 7:1-10, 18-26, 28; and Redaction "B," containing Q 9:57-60; 10:2-11, 16, 21, 23-24. These two compositions were brought together by a third "redaction," containing the materials critical of "this generation."

What escapes Sato's model is a set of materials in Q 11:2-4, 9-13, 33-35; 12:2-12, 22-31, 33-34; 12:49—13:21, and the double-tradition material that falls between Luke 13:35 and 17:23. These texts Sato assigns to various "unsystematic interpolations and additions" (1988:43; see below, p. 174). This solution creates a paradox of some of the Q-materials being highly or-

---

13. See Jacobson 1982b, repr. here, chap. 6.
14. Jacobson 1978:52-66, 95-96. For further discussion see Kloppenborg 1984:51-54.
15. That Q 4:1-13 belongs to the final editing of Q has been argued by several scholars, although not always for the same set of reasons. See Polag 1977:15-17; Zeller 1980; Kloppenborg 1987:246-62; Sato 1988:35-36, 45 (see below, pp. 167-68, 176); Kosch 1989:60, 236-37, 451. For a recent dissent, see Humphrey 1991.

ganized and collected in an intentional framing redaction, and others being added, rather capriciously or, as Sato himself says, "in a completely unmotivated way" (1988:39; see below, p. 171).

The attention given to the framing redaction by both Jacobson and Sato accounts in part for the stress laid on prophetic elements in their characterization of Q, for it is at this compositional level that the appeal to Deuteronomistic preaching patterns, repentance, threats of judgment, and such prophetic heroes as Jonah are common. Other scholars, without denying these elements, concentrate on the composition of materials antecedent to the framing redaction, and it is here that sapiential sayings emerge more prominently.

In his study of Synoptic wisdom admonitions (1977b), Dieter Zeller argued for the existence of six (or seven) complexes of sayings, each formed around the kernel of a monitory saying:

1. Concerning enemies: 6:(20-23), 27-28, 29-30, 31, 32-33, 35c, 36-38, 41-42 (43-46, 47-49)
2. Behavior of missionaries: 10:2-8a, 9-11a, 12 (16)
3. Prayer: 11:(2-4), 9-13
4. Behavior during persecution: 12:(2-3), 4-7, 8-9 (10)
5. Attitude toward possessions: 12:22-31, 33-34
6. Watchfulness: 12:(35-37?), 39-40, 42-46[16]

A seventh complex might be added:

7. Behavior in view of the End: 17:23-24, 37, 26-27, 30, 34-35

Common to at least the first six collections is that they address adherents of the Jesus movement rather than polemicizing against outsiders. Some of the collections may originally have been used and transmitted by wandering charismatics (10:3-12; 12:22-31; 12:2-9?) (1977b:192; 1982:407; see below, p. 128). Not all these collections may be so understood, however: there is no reason to restrict the first collection (Q 6:20-49) to this situation. There is evidence, moreover, that the second and fifth collections underwent redaction from the point of view of sedentary communities: 10:2 and 10:21-22, which address the community as a whole rather than merely the itinerant preachers, have been added to bracket and frame the earlier cluster of sayings, and the addition of Q 12:33-34, encouraging almsgiving, betrays a similar shift in addressees.

Only later in the composition of Q were polemical materials directed at the Baptist's disciples (3:7-9, 16-17; 7:18-28) and "this generation" (11:14-23, 29-32, 39-52) incorporated. While these traditions might have been formulated early on in actual situations of conflict, they were reused in the new situation of a sedentary community. Sayings such as 3:7-9 were now heard as admonitions to catechumens to exhibit repentance, and the polem-

16. Zeller 1977b:191. Sayings enclosed in parentheses are "possibly later expansions."

ical materials helped the community to arrive at a self-identity over against Israel (1982:408–9).

Rather than employing the essentially form-critical method of Zeller, Kloppenborg endorsed the redaction- and literary-critical method of Lührmann, and worked "backward" or "downward" from the latest levels of Q to the earliest. Nonetheless, he arrived at a conclusion similar to that of Zeller: lying beneath the framing redaction was a set of sapiential materials, hortatory and instructional in character. Kloppenborg noted that in form and structure these materials conform to the genre of "instruction," a widely attested Near Eastern wisdom genre (1986; repr. here, chap. 9). This layer of Q includes:

1. Q 6:20b-23b, 27-35, 36-45, 46-49
2. Q 9:57-60, (61-62); 10:2-11, 16
3. Q 11:2-4, 9-13
4. Q 12:2-7, 11-12
5. Q 12:22b-31, 33-34; and probably
6. Q 13:24; 14:26-27; 17:33; 14:34-35

Since some of these blocks contain secondary interpolations that express the perspective of the polemical redaction, it is reasonable to assume that the hortatory instructions were literarily antecedent to the polemical materials and that at some point in the development of Q the instructional material was edited in accordance with the later perspective.

Though more limited in scope, Ronald Piper's 1982 essay (repr. here, chap. 8) and his subsequent dissertation (1989) drew attention not only to the wealth of sapiential materials in Q but to a recurrent compositional structure, observed in several clusters of wisdom sayings:[17] (1) each begins with an admonition of wide or general appeal followed by (2) a supporting maxim; (3) the following section, usually taking the form of a double rhetorical question, introduces new imagery; and (4) a final saying narrows the original general sapiential insight to a specific issue. This structural regularity indicates, according to Piper, that these aphoristic collections are "not haphazard collections of aphoristic sayings" but on the contrary "display a design and argument unique in the synoptic tradition"; it also suggests that these collections are the result of "intentional and unique composition" (1989:64–65). Although Piper stops short of positing a formative stratum of Q containing these clusters, he rightly insists that such regularities result from deliberate *literary* activity.

Extending his analysis to other sapiential clusters (6:27-28, 31-36; 6:29-30; 12:33b-34; 12:58-59; 13:23-24; 17:3b-4), Piper notes elements of deliberate stylizing, even though these do not conform to the same four-part structure outlined above. They cohere, however, with the themes present in

17. Q 6:37-42; 6:43-45; 11:9-13; 12:2-9; and 12:22-31.

the structured collections. Like the structured collections, these units are directed at community members rather than at outsiders; they intend to persuade rather than command; and persuasion has an experiential basis. Neither the Torah nor imminent eschatological awareness plays a role at all in these sayings.

It is because of the striking similarities in structure, tone, and comportment that Piper rejects Jacobson's conclusions that Q 11:9-13; 12:2-9; and 12:22-31 ought to be relegated to a late redaction. Although he did not engage Sato's work, his findings would likewise tell against Sato's suggestion that the Q-material found in Luke 11:2-4, 9-13; 12:2-12, 22-31, 33-34 were "unmotivated" or late additions to Q. Their thematic and general structural coherence shows that they belong together with Q 6:37-42, which on virtually all showings belongs to the formative stage of Q.

The several essays of Heinz Schürmann represent an approach that diverges somewhat from those of Jacobson and Sato on the one hand, and from those of Zeller, Kloppenborg, and Piper on the other, but that has several important points of contact with each. Schürmann adopted a compositional method of analysis, observing the effects of juxtaposing one saying with another or one group of sayings with another. Thus, he was able to detect compositional strategies not simply at a final level but at various stages in the assembling of the Q materials. The model pioneered in his 1975 essay on the Son of Man sayings in Q (repr. here, chap. 5) was refined further in subsequent essays on the kingdom sayings (1982), the woes (1986), and the composition of Q (1991). Beneath the final redaction of Q, Schürmann detected four forms of composition: paired sayings, saying groups, structured compositions, and dominical discourses (*Reden Jesu*) (1991:330). He even concurred with Kloppenborg's hypothesis of six topically organized "speeches" (1991:327). Nevertheless, Schürmann was reluctant to construe these speeches as a discrete layer or stage of composition or to convert the compositional forms that he had identified synchronically into a diachronic compositional history. Moreover, he did not accept the suggestion of Lührmann, adopted by both Jacobson and Kloppenborg, that one stage of redaction was controlled by the motif of the judgment of "this generation," arguing that this motif is found at several stages of composition (see below, p. 84). Indeed, it remains unclear what theological or literary characteristics, if any, Schürmann would ascribe to the final assembling of the various components of Q into a single document.

FUTURE COURSES

Literary-critical investigations of the Sayings Gospel continue. Whereas the phase of Q scholarship represented in the essays in this volume reflects efforts to understand the composition of Q in diachronic terms by isolating redactional strata and compositional units, another phase of Q studies has begun to emerge, addressing composition from a synchronic point of view.

Drawing on the pioneering work of Burton Mack and Vernon K. Robbins (1989) on chria elaboration in ancient rhetoric,[18] several scholars have endeavored to discern patterns of chria elaboration in Q 7:18-35 (Cameron 1990), Q 6:27-36 (Douglas 1990), and Q 11:14-26 (Humphries 1988). These synchronic approaches presuppose the results of diachronic (stratigraphical) analysis but raise further questions regarding the argumentative style of various Q-compositions.

Another type of investigation inquires into the "narrative world" and "mental map" of the document—the way in which the rhetoric of the document creates and conceives temporal and geographical space. The "world" of Q is one bounded by Abel (Q 11:51) and the day of the Lord (Q 17:24, 26-30) and populated by the heroes of Israel's past. Geographically, the mental map is centered on Lower Galilee with a periphery defined by Jerusalem to the south and the gentile cities of Tyre and Sidon (and Nineveh) to the north, the former characterized in highly negative terms, and the latter viewed positively (Kloppenborg 1990a; Reed 1992).

All these efforts reflect a concern to situate the Sayings Gospel theologically, literarily, and socially. Redaction and composition criticism seek to delineate a characteristic theology for Q, while generic analyses situate Q within the range and variety of ancient sayings collections. Rhetorical analyses are concerned not only to discern argumentative patterns but implicitly or explicitly to raise questions about the "rhetorical situation" that the document was designed to address (see Bitzer 1968) as well as questions about the social level of those who framed and transmitted the document. To ask about the "narrative world" or "mental map" of Q is to inquire into the way in which the document attempts to promote a perception of reality in the imagination of the hearer or reader. This is ultimately the question of the politics of the Sayings Gospel.

---

18. On chriae in general, see the collection of texts by Hock and O'Neil 1986 and Robbins 1989, and the analyses by Butts 1986; Colson 1921; R. Taylor, 1946; Nadeau 1952; Mack 1990.

1

What the Saying Source Reveals about the Early Church

[35] We do not possess any firsthand sources about the early church, since the account in Acts is a description edited from the perspective of a later period. To be sure, Acts is based on sources, but apart from a few datable references to external history, it does not tell us much. There is also little to gain from the Pauline letters. The main source for the primitive community should be seen where its main accomplishment was: in the collection of gospel traditions. This source is indirect—even more than that. Since the gospel tradition is not available to us as the early church created it but only as it was reworked by scribes who added to it in varying degrees and who worked under varying degrees of foreign influences, we can get to this indirect source only through inferences. It seems to me that the sayings source (*Spruchquelle*) employed by Matthew and Luke is the nearest to the primitive community. The following study is devoted solely to this material.[1]

THE METHOD OF THIS INVESTIGATION

The investigation is hampered by difficulties:

1. The extent of Q cannot be determined with certainty. It may be debated whether the material that Matthew and Luke have in common[2]

Rudolf Bultmann, "Was lässt die Spruchquelle über die Urgemeinde erkennen," *Oldenburgische Kirchenblatt* 19 (1913) 35–37, 41–44. (Where Bultmann has not given bibliographical and page references, they have been supplied—ED.)

1. The following explication presupposes a definite solution to the Synoptic problem, which obviously I cannot pursue in more detail here. I refer the reader to B. Weiss 1908; Jülicher 1904; and Wellhausen 1905, 1911.

2. Apart from the Markan material used by Matthew and Luke.

was in fact found in Q because there are often serious discrepancies in reporting, for example, in the parables of the banquet (Matt 22:1-10//Luke 14:16-24) and the talents (Matt 25:14-30//Luke 19:12-27). Moreover, much of the material that only one of the evangelists took over may also have come from Q, for example, the command to limit the mission to Jewish villages (Matt 10:5-6).

2. The material that can be ascribed to Q with some certainty—because Matthew and Luke have it in common and because one can recognize some commonality in terms of content and sequence—nevertheless comes to us as interpreted by Matthew and Luke, who undoubtedly often obliterated the original, as far as both wording and sense are concerned. For example, it is obvious that both altered the beatitudes and that we can only tentatively identify the characteristics of each evangelist in order to arrive at the original version. Matthew appears to have altered the comparison of the Pharisees with sepulchers, which Luke gives in its original form (Matt 23:27-28//Luke 11:44). Luke has rearranged the invitation to prayer (Matt 7:7-11//Luke 11:9-13). But who is the more original in reproducing the wording of the sign of Jonah (Matt 12:39-40//Luke 11:29-30)? There is also no evidence at all that permits us to know the original meaning of the sayings about the blind guides (Matt 15:14//Luke 6:39), or the student and the teacher (Matt 10:24-25//Luke 6:40), or the similitude of the salt (Matt 5:13//Luke 14:34-35). The criteria for deciding include linguistic factors and the consideration of the evangelists' favorite usages and favorite concepts.

3. Even if the extent, wording, and meaning of Q are in some instances established securely, one does not thereby arrive at a description of the early church. Instead one has the fragments from a history that predates the early community. But it must be emphasized that every literary work is in the first instance a reflection of the time in that it was written, not of the time that it describes; all the more so if in its composition pragmatic tendencies were determinative, as is the case in the present instance. This principle is, however, to be used with great care. For the closer the source is to the time about which it speaks, and the more powerful the historical event of which it speaks, the greater the weight of historical reality impinges on the initiative of the narrator(s). Despite the tendencies of the narrators, historical reality will force its way through and will form the kernel of the literary work. In contrast, the medium in which it appears may be scanty. Much will be included, despite the fact that it does not accord with the tendencies of the writer. Much will be transmitted without reflection or understanding, and it would obviously be incorrect to use such material for understanding the character of the writer. If one is aware of these limitations, it is possible, in spite of the axiom mentioned above, to proceed and to use Q as a source for the early church. For every historical accomplishment appears in the memoirs of the succeeding generation, although in a subjective reflection. Everything depends on deciding how far one can differentiate

between the subjective medium and the historical reality that is described. But it is not [36] always a matter of differentiation. Indeed, the most revealing perspective for understanding the writer is not obtained from that. Rather, one understands the writer most clearly by recognizing the intention that guided him in his account and by identifying the tendencies active in his selection of his material. Thus in the following it will be possible in many instances to use statements that obviously bring one face-to-face with the subjectivity of the community that provided the account. But in most instances I will use these statements simply for characterization, because they are transmitted by, and hence must have corresponded to some degree to the interests and nature of, the primitive community.

From the outset I must stress most emphatically the uncertainty of the whole investigation that ensues from all of this. Yet this uncertainty does not relieve one of the responsibility to try to read Q from the perspective of the primitive community.[3]

THE EARLY CHURCH ACCORDING TO Q

Q begins with the preaching of the Baptist and ends with an apocalyptic sermon. Thus eschatology is found at the beginning and at the end.[4] Not only that, but eschatology is a pervasive motif in Q: as consolation for the present in the beatitudes, as motivation for admonitions concerning moral behavior, as the means by which to grasp the messiahship of Jesus, and as the keynote of the propaganda and the threat against the unbelieving generation.

But let me clarify the eschatological mood. What are its characteristics?

This eschatological mood is not in fact primarily expectation and calculation, nor longing and anxiety; it is in the first place *the consciousness of being the chosen eschatological people of Israel.* The most important expression of this point is the institution of the Twelve, which did not go back to Jesus and was certainly a creation of the primitive community. That is, it must be understood on the basis of the community's eschatological consciousness: the Twelve are the representatives of the community who will sit on twelve thrones in the coming kingdom, judging the twelve tribes of Israel (Matt 19:28-29 // Luke 22:28-30). The beatitudes, which form the beginning of the main section of Q and follow the introduction (the Baptist, baptism, and temptation) are also significant. The community regarded itself as the pious and the oppressed, friends of God but strangers to the

3. The occasional references that are found concerning the external state and history of the primitive community—insofar as they are not characteristic of its inner life—will be set aside. With these references one has no occasion and justification to limit the study to Q.

4. Both the preaching of repentance and the messianic proclamation of the Baptist have an eschatological character and must have been read by the primitive community in that sense, even if it first understood the messianic prophecy as a prophecy about the earthly Jesus.

world, those of whom Isaiah and the Psalms speak.[5] To them belongs the "salvation" that Jesus proclaimed to the poor. This mood will bestow a feeling of elation. The foundation of the community are the blessed eye-witnesses who saw what the prophets and kings of the past wished to see but could not (Matt 13:16-17 // Luke 10:23-24). Together with this feeling of elation, this foundation lends a mood of exclusivity and unity that is naturally quite distinct from ecclesial exclusivity. It is an eschatological mood pure and simple. They believed themselves to be separate from γενεὰ αὕτη ("this generation").[6] They applied to themselves Jesus' thanksgiving concerning the simple and uneducated (Matt 11:25 // Luke 10:21). They had accepted, as it were, the invitation to the feast that others had scorned (Matt 22:1-10 // Luke 14:16-24). They thought of themselves as the sheep among the wolves (Matt 10:16 // Luke 10:3); they knew that whoever ex-alted himself would be humbled and whoever humbled himself would be exalted (Matt 18:4; 23:12 // Luke 18:14; 14:11); and they knew that the last would be first and the first last (Matt 20:16 // Luke 13:30).

The expectation of the end is not simply a joyful hope; it can also take on the gloomy sound of threat. The threat is directed primarily at γενεὰ αὕτη ("this generation"). The Q-community adopted the repentance ser-mon of the Baptist (Matt 3:7-10 // Luke 3:7-9) for this purpose. They trans-mitted the woes that Jesus pronounced against the Galilean towns (Matt 11:21-24 // Luke 10:13-15).[7] They told one another, whether rightly or wrongly, that Jesus employed a prophecy of the destruction of Jerusalem that was in circulation (Matt 23:37-39 // Luke 13:34-35). Q did not even hesitate to place in his mouth a terrible curse against the towns that refused the message of his apostles (Matt 10:15 // Luke 10:12).

Q, however, also invoked the terrors of the judgment as a warning to its own members. Not everyone who says "Lord, Lord" will in the end be rec-ognized as a servant (Matt 7:21 // Luke 6:46 and Matt 7:22-23 // 13:26-27); the tree that does not produce fruit is thrown into the fire (Matt 3:10 // Luke 3:9; Matt 7:19?). It is important not to lose sight of the end and to become like the negligent people of Noah's day (Matt 24:37-39 // Luke 17:26-27). The judgment tears apart what seems now to belong together (Matt 24:40-41 // Luke 17:34-35). In the life of the community the idea of the judgment motivated in a salutary way the admonition to reconciliation: Who knows how much time remains in which to be reconciled (Matt 5:25-26 // Luke 12:58-59)? Whoever makes judgments about splinters should think about the supreme Judge (Matt 7:1-2 // Luke 6:37-38). Woe to the one who causes scandal (Matt 18:7 // Luke 17:1); woe to the one

5. Isa 61:1-6; 49:13; Pss 9:13; 23:4; 24:9-13; 33:19; 34:10; 36:9, 11; 72:1; 106:9; 125:5 (LXX).

6. Matt 11:16 // Luke 7:31; Matt 12:39, 41-42 // Luke 11:29-32; Matt 23:36 // Luke 11:50-51.

7. According to Wellhausen (1904b:55), the woes were created by the primitive com-munity.

who does not work with his talent (Matt 25:14-30//Luke 19:12-27). Above all, remain faithful. Whoever does not confess the Lord in public will not be acknowledged by him at the judgment (Matt 10:32-33//Luke 12:8-9). **[37]**

Some tension was liable to be inherent in this eschatological mood. The possession of salvation is, in spite of all certainty about its present reality, not yet a full reality. Thus the believer lives in the tension between present assurance and future expectation. The kingdom is at hand. The Messiah has already come; and even if he has not yet exerted his own authority, he has nonetheless let the Baptist know unmistakably both how and in what things his messianic character should be perceived (Matt 11:2-6//Luke 7:18-23). Q transmitted Jesus' saying that, confident of victory, asserted that the kingdom is felt to be already present in the defeat of the demons (Matt 12:28//Luke 11:20). Indeed, Q witnessed the same reality in the fact that the sick were healed and the demons fled (Matt 10:8//Luke 10:9 [Matt 7:22//Luke 13:26 ?]). The preachers were commissioned to hurry throughout the land with the message "the kingdom is near" in order to gather what can still be gathered (Matt 10:7//Luke 10:9). Haste is necessary. The equipment that the missionaries are to have is only for a brief, hurried mission at the last moment, not for a continuous undertaking (Matt 10:9-10//Luke 10:4). They should move quickly from one town to the next (Matt 10:12-14//Luke 10:5-7, 10-11; Matt 10:23?). The Son of Man will come suddenly, as lightning strikes, as the flood at the time of Noah, when no one suspects it, as a thief in the night.[8]

By contrast, some pericopae, including those just cited, suggest that Q had already begun to sense the problem of the nonarrival of the parousia. These pericopae were to corroborate this impression: it is quite true that the Son of Man will come suddenly. Indeed, if these sayings are used in order to warn about deceptive signs or pseudo-messiahs (Matt 24:26-27// Luke 17:23-24), or to warn against carefree attitudes (Matt 24:37-41// Luke 17:26-27, 34-35), or as admonitions to reconciliation (Matt 5:25-26// Luke 12:58-59) and faithfulness (Matt 10:32-33//Luke 12:8-9), that indicates precisely that the tension was beginning to abate. The parable of the wise and faithful servant (and his opposite number) is the clearest indication of this decreasing tension.

Hence the picture is not unitary; but this ambiguity is in fact typical. The eschatological mood that is the foundational motif is permeated by another mood that is focused on the present. The best proof of this focus is not the pericopae which indicate that Q eagerly awaited the parousia, but those in which the parousia is generally ignored and in which the idea of the "reign of God" has lost its eschatological hue and is used to refer to the community itself. It is difficult to tell whether the parables of the mustard

8. Matt 24:27//Luke 17:24; Matt 24:37-39//Luke 17:26-27; Matt 24:43-44//Luke 12:39-40.

seed and the leaven should be interpreted in this way.[9] Even if they originally might have been intended eschatologically, elements in both Matthew
and Luke allow one to ignore the eschatological tone and seem to refer to a
general growth of the reign of God on earth. It is also difficult to interpret
the similitudes of the salt and the lamp (Matt 5:13, 14-16 // Luke 14:34-35;
11:33), which perhaps are already used in Q to admonish the disciples (i.e.,
the Christians) to work in the world. The words of Jesus about the Baptist
(Matt 11:11, 12-13 // Luke 7:28; 16:16) are even clearer in this respect: the
present time, as the period of the kingdom, is already distinguished from
the past to which the Baptist belongs. Q is also concerned with theoretical
questions about the validity of the Law (Matt 5:18 // Luke 16:17). That
concern confirms the general impression of Q. Generally speaking, if
eschatology is pervasive, Q nonetheless contains numerous admonitions in
which the eschatological perspective is completely missing, or admonitions
that are motivated purely by the idea of love, or that have the character of a
completely non-eschatological, thoroughly secular proverbial wisdom. The
main proof of the double-faceted character of the primitive community is
the existence of Q itself. Clearly it must be maintained—and the conclusion (of Q) confirms this point—that Q came into being in an eschatological atmosphere and was imbued with an eschatological mood. But it is
likewise clear that no one would write such a document if he were prepared
for the inbreaking of the kingdom on the very next day. Hence the intense
expectation of the first phase had already subsided.

If one wants to summarize this duality, one could say: it is the duality of
the reign of God and of the emerging church. [41] The same duality pene-
trated other aspects of community life. There was an enthusiastic mood of
being the chosen eschatological community.

First of all, Q places on the Baptist's lips the statement that the Messiah
will baptize with the Spirit (Matt 3:11 // Luke 3:16). Jesus himself received
the Spirit at the baptism (Matt 3:16 // Luke 3:22); being driven into the
wilderness by the Spirit, he struggled with the devil (Matt 4:1 // Luke
4:1-2); and he drove out demons by the power of the Spirit (Matt 12:28 //
Luke 11:20).[10] A few scholars have doubted that enthusiastic experiences
such as those described by the Pentecost narrative could have existed in the
early community and suppose instead that they are a retrojection of phenomena from Gentile Christianity. It seems to me, however, that the awareness of the possession of the Spirit is found in Q. This awareness is present
in the pericopae mentioned above and, in addition, in the saying about blasphemy of the Spirit (Matt 12:32 // Luke 12:10). The saying that the Spirit
speaks through those who are persecuted and those who are subjected to

9. Matt 13:31-32, 33 // Luke 13:18-19, 20-21. Cf. Wellhausen [Bultmann probably refers
to Wellhausen 1904b:68—ED.].

10. Bultmann seems to take the Matthaean form of Matt 12:28 // Luke 11:20 (with "Spirit
of God" instead of "finger of God") as original. Later (1963:162 n. 1) he is undecided—ED.

trials (Matt 10:19-20 // Luke 12:11-12) is also born of the experience of endowment with supernatural power. Yet one must admit that Q seldom has direct statements about the Spirit. Enthusiasm is nonetheless evident. Besides the warning against serving two masters and self-deception (Matt 6:24 // Luke 16:13; Matt 7:21-23 // Luke 6:46; 13:26-27), one should ask to what extent Jesus' enthusiastic instructions on discipleship and on his followers' relationships to their families (Matt 8:18-22 // Luke 9:57-60; Matt 10:37-39 // Luke 14:26-27; 17:33) corresponded in fact to the attitudes of the early church. Nevertheless, a high level of enthusiasm is undoubtedly expressed in the words of the [mission] instruction speech, which certainly derives from the community: the power by which Jesus accomplished healings also lives on in the missionaries of the community. They travel through the countryside without provisions; they regard themselves as the envoys of God, sent into houses; their greeting of peace brings peace, their curse brings judgment (Matt 10:7-8, 9-15 // Luke 10:9, 4, 5, 10-12). Enthusiasm is also expressed in the consciousness of being sent like sheep among the wolves (Matt 10:16 // Luke 10:3), in the blessing pronounced on the persecuted (Matt 5:11-12 // Luke 6:22-23), and in the statement that all wonders are possible for the one who believes (Matt 17:20 // Luke 17:6).

In the area of morals, this Spirit is the spirit of freedom. The old Law no longer plays a role. Of course, it is unclear whether the statement that the period of the Law extended up to John (Matt 11:12-13 // Luke 16:16) was meant in that way in Q. It is clear, however, that according to Q one was freed from unbearable burdens. Jesus' thanksgiving applied to the uneducated, the simple—those who did not comprehend the hairsplitting niceties of παράδοσις ("[Pharisaic] tradition") (Matt 11:25-27 // Luke 10:21-22). His woe was aimed at the scribes who barred the way of salvation to others (Matt 23:13 // Luke 11:52) and who tithed mint, dill, and cumin instead of being disposed in love (Matt 23:23 // Luke 11:42)—inner instead of outer purity (Matt 23:25-26 // Luke 11:39-41)! It is wrong to treat divorce in accordance with the praxis of the Law (Matt 5:32 // Luke 16:18). One can even break the Sabbath if necessity and love require it (Matt 12:11-12 // Luke 14:5). Of course, Q lacks the legal controversies that Mark has, but the continued life of the Spirit that overrides the Law is demonstrated by instances in which the Law is ignored: the beatitudes (Matt 5:3-9 // Luke 6:20-21), the parables of the house builder (Matt 7:24-27 // Luke 6:47-49) and the talents (Matt 25:14-30 // Luke 19:12-27). Above all, it is evidenced by the Spirit that surpasses the Law, warns against judging and retaliation (Matt 7:1-5 // Luke 6:37-38, 41-42), and requires love and reconciliation (Matt 5:38-42 // Luke 6:29-30; Matt 18:21-22 // Luke 17:4), and even love of enemies (Matt 5:43-48 // Luke 6:27-28, 36-37).

Even among the ethical teachings that the early church transmitted, however, one finds some that do not partake of the spirit of freedom. This does not mean that they do not necessarily stand at the summit of Christian ethics, or that they must have been produced by the primitive community.

All of them could doubtless be traced back to Jesus with more or less certainty. But the fact that they do not distinguish themselves significantly from the teachings of Jewish proverbial wisdom indicates again the double character of the community that adopted these sayings, along with those new sayings that breathed the spirit of [42] freedom. There are sentences like the Golden Rule (Matt 7:12 // Luke 6:31), like the rationalizing motivation in the saying on gathering treasures (Matt 6:19-21 // Luke 12:33-34), like the sayings on serving two masters (Matt 6:24 // Luke 16:13), on the worker and his reward (Matt 10:10b // Luke 10:7b), on having and receiving (Matt 25:29 // Luke 19:26), or even the humorous mockery of concern about one's stature (Matt 6:27 // Luke 12:25)—sayings of secular and practical wisdom that contain nothing especially distinctive. In another way the sayings buttressed by the motif of retaliation form a counter-pole to the spirit of freedom and love. These can be combined with sayings of the highest moral content, such as is the case with the admonition about reconciliation (Matt 5:25-26 // Luke 12:57-59). The saying that concerns the eternal validity of the Law (Matt 5:18 // Luke 16:17) displays crass disregard of the spirit of the new restricted view of the Law. It is here that the method of our reconstruction is especially clear. It is by no means improbable that Jesus uttered a saying like Matt 5:18 // Luke 16:17; but it was not characteristic of him. It is, however, characteristic of the community that transmitted it. If one does not go beyond the material common to Matthew and Luke, antinomian sayings are as infrequent in Q as are sayings with a legal character.[11]

The spirit of legality, however, does not reveal itself only in such sayings but also in the handful of indications that we get regarding the style of community life. It is necessary to warn that disputes with brothers must be settled (Matt 18:15 // Luke 17:3); one must forgive not once but repeatedly (Matt 18:21-22 // Luke 17:4). One must not scandalize fellow Christians (Matt 18:7 // Luke 17:1). One should not judge rashly (Matt 7:1-5 // Luke 6:37-38, 41-42). If one takes note of the position that the parable of the builders (Matt 7:24-27 // Luke 6:47-49) occupies in Q—at the conclusion of a complex of moral admonitions—its significance lies in its warning against not taking one's Christian life too lightly.[12]

None of these sayings needs to be taken as a product of the early church: their presence in Q is indicative of the fact that the spirit of order and of communal ethics began to gain ground beside the spirit of freedom. The main evidence for the incursion of the spirit of order is, again, the very existence of Q, which came into being out of a need to have fixed forms for regulating communal life. The principle of order in Q is quite peculiar. Q

11. I hold it to be very possible that many of the legal pronouncements of Matthew that Luke avoided derive from Q. But because of the uncertainty I will not go further than this. See Matt 5:17-20? 5:21-24; (16:17-19); 18:16-18; 23:3, 23b (which is a gloss in Luke).

12. Perhaps one might also mention the lack of Markan controversy stories as an example.

is not arranged according to a chronological perspective as Mark was but follows a catechetical one. That the sayings in Q concerning the eternal validity of the Law and of divorce come immediately after one another (Matt 5:18, 32 // Luke 16:17, 18)[13]—the former positioned to mitigate the antinomian point of the latter—indicates quite clearly that we are not mistaken in affirming a duality. Here again is the duality of the reign of God and the church or, more precisely, the duality of the Spirit and freedom on the one hand and ecclesiality on the other.

Thus we see that, conscious of being the eschatological community, the early church separated itself conceptually from γενεὰ αὕτη ("this generation"). I have already said that this separation in no way involved a break with Judaism or the constituting of a new congregation or the consciousness of being a new religious society. But obviously one could not stop ideological opposition from becoming practical opposition. The opponents themselves took care of this type of separation.

Hostility was above all directed at the representatives of the contemporary trends in the Jewish religion that stood closest to Christianity: the Pharisees and the scribes. Q already included a speech against the Pharisees in which the hate-filled woes were aimed not only at the religious principles of Pharisaism but at their person, their vanity (Matt 23:6-7 // Luke 11:43) and their hypocrisy (Matt 23:27-28 // Luke 11:44). They are the killers of the prophets and the real enemies of the Lord (Matt 23:29-32 // Luke 11:47-48). Sinners streamed to the Baptist, but the Pharisees resisted the will of God (Matt 21:32 // Luke 7:29-30). Perhaps the sayings concerning the first and the last (Matt 20:16 // Luke 13:30) and blind guides (Matt 15:14 // Luke 6:40) are also directed against the Pharisees.

The hostility of the community, however, applies not only to the Jewish leaders.[14] Q expresses opposition to the whole of the Jewish people, who are introduced as γενεὰ αὕτη ("this generation"), to whom God's Wisdom cannot justify herself (Matt 11:16-19 // Luke 7:31-35), who have closed their eyes to the sign of the Son of Man (Matt 12:38-40 // Luke 11:29-30), and who have blasphemed the Spirit working in Jesus and in his church (Matt 12:32 // Luke 12:10). The people of this generation must be judged by the Ninevites and the queen of the South (Matt 12:41-42 // Luke 11:31-32). The instruction speech reveals that the message of the apostles found believers in some households (Matt 10:13 // Luke 10:6), but in general it is permeated by a tone of hostility. At the same time Q complains about the households who have rejected the message (Matt 10:12-15 // Luke 10:5-6, 10-12). Q transmits the woe against the Galilean towns and the lament over Jerusalem (Matt 11:20-24 // Luke 10:13-15; Matt 23:37-39 // Luke

---

13. See Wellhausen 1904b:20, 21; 1904a:89; 1911:69–70.

14. In Q the Pharisees appear as opponents less frequently than in Matthew, who often introduces them: Matt 3:7 (cf. Luke 3:7); Matt 12:38 (cf. Luke 11:29); Matt 19:3 (cf. Mark 10:2).

13:34-35), and we are told that Q was aware that Jesus came not to bring peace [43] for this period of time but strife (Matt 10:34-36//Luke 12:51-53). To be his disciple requires that one be prepared to tear apart the most intimate of family bonds (Matt 10:37//Luke 14:26) and to leave the dead to bury their own dead (Matt 8:21-22//Luke 9:59-60). Many fellow citizens who had been invited to the feast scorned it out of thoughtlessness and hostility (Matt 22:1-10//Luke 14:16-24).

The opposition to Israel gives the impression of having arisen more from the sad experience of resistance than from a theoretical surmounting of nationalistic barriers. Even for the saying about Gentiles in the kingdom (Matt 8:11-12//Luke 13:28-29) this observation holds, and the story of the centurion of Capernaum (Matt 8:5-13//Luke 7:1-10) is told as an exception to the rule. Q is quite clear on the fact that belonging to the Jewish nation does not in itself guarantee participation in the reign of God. The speech of the Baptist that protests against the claims of the children of Abraham has been transmitted by the community (Matt 3:7-10//Luke 3:7-9). It is not that Q had a basically universalist perspective. One should perhaps even consider whether the saying of Matthew that restricts the mission to the Jews derived from Q (Matt 10:5-6).

In any event even here there is clearly a duality: the duality between the sense of opposition to the Jewish people and the consciousness of solidarity with them. For the latter there are obviously no explicit statements, but this lack only affirms the self-evident character of this consciousness. It is further corroborated by the above-mentioned absence of universalist ideas. It is quite clear: Q understood itself as the eschatological Israel. The beatitudes refer to the pious of Israel, and the twelve representatives of the community will sit on twelve thrones and will rule the tribes of Israel (Matt 19:28//Luke 22:28-30). Closely related to this duality is the duality found in Q's relationship to the Baptist. Q begins with an account of his effectiveness and thereby reveals the consciousness that Jesus and the Christian movement had followed his activity. Jesus was baptized by him. Q understood itself to be in solidarity with him, up to a point. The relation of the people to the Baptist mirrors their relationship to Jesus (Matt 11:16-19; 21:32//Luke 7:31-35, 29-30). Q transmits Jesus' saying which explains that John is more than a prophet (Matt 11:7-10//Luke 7:24-27). But in spite of this saying, Q knows that John was not even worthy to render Jesus the lowly service of a slave (Matt 3:11//Luke 3:16) and that the least in the kingdom is greater than John (Matt 11:11//Luke 7:28).

In all these antinomies, what is in fact the cohesive historical force? Its origin and its strength? It is what is most self-evident, it is the consciousness of belonging to Jesus. That point is so self-evident that it never even needs to be formulated, either explicitly or negatively. Jesus is the Lord and to him alone is the address "Lord" offered (Matt 7:21//Luke 6:46). All attention is concentrated on him. Through his coming the eschatological community has been called into existence. It is he who declares the poor to be blessed (Matt 5:3-9 // Luke 6:20-21) and who pronounces the thanksgiving concerning the simple (Matt 11:25-27 // Luke 10:21-22). It is he who initiates the present events: he sends forth the missionaries (Matt 9:37—10:16 // Luke 10:2-16) and sends the strife in which they find themselves (Matt 10:34-36 // Luke 12:51-53). Just as he is Lord of the present, so he will be Lord of the future. He judges between true servants and those who only pay lip service (Matt 7:22-23 // Luke 13:26-27). Ultimately, confessing him will be what matters. His image is strong enough to bear the same duality that permeates all the facets of community life. In his portrait he appears as the duality of Jesus and Christ.

Little is said in Q of Jesus' human existence. There are few stories about him: his baptism and testing, the encounter with the centurion of Capernaum, a controversy on the occasion of an exorcism—that is all there appears to be. In the sayings and speeches of Q Jesus' person for the most part plays no role at all. What this means becomes clear if one remembers that, for example, in the woes against the Pharisees, their attitude toward his person never becomes a matter of reproach for the Pharisees. (One might contrast this with the polemic of the Fourth Gospel!) Nevertheless, the person of Jesus in Q is lively, and indeed the fact of the existence of Q testifies to the power of his person in the primitive community. Jesus' image was kept alive not by describing him but by characterizing him by what he said and by placing on his lips new experiences and realizations that accrued to the church. Q contains the Sermon on the Mount in its essential components. That alone is a sufficient indication of the power of Jesus in the primitive community, and of what the first Christians had experienced of him and were capable of maintaining of him. He preached reconciliation and love in an unprecedented manner (Matt 5:43-48 // Luke 6:27-28, 32-36; Matt 7:1-5 // Luke 6:37-38, 41-42; Matt 18:21-22 // Luke 17:4). He taught absolute honesty and simplicity in the submission to God's will.[15] And he did not only teach this! In him one learns that God reveals himself to the uneducated (Matt 11:25-27 // Luke 10:21-22) and that he has more joy over the recovery of one lost sheep than over the ninety-nine that were not lost (Matt 18:12-13 // Luke 15:3-7). He showed that God [44] can be seen as father (Matt 7:7-11 // Luke 11:9-13) and can be petitioned as a father (Matt 6:9-13 // Luke 11:2-4), and how one can be aware of being a child of God (Matt 5:45, 38 // Luke 6:35-36). When the Spirit, freedom, and love are alive in the community, it is due to his influence.

Yet his image is not monolithic. Into the image of the person filled with God's power are added elements of the Jewish Messiah, the Christ of the church. This addition already happened to some extent in the same sayings that disclose the power of his historical person. The fact that such additions

15. Matt 7:3-5 // Luke 6:41-42; Matt 6:24 // Luke 16:13; Matt 10:37, 39 // Luke 14:26; 17:33; Matt 18:4; 23:12 // Luke 14:11; 18:14. He himself is the model: Matt 8:18-20 // Luke 9:57-58.

occurred shows that the duality that I have described is not something nonorganic, but is historically unitary and essential. Jesus as the model of absolute self-surrender bears the title Son of Man (Matt 8:20 // Luke 9:58). The life that the disciple ought to lead in self-sacrificing surrender is depicted as "discipleship" (Matt 8:18-22 // Luke 9:57-60). To belong to him, to be worthy of being his disciple, is what matters (Matt 10:37-39 // Luke 14:26-27).

Other sayings and stories fully bear the character of a messianic portrait. Jesus is consecrated as Messiah at his baptism. His struggle in the wilderness with the devil is a messianic testing. Elijah is his precursor; Jesus is the Messiah.[16] His deeds are those of the Messiah (Matt 11:2-6 // Luke 7:18-23). He is the apocalyptic Son of Man and he will one day pronounce judgment—for some salvation, and for others condemnation (Matt 10:32-33 // Luke 12:8-9; Matt 23:39 // Luke 13:35; Matt 24:27, 44 // Luke 17:24; 12:40). Indeed, the title "Son of Man" adheres so tightly to him that it is attested of him even apart from his apocalyptic role.[17]

Reign of God versus church; Spirit and freedom versus order; the chosen Israel versus the new church; Jesus versus the Christ—within these antinomies moves the primitive community. This strange ambivalence is what is characteristic of the community; it is characteristic of it as a seedbed is of new growth. Such growth can be preserved historically only through its connection with old forms and by producing new forms. Nevertheless, it bursts the old forms and recognizes the new as inadequate from the start. I have already stated what is new and what is really impelling the process: it is the person of Jesus with his spiritual content. The importance of the primitive community lies in the fact that it comprehended and maintained this new insight.

16. Matt 3:4 (in Q?); Matt 11:10 // Luke 7:27; Matt 11:14 (in Q?).
17. Matt 8:20 // Luke 9:58; Matt 11:19 // Luke 7:34; Matt 12:32 // Luke 12:10; Matt 12:40 // Luke 11:30.

2

The Synoptic Sayings Source and the *Gospel of Thomas*

HELMUT KOESTER

COLLECTIONS OF SAYINGS

James M. Robinson, in his article "*LOGOI SOPHON*" (1971b), has brought about a basic shift in the investigation of the Coptic *Gospel of Thomas*.[1] He neither strains to isolate certain sayings as possibly genuine, nor does he concentrate on the question whether or not this newly discovered Gospel is dependent on the canonical Gospels.[2] Rather he tries to determine the character and genre of this "Gospel" as a whole, a work which is, in fact, nothing other than a collection of sayings.

[167] How and why was such a writing composed? What was the theological principle presiding over the formation of this type of "Gospel"? How is Christian faith understood, and how does it relate to the earthly

Excerpted from Helmut Koester, "One Jesus and Four Primitive Gospels," *HTR* 61 (1968) 203–47; repr. as pp. 158–204 in James M. Robinson and Helmut Koester, *Trajectories through Early Christianity* (Philadelphia: Fortress, 1971).

1. For literature on the *Gospel of Thomas*, see Haenchen 1961a; further in Hennecke 1963:278–83 and 307; also Koester 1971a:129–43.
2. On this question, see Grant, Freedman 1960; Gärtner 1961; H. Turner 1962; McArthur 1960, 1959–60. The wisdom of the methodological procedure of the latest and most extensive publication on this question is beyond my comprehension. Schrage (1964b) tries to prove the secondary character of the tradition contained in the *Gospel of Thomas* by a comparison with the Sahidic translation of the Synoptic Gospels (and John). However, the Sahidic translation of the NT was not made until the third century at the earliest; cf. Metzger 1964:79–81. Thus, any agreements could only prove that the Sahidic version was influenced by the *Gospel of Thomas*, which was certainly known in Egypt by the end of the second century, as is evidenced by the Oxyrhynchus Logia. Moreover, Schrage's understanding of form-critical method is glaringly evident in comments such as the following (on Saying 31, i.e., *P. Oxy.* 1,6): "Thomas has detached the saying from this historical situation to which it was assigned by the Synoptic Gospels, and has again made it a 'free logion'" (p. 76). See also Bartsch, 1959–60; Cullmann 1960, ET 1962; Hunzinger 1960a, 1960b; Montefiore 1962; Wilson 1960a, 1960b, 1960–61; Spivey 1962; Saunders 1963; North 1962.

35

Jesus, if the work contains nothing but "words of Jesus"? These are the primary questions which are asked in Robinson's article.

The *Gospel of Thomas*[3] contains a variety of sayings, thematically only loosely connected with each other; "word association," however, as a principle of composition, is frequent. It is not possible to discover any overriding theological concern in the order and arrangement of the sayings, or in the setting of the whole Gospel. In spite of the designation of Jesus as the "Living One" in the incipit, and in spite of the designation of the sayings as "secret words," there are no features compelling us to understand the work as a secret revelation after the resurrection.[4] Scenes where Jesus gives instructions privately to his disciples are not uncommon in the canonical Gospels,[5] and all the technical nomenclature of the typical "revelation discourse after the resurrection"[6] is missing in the *Gospel of Thomas*. Moreover, the sayings are, at least in part, sayings of Jesus, or modifications of such sayings. Thus, for the *Gospel of Thomas*, "Jesus the Living One" may well be the earthly Jesus, who at some time in his ministry is assumed to have spoken these words to Judas Thomas. However, this Gospel was written and read in a Christian community after Jesus' death. Therefore, these sayings are now understood in terms of a new context and situation, even though no such new "situation" is expressed by the framework of this Gospel itself (i.e., a "situation" after Easter, such as is indicated by the passion-resurrection framework of the resurrection appearances of the canonical Gospels, or by the situation of a special revelation of Jesus appearing from heaven). What has happened to the [168] words of the earthly Jesus after his death, when they are repeated without an externally visible break in continuity? For the death of Jesus, his resurrection, and his ascension never explicitly appear. Jesus is always represented as the "Living One," without any concern for the problem of his death, and without any recognition of the fact that his life has become past history.

The sayings themselves, their forms, alterations, and accretions, are our only guides. It is advisable to consider examples from each form-critical category of sayings separately. Any category of sayings has its particular structure and inherent theological tendency. This enables us to discern changes and evaluate them theologically, once such sayings have been detached from their original function in Jesus' proclamation and have been given a new *Sitz im Leben* as words of Jesus "the Living One," in the life of the church after his death. The way in which particular categories of sayings were interpreted, further developed, augmented, and multiplied

3. Quotations are from the edition of Guillaumont 1959. The numbering of the individual sayings in this edition is the same as in Hennecke 1963:511–22.

4. The case is quite different with the closely related *Book of Thomas the Contender*, where Thomas requests Jesus to impart revelations to him before his ascension; cf. H.-C. Puech in Hennecke 1963:308.

5. See Matt 5:1-2; Mark 4:10-11, 34; 7:17; 13:3; etc.

6. On the revelation discourse source, see Koester 1971b:193–98.

should reveal the theological tendency which dominated this tradition as a whole.

Generally speaking, the types of sayings represented in the *Gospel of Thomas* correspond to those found in the Synoptic Gospels (with occasional parallels in John). They reflect, at least partly, the types and forms used by Jesus in his proclamation.[7]

1. Prophetic and Apocalyptic Sayings

Next to the parables of Jesus, we find the largest number of sayings of Jesus among prophetic and apocalyptic sayings. Furthermore, these sayings, as found in the Synoptic Gospels, also include a great number of sayings which clearly reflect various stages in the church's eschatology and can readily be distinguished from Jesus' own proclamation.

Thus, I have chosen to treat this category of sayings in more detail than others, in order to determine with more precision the *Sitz im Leben* of the saying in *Thomas* and their relation both to the Synoptic tradition and to Jesus' original proclamation.

It may be argued that the category of prophetic and apocalyptic [**169**] sayings is least typical of the genre of Gospel literature represented by *Thomas*, a genre which James M. Robinson has called "words of the wise." But, first, it is often extremely difficult to assign wisdom sayings and proverbs to a particular person, or time, or stage in the development of the tradition;[8] second, as we will see, the *Gospel of Thomas* lacks such apocalyptic sayings as are characteristic of another type of tradition and Gospel literature, namely that of "revelation" or "apocalypse"; third, the designation "words of the wise," if I understand Robinson correctly, should not mislead us to narrow our quest down to the investigation of only sapiential sayings.

On first reading the *Gospel of Thomas*, one gets the impression of its treatment of apocalyptic sayings that they are a secondary spiritualization of canonical apocalyptic material, a view well formulated by Robert M. Grant, who represents the common opinion:

> He has substituted a kind of spiritual understanding for the Gospel of Jesus ... Thomas lacks the connection with the past ... as well as an emphasis upon the importance of the future which was given by Jesus' statements about things to come. He has made the Kingdom almost exclusively present, while in our Gospels it is partly present but will be fully realized only in the future. (Grant, Freedman 1960:113)

I myself once shared this understanding of the apocalyptic sayings in the

---

7. In the classification I follow Bultmann 1931; ET 1968:passim.

8. Robinson's assessment of the genre of the *Gospel of Thomas* is quite correct. It is, indeed, the category of the "wisdom saying" which gives the *Gospel of Thomas* its peculiar character. However, the sapiential material would yield but little evidence for the question whether or not *Thomas* is independent of the Synoptic Gospels.

Gospel of Thomas. However, closer consideration of the prophetic and apocalyptic sayings in the *Gospel of Thomas* requires a basic modification of this
view.

First of all, among the apocalyptic sayings of *Thomas* which have parallels in the Synoptic Gospels, there is not a single one which corresponds to
the so-called Synoptic apocalypse (Mark 13; Matt 24–25; Luke 21).[9] Most
of the apocalyptic sayings of [170] *Thomas* have their Synoptic parallels in
the major Q-collection of eschatological sayings which is reproduced in
Luke 12:35-56; cf. the *Gospel of Thomas* 21c (Luke 12:35),[10] 21b and 103
(Q 12:39), 16b (Q 12:52-53), 91 (Q 12:54-56).[11] Several others are certainly Q-sayings: the *Gospel of Thomas* 54, 69, 68 (Q 6:20, 21a, 22), 46 (Q
7:28), 61a (Q 17:34). The other sayings of this type have parallels either in
the Markan sayings collection in the parable chapter—the *Gospel of Thomas*
5 and 6 (Mark 4:22), 41 (Mark 4:25)—or in sayings peculiar to Luke: the
Gospel of Thomas 3 (Luke 17:20-21) and 79 (Luke 11:27-28).

The predominance of Q-sayings among these prophetic and apocalyptic
sayings of *Thomas* raises the question whether *Thomas* presupposes the particular apocalyptic expectation of Q which is epitomized in the sayings
about the coming Son of Man.[12] But *Thomas* neither reproduces any of the
typical Q-sayings about the coming of the Son of Man or of his "day" (Q
12:40; 17:24, 26-27, 28-30; cf. Q 12:8-9; Q/Matt 19:28) nor uses the title
"Son of Man"[13] for Jesus or for any other figure.[14] [171] This allows for either of two explanations: (1) *Thomas* may have carefully avoided this term,

---

9. There are only a few remote contacts with the Synoptic apocalypse. One of these is the
parable of the thief (Matt 24:43), which occurs in two variants in the *Gospel of Thomas*, in Sayings 21 and 103. However, this parable (to be distinguished from the parable of the landlord's
return, Mark 13:34-36) is part of the Synoptic Saying source Q (Q 12:39); it was the author of
Matthew who introduced this and similar Q-material into the Synoptic apocalypse (Matt
24:37-51 // Luke 17:26-27, 34-35; 12:39-40, 42-46). A second instance is the *Gospel of Thomas*
61a ("Two will rest on a bed . . ."); the Synoptic parallel is found in Luke 17:34, i.e., again
within a Q-context (Luke 17:22-37) which was in part incorporated into the Synoptic apocalypse first by Matthew (24:26-27, 37-39, 40-41).

10. There is no parallel in Matthew. It is difficult to determine whether it was Luke or Q
that added this well-known eschatological admonition (cf. 1 Pet 1:13; *Did.* 16.1).

11. Two of the prophetic sayings, formulated as "I-sayings," come from the same context:
Sayings 10 (Luke 12:49) and 16 (Q 12:51). Only the latter can be assigned to Q with certainty
(cf. Matt 10:34), whereas the former has no parallel in Matthew and may come from Luke's
special source rather than from Q.

12. On the Christology of the coming Son of Man, see Tödt 1959:44–62; ET 1965:47–67;
Hahn 1974:32–42; ET 1969:28–34.

13. Only once does *Thomas* speak of Jesus as the Son of Man: "The foxes have their holes
and the birds have their nest, but the Son of Man has no place to lay his head and rest" (Saying
86; cf. Q 9:58). Bultmann (1968:98; also Tödt 1965:122) has argued that this saying is a proverb in which *Son of Man* is no honorific title, but simply means "man," as contrasted with the
animals. Even though this explanation has not been widely accepted (see, against Bultmann:
Bornkamm 1960:229–30; Hahn 1969:36), the *Gospel of Thomas*, which does not use the term
as a title, seems to confirm Bultmann's suggestion. The decisive question is whether *Thomas*
presupposes a stage of the Synoptic tradition in which a titular usage of the term *Son of Man*
had not yet developed; on this, see below.

14. Saying 106: "When you make the two one, you shall become sons of man." Whatever

and the sayings in which it occurred;[15] but in view of the *Gospel of Thomas* 86,[16] this is not very likely; (2) *Thomas* presupposes a stage and form of the tradition of eschatological sayings which did not yet contain an apocalyptic expectation of the Son of Man. Did such a stage ever exist in the early church's transmission and expansion of Jesus' eschatological sayings?

Rudolf Bultmann was still prepared to ascribe to Jesus those Son of Man sayings in which Jesus distinguished between himself and the future Son of Man (1968:151–52). But, more recently, Philipp Vielhauer and others have forcefully and persuasively challenged this assumption.[17] Vielhauer argues that the proclamation of the kingdom and the expectation of the Son of Man are mutually exclusive concepts with respect to their content and history-of-religions background; and he proves that all sayings about the Son of Man **[172]** disclose certain features of a christological development which are absent in the most primitive stage of the Synoptic tradition and its eschatology.

For our evaluation of the apocalyptic sayings of Jesus, this implies that there were at least three different concepts of eschatology which occur in gospel literature side by side, often conflated with each other: (1) a developed, and even elaborate, "revelation" about future events, as it occurs in the Synoptic apocalypse of Mark 13; (2) the expectation of the Son of Man and of "his day," as it is represented in Q, but which is also evident in isolated sayings of Mark (e.g., Mark 8:38) and in the Synoptic apocalypse in its present form;[18] (3) the proclamation of the coming of the kingdom, which is older than the two other apocalyptic theories and ultimately has its roots in the preaching of Jesus.

"sons of man" means here, it is not used as a title for a specific figure. Certainly the suggestions that " 'man' . . . refers to the first immortal figure, the Saviour" (Gärtner 1961:246) presupposes too much of a gnostic redeemer mythology. A penetrating attempt to distinguish various layers of traditions and redaction within the Synoptic Sayings source has been published by Dieter Lührmann (1969). Lührmann assigns the sayings about the coming Son of Man to a comparatively early stage of the tradition of Q, but he questions their historicity. Further elaboration of the stages of tradition which led to the composition of Q must include the *Gospel of Thomas* and its traditions in such a trajectory of the Synoptic Sayings source. This would also shed more light on the place of the Son of Man sayings in this trajectory.

15. Saying 44 presents a variant of the Synoptic saying about "the sin that cannot be forgiven." But whereas the Q-version of this saying (Q 12:10) contrasts the blasphemy against the Holy Spirit with the blasphemy against the Son of Man, *Thomas* distinguishes between blasphemies against the Father, the Son, and the Holy Spirit. It is difficult to determine whether this "trinitarian version" of the injunction presupposes Q or rather the more original form of Mark 3:28-29 (Matt 12:31) and *Did.* 11.7. It is not unlikely that the *Son of Man* was introduced into this saying by the author of Q. The twofold tradition in the Synoptic Gospels and the reference in the *Didache* proves that this saying circulated freely; cf. Koester 1957: 215–17.

16. See above, n. 13.

17. Vielhauer 1965a, 1965b; a similar view is found in Perrin 1967:164–73.

18. In the parallels to the Synoptic apocalypse in 1 Thess 4:15-17 and *Did.* 16, the title used is not *Son of Man* but *Lord*, which may be the more original title for this tradition of apocalyptic revelation.

The *Gospel of Thomas* does not reveal any acquaintance with either the Synoptic apocalypse or Q's Son of Man expectation. It does contain, however, a number of apocalyptic sayings. The most conspicuous term in these sayings, as well as in the *Gospel of Thomas* as a whole, is *kingdom*,[19] or *kingdom of heaven*,[20] or *kingdom of the Father*.[21] To be sure, these sayings in the *Gospel of Thomas* almost always show a tendency to emphasize the presence of the kingdom for the believer rather than its future coming. But it is very questionable whether such eschatology of the kingdom is a later gnostic spiritualization of early Christian apocalyptic expectation, or rather an interpretation and elaboration of Jesus' most original proclamation.

The *Gospel of Thomas* preserves Jesus' emphasis that the coming of the kingdom cannot be timed or located:

Saying 3: (The kingdom is not in heaven, nor in the sea . . .) the kingdom is within you and is without you.

[173] Cf. Luke 17:20-21: The kingdom of God does not come with signs to be observed; nor will they say: "Here it is," or "there"; behold, the kingdom of God is among you.[22]

To the saying against those who test the face of the sky and the earth but do not test the time (Q 12:56), the *Gospel of Thomas* 91 adds: "and him who is before your face you have not known." This addition to an original saying of Jesus simply makes explicit what is already implied in Jesus' proclamation: one should not look into the future, nor into the past, but believe in the kingdom which is already present in his message.

Thomas condenses this original impact of Jesus' words into the christological title "the Living One," which occurs in sayings formulated in analogy to prophetic sayings of Jesus:

Saying 52: (With respect to the twenty-four prophets in Israel who spoke about Jesus) You have dismissed the Living One who is before you and you have spoken about the dead.

Saying 111: The heavens will be rolled up and the earth in your presence, and he who lives on the Living One shall see neither death nor fear.

It is quite obvious that Thomas interprets the kingdom's presence in such a way that he eliminates the tension between present and future which

19. Sayings 3, 22, 27, 46, 49, 82, 107, 109, 113.
20. Sayings 20, 54, 114.
21. Sayings 57, 76, 96–99, 113.
22. Cf. also the *Gospel of Thomas* 113: "(The kingdom . . .) will not come by expectation; they will not say: 'See here,' or 'See there.' But the kingdom of the Father is spread upon the earth and men do not see it."

characterizes Jesus' proclamation; past and future can become a unity in the present religious experience:

> Saying 18: Where the beginning is, there shall be the end. Blessed is he who shall stand at the beginning, and he shall know the end and he shall not taste death. [174]

The kingdom is not only the believer's destiny, it is also his origin:

> Saying 49: Blessed are the solitary and elect, for they shall find the kingdom; because you come from it, you shall go there again.

This saying is parallel to Saying 50:

> We have come from the light, where the light has originated through itself.

The metaphor of the "child"—again derived from a genuine saying of Jesus (Mark 10:15 par.)—becomes an important symbol for the true believer in whose religious experience the opposites are reconciled:

> Saying 22: These children who are being suckled are like those who enter the kingdom. . . . When you make the two one, and when you make the inner as the outer . . . and the above as the below . . . the male and the female into a single one . . . then you shall enter the kingdom.[23]

Other prophetic sayings of Jesus in the form of beatitudes, some of them quoted without significant alterations (Sayings 54, 68, 69 = Matt 5:3, 6, 11), are used to describe this same state of present blessedness; thus, all these designations by which Jesus identified the heirs of the kingdom—the children, the poor, the hungry, those who suffer persecution—ultimately mean in the *Gospel of Thomas* the "Solitary One." In the agonizing eschatological divisions which have been ushered in by Jesus (Q 12:51-53,[24] quoted in Saying 16), the believers stand as the "Solitaries."[25] [175]

Jesus radicalized the traditional apocalyptic expectations of the kingdom; his message demands that the mysterious presence of the kingdom in his words be recognized. The Gnosticism of the *Gospel of Thomas* appears to be

23. On Saying 22, see Kee 1963 and the critical discussion of Kee's article in Robinson 1960:230-33.

24. This saying does not belong to the context of the Synoptic apocalypse; it does not speak about the divisions which will occur before the coming of the Son of Man, but about those which Jesus causes through his ministry. Thus it represents an eschatological orientation which is probably more primitive than either Q's expectation of the Son of Man or of the eschatology of Mark 13.

25. The Solitaries as the possessors of the kingdom also appear in Sayings 4, 23, 49, 75; Klijn (1962) has argued that this term describes the primordial "One-ness," regained in the eschatological experience of the believer.

a direct continuation of the eschatological sayings of Jesus. But the disclosure of the mysterious presence of the kingdom is no longer an eschatological event; it has become a matter of the interpretation of Jesus' words: "The repose of the dead and . . . the new world . . . has come, but you know it not" (Saying 51); thus, "whoever finds the explanation of these words will not taste death" (Saying 1). It is as this discovery of the secret presence of "Life,"[26] "Light,"[27] and "Repose"[28] in Jesus' words that "everything that is hidden will be revealed" (Sayings 5, 6 = Mark 4:22).[29]

2. Parables

The *Gospel of Thomas* has preserved a large number of parables.[30] Most of these have direct parallels in the Synoptic Gospels,[31] and perhaps all are original parables of Jesus.[32] As a rule, these parables are rather brief; exceptions are Sayings 64 and 65 (parables of the great supper, Matt 22:1-10, and the evil husbandmen, Mark 12:1-12). Allegorical embellishments and [176] interpretations are rare,[33] but indicative of *Thomas's* gnosticizing tendencies.[34]

I presuppose that the parables of *Thomas* are not taken from the Synoptic Gospels, but derive from an earlier stage of tradition of Synoptic parables.

In Jesus' proclamation, the parables speak about the kingdom of God and about man's situation in view of its coming. In the *Gospel of Thomas* they speak about the man who has found a great religious treasure:

Saying 8: The man is like a wise fisherman who cast his net into the sea; he drew it up from the sea full of small fish. Among them he found a large and good fish; that wise fisherman, he threw all the small fish down into the sea; he chose the large fish without regret.

26. Saying 4.
27. Sayings 61c, 83.
28. Sayings 50, 51, 60, 90.
29. The "days in which the disciples will seek Jesus and not find him" (Saying 38b) are not the days after Jesus' death, nor the time before his parousia, but the "time" in which men may not be able to understand his words (cf. Sayings 38a, 39).
30. I have not included here the numerous metaphors, since they belong to the wisdom sayings.
31. Sayings 8, 9, 20, 57, 63–65, 76, 107; cf. 21b, 103.
32. This is also not improbable for the parables which lack parallels in the Synoptic Gospels (Sayings 96, 97, 98, 109); cf. Hunzinger 1960b.
33. There is no trace in *Thomas* of the allegorical interpretations which some of the parables he quotes have received in the Synoptic Gospels; cf. Sayings 9 (the "sower," Mark 4:3-9, 13-20), 57 (parable of the tares, Matt 13:24-30, 36-43). Perhaps Saying 65 also preserves a version of the parable of the evil husbandmen which is more original and less allegorical than Mark 12:1-12.
34. There are two instances in which the allegorical interpretation makes it difficult to determine whether there was once a more primitive parable and, if so, what it meant: Sayings 21a (the little children in the field who take off their clothes) and 60 (the Samaritan carrying a lamb).

The point is quite different from the judgment parable in Matt 13:47-48.[35] In *Thomas* we have a wisdom parable which praises the wisdom of the fisherman—the term *wise* occurs twice—as an example of wise discrimination.[36] In the parable of the pearl [**177**] (Saying 76 = Matt 13:45-46) *Thomas* underlines the admonition to seek enduring treasure by adding another wisdom saying from the Synoptic tradition: "Do you also seek for the treasure which fails not, which endures, there where no moth comes near . . ." (Q 12:33).

The remarkable feature of these parables in *Thomas* is that they are never understood as eschatological parables but rather as admonitions to find the mysterious treasure in Jesus' words and in one's own self.

3. I-Sayings

I-sayings are more numerous than in the Synoptic Gospels. Some of them differ only slightly from their Synoptic parallels (e.g., Saying 10 = Luke 12:49),[37] but most of them are independent formulations. They do not show Jesus presenting himself in the role of an apocalyptic prophet; nor do we find any trace of the development typical of the Synoptic Sayings source Q, where the "I" of Jesus corresponds to the future coming of the Son of Man;[38] nor is there any sign that *Thomas* knew of the Markan I-sayings which predict the passion and resurrection of Jesus.[39] Rather, Jesus appears as the divine revealer who makes his disciples "Single Ones" (Saying 23).

---

35. Matt 13:49-50 is a secondary allegory of judgment which seems not yet to have become a part of the version which *Thomas* knew.

36. One may wonder whether Thomas refers to the Synoptic parable of Matt 13:47-48 at all. There is an almost exact parallel to Saying 8 in the poetic version of the Aesopic fables by Babrius, who, in the first century C.E., dedicated his work to the son of King Alexander, whose tutor he was. This Alexander seems to have been a petty king in Cilicia, grandson of Herod's son Alexander, mentioned by Josephus (*Ant.* 18.140). Fable 4 of Babrius reads:

> "A fisherman drew in the net which he had cast a short time before and, as luck would have it, it was full of all kinds of delectable fish. But the little ones fled to the bottom of the net and slipped out through its many meshes, whereas the big ones were caught and lay stretched out in the boat." (LCL)

This is almost an exact parallel from the secular tradition of fables, and at least opens up the possibility that in other instances as well *Thomas* may have drawn upon the wisdom tradition of his time—even if the application is quite different in Babrius:

> It's one way to be insured and out of trouble, to be small; but you will seldom see a man who enjoys a great reputation and has the luck to evade all risks.

It is, of course, not unlikely that Matt 13:47-48 used the same fable and turned it into a parable of judgment.

37. Only four of the seventeen I-sayings have Synoptic parallels (Sayings 10, 16, 55, 90 = Luke 12:49; Q 12:51a; Q 14:26, 27; cf. Mark 8:34; Matt 11:28-30).

38. See above, pp. 16–17.

39. Cf. Mark 8:31 par.; 9:31 par.; 10:33-34 par.; also Mark 9:9; 14:21, etc. Ever since Wrede (1901:82–92; ET 1971:82–114) many critical scholars have maintained that all of these sayings are secondary formulations (*vaticinia ex eventu*).

That is to say, he brings them into an existence that is independent of the historical circumstances of life. Or Jesus, characteristically, is Wisdom, inviting people to bear his yoke (Saying 90 = Matt 11:28-30). [178]

Thus, the I-sayings of the *Gospel of Thomas* are primarily revelation sayings which have little basis in the historical teaching of Jesus.[40] Indicative of this type of revelation sayings in the I-style are those sayings in which the revealer presents himself as the divine savior (or Wisdom!) who has come to the world: Saying 28: "I stood in the midst of the world and in flesh I appeared to them. . . ."[41]

The fact that some of these sayings are formulated in the "I am" style suggests a comparison with the "I am" sayings of the Gospel of John. Here, however, one discovers a very remarkable difference. In the *Gospel of Thomas*, these "I am" sayings answer the question "Who are you?"—a question which is even explicitly asked by Salome in Saying 61: "Who are you, man, and whose son?" Jesus answers: "I am he who is from the same; to me was given from the things of the father"; cf. Saying 77: "I am the light that is above, I am the all. . . ." Thus, these sayings are examples of "I am" as an identification formula. This belongs to the category of revelatory language in which the divine qualities of the revealer are emphasized.[42]

By contrast, the "I am" sayings in the Gospel of John are instances of the recognition formula, as Bultmann has shown.[43] The "I" is the predicate of the sentence, answering the question: "Who is (or where is) the one whom we expect?" In the Gospel of John, the answer ". . . it is I" claims that all this has now come and is present in Jesus of Nazareth. In this way, the stress is upon the appearance among men of the divine revelation (Logos, Father). The identification formula could shift into a recognition formula, because the basic structure of John's Gospel derives from [179] the cross-resurrection kerygma.[44] The narrative context of the Gospel, and the fact that the Gospel as a whole is directed toward Jesus' glorification on the cross, forced the "I am" sayings into the category of the recognition formula. Whatever was expected as the salvation (the Life, the Light, the Way, the Truth) is present in the story of a particular human being. The *Gospel of Thomas*, on the other hand, does not present the story of Jesus' life, nor is Jesus proclaimed as a man who suffered on the cross "under

40. Cf. Bultmann 1931:161-79; ET 1968:150-66.
41. Equally significant are I-sayings which speak of the revelation of the divine mysteries; cf. Sayings 62, 108; see also Saying 17: "I shall give you what eye has not seen." This saying is missing in the canonical Gospels, but is quoted, introduced by "it is written," in 1 Cor 2:9.
42. For example, see Bultmann 1971b:225-26 n. 3, where the various forms of the "I am" formula are analyzed. In the *Gospel of Thomas*, as elsewhere, there is not a clear-cut distinction between the identification formula on the one hand and the presentation and qualification formulae on the other.
43. Bultmann 1971b:225-26 n. 3. Bultmann considers John 11:25 and 14:6 possible exceptions.
44. Bultmann (1971b:226 n. 3) suggests that some of the "I am" sayings of John originally were presentation [or qualification] formulae.

Pontius Pilate." The concern is exclusively with his words. For these, the historical origin is quite irrelevant. Who Jesus was or that he once lived and died is without any importance. Thus, the recognition formula is not relevant, since this formula is used to recognize the presence of the revelation in a particular historical man and in his fate. The absence of the recognition formula implies that the sayings collection in itself had no inherent principle by which such sayings could be made to witness to a particular historical event. The sayings collection explains that Jesus and his words—whoever he may have been in his historical appearance—have divine quality. By way of contrast, the Gospel of the passion-kerygma witnesses that whatever is divine has become a historical and human reality in the earthly Jesus of Nazareth.

4. Wisdom Sayings and Proverbs

Wisdom sayings and proverbs are numerous in the *Gospel of Thomas*. Most of these sayings have exact parallels in the Synoptic Gospels. They are often expressions of general truths which have no relation to any particular historical situation or person:

> Saying 31: Prophet in his fatherland (Mark 6:4-5[45] par.)
> 32: The city built on a mountain (Matt 5:14b)
> 33a: What you hear in your ear (Q 12:3)[46] **[180]**
> 33b: Light under a bushel (Mark 4:21; Matt 5:15 par.)
> 34: Blind leading the blind (Q 6:39)
> 35: House of the strong man (Mark 3:27)
> 45a: No grapes from thorns (Q 6:44)
> 45b: Good heart—good words (Q 6:45)
> 47a: Serving two masters (Q 16:13)
> 47b: Old and new wine (Luke 5:39)
> 47c: New wine in old wineskins (Mark 2:22; cf. Matt 9:17; Luke 5:37)[47]
> 47d: Old patch on new garment (Mark 2:21; cf. Matt 9:16; Luke 5:36)[48]
> 67: Whoever knows the all (cf. Mark 8:36; Matt 16:26; Luke 9:25)
> 94: Whoever seeks, will find (Matt 7:8; cf. Luke 11:10)

45. On this proverb (*P.Oxy.* 1,6) see Koester 1971a:129-32.

46. See below, n. 53

47. The *Gospel of Thomas* adds "and they do not put old wine into a new wineskin, lest it spoil it." This may be a secondary addition in analogy to the first sentence; cf. Bartsch 1959-60:251-53. But some of these parallelisms in the *Gospel of Thomas* are probably original, as, e.g., in Saying 31 (cf. nn. 45, 55).

48. The reversal of the order "old patch on new garment" instead of "new patch on old garment" (as in the Synoptic Gospels) is most peculiar. Quispel quite ingeniously reconstructs an old (Aramaic) parallelism which, he says, was the basis of both versions: "They do not put an old patch on a new garment, because it does not match the new, and they do not sew a new patch on an old garment, because there would be a rent." See Quispel 1958-59:281; 1957:194-95. Perhaps the reversal is caused simply by the second half of the preceding saying, 47c.

There are also some general admonitions:

Saying 26: The beam in your brother's eye (Q 6:41-42)
39b: Wise as serpents (Matt 10:16)
92: Seek and you will find (Q 11:9)
93: On not profaning the holy (Matt 7:6)

The relationship of these proverbial sayings to their Synoptic parallels is most peculiar. To the extent that they represent sayings which Matthew and Luke drew from Q, their Synoptic parallels [181] are usually found either in the "Sermon on the Mount" (Matt 5–7) or the "Sermon on the Plain" (Luke 6). In both of these Synoptic contexts we find Sayings 26 and 45a.[49] The parallels of Sayings 33b, 47a, 92, and 94 occur only in the Sermon on the Mount,[50] whereas Luke has the same sayings in different contexts.[51] For Sayings 32 and 93[52] there are no parallels in Luke at all. On the other hand, Sayings 34 and 45b are paralleled only in Luke's Sermon on the Plain (Luke 6:39, 45), whereas Matthew's parallels are found outside the Sermon on the Mount (Matt 15:14; 12:34-35). However, if any of these wisdom sayings of *Thomas* with parallels in the Synoptic Gospels have no parallels in either Matthew 5–7 or Luke 6, there is always a parallel in the Gospel of Mark.[53] Sayings 31, 35, 47c, 47d, and 67 are found in Mark 6:4-5; 3:27; 2:22; 2:21; and 8:36.[54]

Since no peculiarities of the editorial work of Matthew, Mark, or Luke are recognizable in these proverbial sayings of *Thomas*,[55] [182] there is no

49. Matt 7:3, 5 // Luke 6:41-42; Matt 7:16 // Luke 6:44.
50. Matt 5:15; 6:24; 7:7; 7:8.
51. Luke 11:33; 16:13; 11:9; 11:10.
52. Matt 5:14; 7:6.
53 The only exceptions are Saying 47b = Luke 5:39, though this saying belongs together with others which Luke drew from Mark: Mark 2:21-22 // Luke 5:36-39 (= Sayings 47c, d); Saying 33a ("What you shall hear in your ear . . .") = Matt 10:27 // Luke 12:3, though again this saying is closely connected with the sayings in Mark 4:21-25; Mark 4:21 = Saying 33b; Mark 4:22 // Matt 10:26 // Luke 12:2 = Saying 5.
54. Saying 33b occurs in Mark 4:21 as well as in the Sermon on the Mount (Matt 5:15). Mark 4:21 is part of the small collection of Q-sayings in Mark's Gospel (Mark 4:21-25) which has relations also to other sayings in *Thomas* (cf. Sayings 5, 41). Matt 5:15 also proves that this saying was in an original part of the tradition which has been expanded into the Sermons "on the Mount" and "on the Plain" by Matthew and Luke. It is noteworthy, however, that the form of this saying in *Thomas* corresponds most closely to Luke 11:33 rather than to Matt 5:15 and Mark 4:21 // Luke 8:16.
55. On the contrary, some of these sayings, as they occur in the *Gospel of Thomas*, have a more primitive form than their Synoptic parallels. Cf., e.g., Saying 31, which has preserved the original parallelism, whereas Mark 6:4, 5 transformed the second half of the saying ("no physician heals those who know him") into narrative ("and he could not perform any miracles there"). Saying 26 reproduces Matt 7:3 and 5, but does not have Matt 7:4 par. "Or how can you say to your brother, 'Let me take the speck out of your eye . . .'?" This saying provides, nota bene, a good example of the irresponsible way in which some scholars try to prove that *Thomas* introduced secondary alterations into Synoptic sayings: Bartsch (1959–60:255) calls "and then you will see clearly" a secondary addition; but this phrase (in *P.Oxy.* 1,1) is the exact equivalent of the phrase which is found in both Matt 7:5 and Luke 6:42! Saying 45b =

reason to assume that they were drawn from the Synoptic Gospels.[56] Rather, *Thomas*'s source must have been a very primitive collection of proverbs, a collection which was incorporated into Matthew's and Luke's common source Q and thus became the basis of the materials used by Matt 5–7 and Luke 6 for their "Sermons," and which was also known by Mark.

It is not surprising to find some signs of secondary growth in these wisdom sayings of *Thomas*. They are, in part, natural developments of such proverbial material.[57] Only rarely does Thomas express any secondary tendentious interpretations in the formulations of the proverbs themselves.[58] His theological bias is explicit in the sayings about seeking and finding:

Saying 92 reproduces the well-known exhortation "Seek and you will find" (Q 11:9), but adds a tendentious I-saying: "But those things which you asked me in those days, I did not tell you then; now I desire to tell them, but you do not inquire after them."

[183] Saying 2: "Let him who seeks, not cease seeking until he finds; and when he finds, he will be troubled, and when he has been troubled, he will marvel and he will reign over the All."[59]

Luke 6:45 preserves the original emphasis upon "good heart—good words"; cf. the rabbinic saying, "What was in the heart, was in the mouth" (*Midr. Ps.* 28.4.115b; Strack and Billerbeck 1922–61:1.639; Bultmann 1931:87; ET 1968:84). Cf. also above, nn. 45 and 47.

56. In some instances (e.g., Saying 45), the proverbs of *Thomas* reveal that they were transmitted in the same combinations in which they occur in the Synoptic Gospels; cf. Bartsch 1959–60:253–54. This, however, is no argument for dependence upon the Synoptics, since some of these sayings were certainly combined and confused already in the earliest stages of the tradition.

57. Cf. such additions according to analogy, as Saying 47a: "It is impossible for a man to mount two horses and to stretch two bows"; Saying 33: "What you shall hear in your ear, preach from your housetops" (added to "city on a mountain" and "light not under a bushel"); but this may be an older Q-tradition; see above, n. 53.

58. In some instances, scholars have been overly quick to identify *Thomas*'s text as secondary; e.g., Saying 93:

"Give not what is holy to the dogs,
lest they cast it on the dung heap.
Throw not the pearls to the swine,
lest they make it [. . .]."

This is a perfect form of a proverb without any religious or Christian application, whereas Matt 7:6 shows signs of an application of this proverb to the situation of the church. When Bartsch (1959–60:255) remarks that "Matthew's interpretation, which was determined by the subject matter, i.e., by the situation of the church, has been replaced by an interpretation which is determined by the metaphorical content" of the Logion, he turns all form-critical standards upside down.

59. This is most certainly a secondary and gnosticizing version of the exhortation to seek and to find. In the Greek version of *Thomas* (*P.Oxy.* 654, 2), as well as in the parallel of this saying which Clement of Alexandria quotes from the *Gospel of the Hebrews* (*Stromateis* 2.9.45.5 and 5.14.96.3), the chain is better preserved, and another line is added: "and on reigning he will rest." Thereby, the saying reveals even more clearly its connection with the theological

Thomas explains what is meant by "finding" in another alteration of a Synoptic wisdom saying (Mark 8:36 par.):

> Saying 67: "Whoever knows the All but fails himself, fails everything."[60]
> Cf. Saying 111b: "Whoever finds himself, of him the world is not worthy."[61]

Speculation about the relation of the self to the origin of being is added to this emphasis upon knowing oneself. This is expressed in several sayings of this type, although they are no longer wisdom sayings of proverbial character. Instead of speaking about the nature of man in general, they contemplate the true nature of the gnostic's self:

> Saying 29: "If the flesh has come into existence because of the spirit, it is a marvel; but if the spirit (has come into existence) because of the body, it is a marvel of marvels. But I marvel how this great wealth has made its home in such poverty."[62]

[**184**] It is only here that the tradition of wisdom sayings takes its characteristic turn into gnostic theology. Throughout the tradition of these sayings their truth does not depend upon the authority of Jesus. Whether the wisdom saying envisages man's being in general, or whether it discloses man's spiritual nature and origin, its truth is vindicated whenever he finds this truth in himself.

5. Rules for the Community

Several rules for the community from the Synoptic tradition have parallels in the *Gospel of Thomas*. But most of them have been modified considerably.

In the Synoptic Gospels, as well as in the epistles of the NT, or in the *Didache*, such rules reflect the attempt of the early Christian church to enable the Christians to live in this world and to regulate the life of the community accordingly. On the whole, the paraenetic tradition of Judaism was utilized, and became the basis for early Christian paraeneses and community regulations. Words of Jesus found only occasional usage in such contexts; for this, Paul's letters, the *Didache*, and *1 Clement* are typical witnesses. Quite a few of these regulations were only subsequently made "say-

---

expectation of the wisdom tradition, namely to find rest; cf. Sir 6:28; Matt 11:28-30, which is quoted in the *Gospel of Thomas* 90.

60. Literally: "fails the whole [or: every] place." The translation of Guillaumont et al. reads: "but fails (*to know*) himself, *lacks* everything." Following Haenchen (1961a:27) I prefer to repeat the word *fail*, since the Coptic text also has the same verb in both instances.

61. Cf. also the gnostic sayings on finding, Sayings 56 and 80. They are certainly secondary extensions of the more primitive Synoptic proverbs on seeking and finding.

62. Cf. also Sayings 84, 87, and 77b.

ings of Jesus," and were introduced into the Synoptic tradition at a secondary stage.

The rules for the community in the *Gospel of Thomas*, whether based upon original words of Jesus or not, always request that the disciple divorce himself from the traditional religious behavior of Judaism and that he separate himself from any concerns with this world. Sayings against fasting, praying, and almsgiving occur several times:

> Saying 14a: "If you fast, you will beget sin for yourselves, and if you pray, you will be condemned, and if you give alms, you will do evil to your spirit."[63]

If fasting and keeping of the Sabbath and circumcision are rejected, they are nevertheless valid symbols for the separation from the world (cf. Sayings 27, 53). Jesus' words on "clean and unclean," [185] preserved in Saying 14c in a form that is probably more original than Mark 7:18-19 par., are perhaps intended to emphasize the importance of the inner man.[64] But it is not just that Thomas spiritualizes religious observance. Rather he understands the commands of Jesus to break with established family ties as demanding a complete separation from society and an acceptance of only the "family" of the truly redeemed. Compare the sayings of Jesus' true relatives (Saying 99)[65] and on hating one's father and mother (Saying 101).[66] A number of sayings imply the rejection of worldly possessions.[67]

The disciples are wanderers who have no home (Saying 42). They heal the sick and accept what is set before them (Saying 14b).[68] If, in this way, they imitate Jesus' own experience of homelessness (Saying 86)—and indeed, this motif was destined to have a powerful influence upon Syrian Christianity—then Jesus' radical divorce from the accepted Jewish interpretation of the law has become a new set of religious rules. They have become test cases for the separation from this world and time. Otherworldliness is the new ideology.

Because of the relation of this Gospel to Jesus' *ipsissima vox*, it is an urgent question whether or not this tradition maintains its original integrity

---

63. Cf. Matt 6:1-18; *Didache* 8. See further, Sayings 6a, 104.

64. See the saying about the "outside and inside of the cup," Saying 89 (Luke 11:39, 40); *Thomas* presents this saying in agreement with Luke 11:40 and with the reversal of "outside" and "inside" found only in 𝔓⁴⁵ C D T a e c, which is usually considered to be a secondary variant of Luke's texts. As long as the meaning of this saying is not quite clear, it is impossible to decide whether *Thomas*'s text represents a more original version which was the original version of Luke too, or whether *Thomas*'s version has subsequently influenced the Lukan manuscript tradition, or whether *Thomas* is dependent upon a variant of Luke's text. On the meaning of this saying, see Haenchen 1961a:53; Quispel 1957:200.

65. Mark 3:33-35 par.

66. Matt 10:37 // Luke 14:26.

67. Saying 95 forbids the lending of money at profit or with the hope to receive it back (Luke 6:34-35); cf. Sayings 81 and 110. Also *Thomas*'s conclusion of the parable of the banquet (Matt 22:1-10; Luke 14:15-24): "Tradesmen and merchants shall not enter the places of my Father" (Saying 64).

68. Luke 10:8, 9 (Matthew's parallel is different and secondary).

once its *Sitz im Leben* has been transferred from the eschatological proclamation of Jesus to the theology of the church. It seems that the sayings of
Jesus were in this case a vital element in the development of a religious
self-understanding [186] for which the historical Jesus of Nazareth became
ultimately irrelevant as a criterion of true faith.

The basis of the *Gospel of Thomas* is a sayings collection which is more
primitive than the canonical Gospels, even though its basic principle is not
related to the creed of the passion and resurrection. Its principle is nonetheless theological. Faith is understood as belief in Jesus' words, a belief which
makes what Jesus proclaimed present and real for the believer. The catalyst
which caused the crystallization of these sayings into a "Gospel" is the
view that the kingdom is uniquely present in Jesus' eschatological preaching and that eternal wisdom about man's true self is disclosed in his words.
The gnostic proclivity of this concept needs no further elaboration.[69]

The relation of this "sayings Gospel," from which the *Gospel of Thomas*
is derived, to the Synoptic Sayings source Q is an open question. Without
doubt, most of its materials are Q-sayings (including some sayings which
appear occasionally in Mark). But it must have been a version of Q in
which the apocalyptic expectation of the Son of Man was missing, and in
which Jesus' radicalized eschatology of the kingdom and his revelation of
divine wisdom in his own words were dominant motifs.

Such a version of Q is, however, not secondary, but very primitive. At
least Paul's debate with his opponents in 1 Corinthians seems to suggest
that the wisdom theology which Paul attacked relied on this understanding
of Jesus' message.[70] These opponents propagated a realized eschatology.
They claimed that divine wisdom was revealed through Jesus. And at least
one saying which Paul quotes in the context of his refutation is indeed
found in the *Gospel of Thomas* 17 (1 Cor 2:9).

This would prove that such sayings collections with explicit theological
tendencies were in use quite early, and not only in Aramaic-speaking circles
in Syria; that the source "Q," used by Matthew and Luke, was a secondary
version of such a "Gospel," [187] into which the apocalyptic expectation of
the Son of Man had been introduced to check the gnosticizing tendencies
of this sayings Gospel; and that the *Gospel of Thomas*, stemming from a
more primitive stage of such a "Gospel," attests its further growth into a
gnostic theology.

---

69. Cf. Robinson 1971b (see below, pp. 51–58), 1965.
70. See further Robinson 1971a; H.-W. Kuhn 1970.

Jewish Wisdom Literature
and the Gattung,
LOGOI SOPHON

JAMES M. ROBINSON

The history of the early Christian designation for the "sayings" gattung came first into view in its gnostic variant, as "hidden sayings."[1] This poses the question as to what there may have been in the tendency of the gattung itself that contributed to this outcome. Bultmann provided a useful suggestion, when he sensed in Q 11:49-51; 13:34-35 a speech by Sophia cited from some lost wisdom document, whose conclusion, "you will not see me again until . . ." was explained in terms of "the myth of the divine Wisdom, . . . who, after tarrying in vain on earth and calling men to herself, takes departure from earth, so that one now seeks her in vain" (1968:115). For this myth [104] does seem to be presupposed in the *Gospel of Thomas*, to judge by Saying 38: "many times have you desired to hear these sayings that I say to you, and you have no other from whom to hear them. There will be days when you will seek me (and) you will not find me" (cf. Q 10:24; 13:34-35). Thus Bultmann's suggestion of an early Christian association of Jewish wisdom literature's personified Sophia with Jesus and of the absorption of part of a collection of wisdom sayings into a collection of Jesus' sayings may in their way point to the prehistory of a gattung that, though apparently not gnostic in origin, was open to a development in that direction, once a general drift toward Gnosticism had set in.

If the *Gospel of Thomas* shows the way in which the Sophia tradition used in Q ends in Gnosticism, an early catholic theologian attests equally

From James M. Robinson, "LOGOI SOPHON: On the Gattung of Q," pp. 103–13 in James M. Robinson and Helmut Koester, *Trajectories through Early Christianity* (Philadelphia: Fortress, 1971).

1. Robinson begins by considering the references to "hidden sayings" in the incipit of the Gospel of Thomas and *P.Oxy.* 654, and then compares similar formations in *Thomas the Contender* (CG II, 7.145.17–19) and *Pistis Sophia*.—Ed.

clearly its origin in Jewish wisdom literature. "The All-virtuous Wisdom said thus: 'Behold I will bring forth to you the expression of my spirit, and I will teach you my *logos*, since I called and you did not obey, and I put forth *logoi* and you did not attend. . . . For it shall come to pass when you call upon me, I will not hear you. The evil shall seek me and they shall not find me. For they hated wisdom'" (*1 Clem.* 57.3-7). Here one has much the same content as in the *Gospel of Thomas*, Saying 38, and in Q (11:49-51; 13:34-35), with a quotation formula reminiscent of that in Q (11:49), "Therefore the Wisdom of God said." Yet in fact what we have is a verbal quotation from the LXX of Prov 1:23-33, and the quotation formula is simply making use of the primitive Christian name for the book of Prov-erbs. Yet the OT origin of the passage neither separates it from Jesus, "who is called Sophia . . . in the *logoi* of the prophets" (Justin, *Dial.* 100.4), nor from the *Gospel of Thomas*. When Bultmann first worked out the gnostic redeemer myth, he appealed to Prov 1:23-33 as "the most important pas-sage, . . . in which the whole myth is reflected."[2] The personified Wisdom [105] of OT wisdom literature developed into the gnostic redeemer myth, especially as it identified Jesus with that redeemer, and thus understood Jesus as bringer of the secret redemptive *gnōsis* or *logoi*.

That such a development comes into view especially in the sayings tradi-tion is more comprehensible when one has noted the close connection be-tween sayings collections and the sages, the *sophoi*. It is partly because the gattung was itself associated with the "wise" that it could easily be swept into the christological development moving from personified Wisdom to the gnostic redeemer. It is this relation with the "wise" that becomes clear from the antecedent history of the gattung within Judaism, as *logoi sophōn*, "words of the wise" or "sayings of the sages."

Already in *Pirke Aboth* one has to do with a collection of sayings that (especially in its first parts) corresponds formally to this gattung. One finds here a chain of loosely connected sayings. In distinction from most of the material studied thus far, the sayings are attributed to different rabbis, rather than to a single sage. Nonetheless, the common designation *Pirke Aboth* ("Chapters of the Fathers") is misleading. For these six *perakim* or "chap-ters" from the Mishnah, when they contain references to themselves, use only the term *debarim*, "sayings." The critical edition by C. Taylor (1897) begins with the title "Sayings of the Ancient Fathers" and ends with the subscription of the title to chapter 6 as "Sayings of Meir," rather than the frequently heard title *Pirke R. Meir.* Also, the oldest rabbinic reference to *Pirke Aboth*, found in the Gemara, *b. B. Qam.* 30a, cites Rabbi Jehudah (d. 299 C.E.) as referring to "the *sayings* of 'Nezikin'" and Raba (d. 352 C.E.) as

---

2. Bultmann 1923:9 (ET 1986:23). The unwillingness of Ralph Marcus (1950–51) to as-sume a move beyond "poetic personification" to "hypostatization" for Sophia in Judaism, in criticism of Helmer Ringgren (1947), seems based on an idealized view of early Judaism (see Marcus 1950–51:169–71).

referring to "the *sayings* of the fathers" (Herford 1962:4). Here the Aramaic term translated "sayings" refers to the Hebrew equivalent that is found in the source itself. For *Pirke Aboth* speaks not only of "the words of the law" (2:5, 8; 3:3-4; 4:7) but also of the "sayings" of a given rabbi, for example, "the sayings of Eleazar ben Arach" (2:13-14; see also 5:10; 6:6).

Furthermore, the quotation formulae do not refer to the rabbis [106] as "father," and the title *rabban* does not occur there until Gamaliel I (1:16; middle of the first century C.E.); not until Jehudah (2:1; ca. 200 C.E.) does the title *rabbi* enter a quotation formula. In the sayings themselves the title *rab* is mentioned in passing in 1:6, 16; 6:3; and "fathers" are mentioned in 2:2. But the sayings refer to the bearers of the sayings tradition predominantly as "sages": "May your house be a meeting place for the sages, and cover yourself with dust of their feet and drink thirstily their sayings" (1:4). The "wise" are exhorted to watch their "words" (1:11). When a person challenges this way of life, he does so with the comment that he has lived his whole life among the "wise" and has learned to prefer silence to the many "words" that only give rise to sin (1:17). Hence the bearers of this tradition are called "sages" in a quotation formula (1:5) and at the opening of the subsequently added sixth chapter. The inference seems unavoidable that the sayings tradition recorded in *Pirke Aboth* would have considered itself "words of the wise," "sayings of the sages," even though this formulation does not occur as such in the *Pirke Aboth*.

One also finds elsewhere in the Judaism of this period such an association of "sayings" with the "sages." The *Testaments of the Twelve Patriarchs* are of course regarded as testaments, as the incipit, "Copy of the testament of Naphthali that he gave at the time of his departure" and the like attest. But in seven of the twelve cases the incipit is varied to refer to *logoi*, e.g., "Copy of the *logoi* of Dan which he spoke to his sons in his last days." Then follows the exhortation to hearken to the *logoi* (*T. Dan* 1.2; *T. Naph.* 1.5; *T. Gad* 3.1 v.l.; *T. Reu.* 3.9; *T. Jud.* 13.1); when *logoi* has already been used in the incipit, the synonym *rhēmata* is used in the exhortation (*T. Iss.* 1.1b; *T. Zeb.* 1.2; *T. Jos.* 1.2). Then the patriarch's experiential wisdom is given in analogy to wisdom literature. One may compare the common form of address "my sons," the speech in praise of "the wisdom of the wise" (*T. Levi* 13.7), the exhortation "become then sages in God, my sons" (*T. Naph.* 8.10), and the parallels to Ahikar.[3] Thus there seems [107] to be some overlapping between the gattung of the "testament" and that of "sayings of the sages." Just as the gattung "sayings collection" can gain profile by more thorough correlation

---

3. See Charles 1912–13:2.291. The form of address "my son(s)" fits of course the imagined situation of a testament, where a father addresses his son(s). Yet this situation itself is characteristic of wisdom literature (Ahikar; Proverbs 31); and the sonship is readily spiritualized and thus made generally applicable (*Corpus Hermeticum* 13). To be sure, the testaments are less collections of transmitted sayings than invented discourse. Hence these *logoi* are in form more comparable to the gnostic and apologetic *logoi*, where the collector has been replaced by the author and the sayings collection by the dialogue, discourse, or tractate.

with the trajectory of the gattung of revelatory discourses of the Resurrected with his disciples, both would gain in profile if the course of the gattung of testament in this period were to be fully plotted.

Much the same situation is found in the *Apocalypse of Adam*. To be sure, this document is from Nag Hammadi's gnostic library (CG, V,5), and hence could have been treated above in the section dealing with the Coptic gnostic library [1971b:74–85]. Yet it is regarded by the editor Alexander Böhlig (1963:95) and by Kurt Rudolph[4] as an outgrowth of Syrian-Palestinian baptismal sects, documentation for pre- and non-Christian Jewish gnosticism.[5] Although the work is designated "The Apocalypse of Adam" in the title found both before (64.1) and after (85.2) the text, and has an incipit (64.2-4) using the loanword *apocalypse* ("The revelation that Adam taught his son Seth in the 700th year"), it is in form much like the *Testaments of the Twelve Patriarchs*. The text continues immediately (64.4-5): "And he said, 'Hear my words, my son Seth.' " Adam says (64.12-13) that Eve taught him "a word of knowledge of God," and that he heard "words" from the three great men (66.9-10), namely, the revelation he gives Seth (67.14-21). When Adam's narration of the future arrives at Noah, the latter's testament is similarly introduced (72.18-19): "He [Noah] will say to them, 'My sons, hear my words.' " And at the end of the work Adam's speech closes (85.3-18): "The words of the God of the aeons that they [those with *gnōsis*] have preserved did not [of themselves] come into the book nor are they written [at all]. Rather angelic ones will bring them, whom all generations of men will not recognize. [**108**] For they will come on a high mountain of a rock of truth. Hence they will be called 'the words of incorruption and of truth,' of those who know the eternal God with wisdom, gnosis, and doctrine from angels for eternity. For he knows everything." In the concluding framework the concept "apocalypse" recurs (85.19-29): "These are the revelations that Adam revealed to Seth his son and that his son taught his seed. This is the hidden *gnōsis* of Adam that he gave to Seth, the holy baptism of those who know the eternal *gnōsis* through those born of *logos*, [and] the imperishable luminaries who came forth from the holy seed." Here those "with wisdom," called "luminaries,"[6] could well be a gnosticized and mythologized development of the concept of the sages as the bearers of the saving "words."

---

4. See Kurt Rudolph, in his book review in *TLZ* 90 (1975) 361–62.

5. See my report in Robinson 1968:377–78.

6. The gnostic redeemer is named "luminary" (*phōstēr*) (76.9–10, 28; 77.15; 82.28); so are his parents (82.7), who, according to Böhlig (1963:93), are the sun and the moon (cf. Gen 1:16 and Rev 12:1), and the Gnostics themselves (75.14–15; 85.28). Cf. also the four "luminaries" of the *Apocryphon of John*, CG, II, 7.33ff. (Krause and Labib 1962:129ff.). This term *luminaries* (Gen 1:14-16 LXX) occurs in the title, preserved on a fragment, of a Qumran document, "Words of the Luminaries" (4QDibHam). Both the meaning of the title and its relation to the liturgical contents are unclear. Baillet (1961, esp. 249) conjectures that the title does not refer to the contents, but rather to the occasion when the material was used. On this assumption he arrives at the translation, "liturgie d'après les luminaires," i.e., "office selon les jours de la semaine." Such a translation seems, however, to be quite strained.

The situation is similar with another "apocalypse," the Ethiopic *Enoch*, which according to the oldest documentation was called the "Words of Enoch the Righteous" (*T. Benj.* 9.1; cf. *Jub.* 21.10, "In the words of Enoch and the words of Noah"). The incipit reads: "Words of the blessing of Enoch," and a superscription in 14.1 reads: "The Book of the Words of Righteousness" (cf. 14.3: "words of wisdom"), just as at the end of the paraenetic book in chapters 91–105 the term *words* and *wisdom* recur. This relationship of words to wisdom is especially clear in the *Similitudes*, chapters 37–71, whose origin as an independent work is recognizable by means of the superscription in 37.1-2 (Eissfeldt 1965:618). Here the work is introduced as "Words of Wisdom," as well as with the exhortation to listen to the "words of the holy one" (*v.l.*, "holy words"), since the Lord of spirits has never before granted such "wisdom." Hence is it not surprising to find in **[109]** chapter 42 the locus classicus for the Sophia myth, attesting the otherwise only "conjectured view that the hiddenness of wisdom [alluded to in wisdom literature] is the consequence of her rejection by men" (Bultmann 1923:9; ET 1986:23). Thus we are directed a step further back, into the wisdom literature in the narrower sense.

The term *wisdom literature* is itself a reflection of an early Christian title for the book of Proverbs. For Eusebius (*Eccl. hist.* 4.22.9) in discussing Hegesippus, says: "And not only he but also Irenaeus and the whole company of the ancients called the Proverbs of Solomon All-Virtuous Wisdom." The use of this title in *1 Clem.* 57.3 has already been noted [above, p. 52].

The book of Proverbs "bears the marks of its origin more plainly than other Old Testament books. Its separate sections have in fact special titles, which reveal that the passages which now follow them once formed separate collections" (Eissfeldt 1965:471). Since the first collection, 1:1—9:18 (like the second, 10:1—22:16, and fifth, chaps. 25–29), bears the superscription "Proverbs of Solomon," the whole book was subsequently given this name. Hence the term *proverb* has been the basic term used in discussing the sayings in wisdom literature. Less noticed is the term used in other collections in the book of Proverbs. Chapter 30 bears the superscription, "The Sayings of Agur Son of Jakeh of Massa," and chapter 31, the superscription, "The Sayings of Lemuel, King of Massah, which his mother taught him." Both superscriptions are less clearly set apart as superscriptions in the LXX than in the Hebrew, which may account for their having been less noted than the term *proverb*.

Already in the Hebrew text the superscription of the collection in Prov 22:17—24:22 "has come now into the first verse (xxii, 17) of the collection which it introduces, but, as [the LXX] shows, it belongs before this verse" (Eissfeldt 1965:471). This superscription reads "The Sayings of the Sages"[7]

---

7. It is unclear whether in the superscription to 23:23-34, "also these are of the wise," the term *proverbs* is to be understood, or, as the preceding superscription, 22:17 (LXX, 30:1) would

(cf. the incipit of the LXX: "To the *logoi* [**110**] of the sages lend your ear and hear my *logoi*"). Here the superscription "Sayings of [a given sage]" used for Proverbs 30 and 31 is generalized into "Sayings of the Sages" (LXX: *logoi sophōn*), and so presents itself as the fitting designation for the gattung that the sources here investigated have tended to put in profile.

The designation "sayings" occurs in a superscription again in Eccl 1:1, "The Words of the Preacher, the Son of David, King of Jerusalem," although to be sure the LXX here uses the translational variant *rhēmata* in place of *logoi*. Toward the conclusion (12:10) the book speaks again of the preacher's "sayings of delight" and "sayings of truth." Then in 12:11 one finds praise of the "sayings of the sages," the same expression as at Prov 22:17. Even though Eccl 12:11 is not readily translatable[8] (RSV: "The sayings of the sages are like goads, and like nails firmly fixed are the collected sayings which are given by one Shepherd"), we seem to have to do with the designation for a gattung that is recognizable as such.

When one inquires behind Jewish wisdom literature, one finds similar collections in Egypt and Mesopotamia. In Egypt the common incipit of such collections of sayings is "Beginning of the instruction." Hence the expression "Sayings of the Sages" at the opening of the sayings collection in Prov 22:17—24:22, a source that has been shown to go back to the book of wisdom of Amen-em-Opet, cannot itself be attributed to the Egyptian *Vorlage*.[9] Perhaps an antecedent for the title can more clearly be found in Mesopotamia. For the Ahikar collection, from which Prov 23:13-14 seems to have been borrowed (Eissfeldt 1965:475), may have been designated as "sayings." To be sure, the Ethiopian fragments, [**111**] preserved in the "Book of the Wise Philosophers," reflect Egyptian usage in the superscription, "Instruction of Ahikar the Sage" (Conybeare, Harris, and Lewis 1913:xxiv–xxv, 128–29). But Ahikar's collection of sayings in the Syrian version A begins by calling upon his son Nadan to regard Ahikar's "sayings" as he would God's words (Conybeare, Harris, and Lewis 1913:103). And the Aramaic version (fifth century B.C.E.) speaks occasionally of Ahikar's "counsel and sayings."[10] The Ahikar collection is also relevant in

---

suggest, the terms *saying*. Cf. RSV: "These also are sayings of the wise."

8. The obscure words could mean "collected sayings" (RSV), "(Spruch)sammlung" (Zimmerli and Ringgren 1962:ad loc.), and thus could be understood as a description of the gattung. Yet the LXX has here a different reading and commentators have emended the text in various ways. Further, it is unclear whether the one shepherd to whom the sayings of the sages are attributed is God (RSV) or Solomon (so Eissfeldt 1965:493, who takes the phrase to allude to the book of Proverbs). In the latter case the use of the plural ("sages") to designate the sayings of an individual sage would be intelligible best on the assumption that a current designation for a gattung is simply taken over without adaptation.

9. See the section "Egyptian Instructions" in Pritchard 1969:412–25, esp. "The Instruction of Amen-em-Opet," pp. 421–24.

10. To be sure, Karl Ludwig Schmidt (1923:63) seems to go too far in claiming that the Aramaic title read: "Sayings of a wise and instructed scribe named Ahikar, which he taught his son." The decisive first word is lacking in the fragmentary text and is not presupposed in the

terms of its contents, in that parallels with various other collections, including Q, occur (Q 12:45-46); the Syrian version also shows affinities of style with the "Sayings of Agur" (Proverbs 30).[11]

It should be well-known that designations for gattungen are less precisely and consistently used as technical terms in the sources themselves than in modern scholarship. Furthermore, we are not obliged to derive our designations for gattungen from the sources. It is enough that the gattungen themselves have been shown to exist there. However, the tendency or direction of a gattung comes more readily to our attention if a movement of language can be found in the sources that names what is constitutive of the gattung and thus brings its tendency to expression. The fact that the sayings collection as a gattung tended to associate the speaker of sayings with the sage has become audible in noting the connection between "sayings," *logoi*, and "sages," *sophoi*, which in substance leads to *logoi sophōn*, "sayings of the sages" or "words of the wise," as a designation for the gattung.[12] [**112**]

The movement of the sayings of Jesus into collections of sayings has already been discussed [1971b:85–103]. There remains only the question as to what effect there would be upon such collections in view of the wisdom implications they bore. It can be presupposed that some wisdom sayings were among Jesus' sayings from the beginning, which could of course have facilitated the collection of his sayings into this gattung. The addition of further wisdom sayings would be facilitated within this gattung, whose proclivities were to be more concerned with the validity or "truth" of the sayings incorporated than with their human authorship or "authenticity." Ulrich Luck has sketched the development from the apocalyptic context predominating in the sayings of Matthew, who of all the canonical evangelists retains closest affinities with the gattung of sayings collections, in spite of his having embedded Q in the Gospel gattung of Mark (Luck 1968). This movement is made all the more comprehensible in view of the emerging scholarly awareness that apocalypticism and wisdom, rather than being

---

English translation (Conybeare, Harris, and Lewis 1913:168).

11. For example, Prov 30:21: "three things ... and four"; 30:24: "four things are ..."; cf. Conybeare, Harris, and Lewis 1913:lvii; Eissfeldt 1965:85–86.

12. To be sure, the term *words* seems to occur in the incipit of various kinds of Hebrew works, such as Deut 1:1; 28:69; Amos 1:1; Neh 1:1; Bar 1:1. It figures in the superscriptions of the Ten Commandments (Exod 20:1; 34:28; cf. 24:3, 4, 8). In the titles of the historical sources of the books of Kings the term *debarim of days* occurs, with quite a different meaning from *words*, i.e., the whole phrase means "history," or (RSV) "chronicles." In the case of Solomon, 1 Kgs 11:41, "The Book of the History [or Chronicles] of Solomon" is a title to which the content, as established by Noth (1967:66–67, ET 1981:57–58) would be well suited. Yet in this one instance "of days" has been omitted, either in deference to the usage of *debarim* at the opening of the verse to embrace both action and wisdom, or as a scribal error. Hence not only could the dangling "*debarim* of ..." be taken to mean "The Book of the *Acts* of Solomon" (RSV), in analogy to other such historical works, but it could also be mistaken as analogous to the other Solomon literature, i.e., wisdom literature. Hence the shortened title could be taken to mean "Book of the *Sayings* of Solomon." Such a misunderstanding would be a further reflection of the association of *words* and *sages*.

at almost exclusive extremes within the spectrum of Jewish alternatives, share certain affinities and congruences that encourage a transition from one to the other.

There are in the Synoptic Gospels peripheral indications of an association of Jesus with personified Wisdom. In Q (7:35) Jesus and John the Baptist seem to function as bearers of or spokesmen for Wisdom; in Luke 11:49 a Q-saying is introduced as spoken by Wisdom, which in Matt 23:34 is spoken by Jesus himself. M. Jack Suggs has worked out this christological development from Q, which regarded Jesus [113] merely as Wisdom's envoy, to Matthew, which identified Jesus directly as Wisdom (Suggs 1970:137ff.). Thus, prior to the elimination of the gattung of sayings collections completely from emergent orthodoxy, one can sense a development whose more radical correlative and ultimate outcome can be seen only in Gnosticism.[13]

Q's association of Jesus with Wisdom, together with its criticism of the sages (Q 10:21), provides a foretaste of the debate to come. The *Gospel of Thomas* indicates the gnosticizing distortion of sayings that took place readily within this gattung. Hence the ongoing orthodox criticism of this distortion provides something of a context for understanding the process in which Q[14] is imbedded in the Markan outline by Matthew and Luke and continues to be acceptable in the orthodox church only in the context of this other gattung, that of "Gospel."

The tendency at work in the gattung *logoi sophōn* was coordinated to the trajectory from the hypostatized Sophia to the gnostic redeemer. As "hidden sayings," this gattung found a place in Gnosticism. But with the dying out of the oral tradition of Jesus' sayings, it fell into disuse even here, for the gattung of dialogues of the Resurrected with his disciples provided a freer context for the imaginary gnostic speculations attributed to Jesus.

13. It is hoped that the revised publication has here overcome the ambiguity of the 1964 German text responsible for the critical question of Wilhelm Wuellner (*JBL* 84 [1965] 302): "I question the view that the *Gattung* 'as such' provoked subsequent association of Jesus with the *sophos/ḥākām* tradition, and wonder whether it was not the other way around." The article does not presuppose the absence of such an association prior to the time Jesus' sayings were brought into collections. Wisdom sayings may well have been transmitted as individual sayings of Jesus prior to their incorporation in a collection (just as Matt 11:19 par. may be older than Q); and there were early christological developments related to wisdom outside the sayings tradition (see my remarks in Robinson 1957, esp. 277–80). The purpose of the present essay is to draw attention to the gattung and the tendency at work in it, and thus to gain some awareness of the influence that would be at work upon the sayings tradition by being transmitted in this gattung. This is intended to help make intelligible the development from Q to the *Gospel of Thomas*, as an aspect of the general development from Jewish wisdom to Hellenistic Gnosticism, from God's Sophia to the gnostic redeemer. This scope is well sensed by Koester (1971b:166–87; see above, pp. 35–50).

14. See with regard to Q my papers, Robinson 1962, esp. 82–86; 1966 (repr. Robinson 1967).

4

Q in the History of
Early Christianity

DIETER LÜHRMANN

"REDACTION" AND "COLLECTION" IN Q

[**84**] The analyses of the large individual sections of Q have shown the like-lihood that there was a final redaction of Q—redaction in the sense of de-liberate composition with a particular theological point of view, to be distinguished from the "collecting" of materials by catchword and by com-mon topic.[1] Collecting of this sort is found in other parts of the Synoptic tradition as well as in Q, for example, in the programmatic speech that forms the basis of the Lukan Sermon on the Plain and the Matthaean Ser-mon on the Mount (Luke 6:20-49 // Matt 5:1—7:29), in Q 12:22-32, 33-34, in Q 12:2-7, or in Luke 11:33, 34-36, where sayings that appear in Matthew in two different parts of the Sermon on the Mount (Matt 5:15; 6:22-23) are here placed together because of the theme of "light." Exam-ples of this kind could be multiplied.

The presence of such collections suggests that Q is already the (provi-sional) result of a long process of tradition and that, correspondingly, the content of Q is not homogeneous. Rather, just as is the case elsewhere in the Synoptic tradition, Q reflects various stages in the assimilation of the preaching of Jesus by the early church.

In contrast to this type of compilation is the use of traditional materials for definite redactional aims. This use can be seen especially with the leit-motif of the opposition between Jesus and "this generation," and the re-

From Dieter Lührmann, "Q in der Geschichte des Urchristentums," pp. 84–104 in *Die Redaktion der Logienquelle*, WMANT 33 (Neukirchen-Vluyn: Neukirchener Verlag, 1969). (Most of the cross references to other parts of the book have been omitted from the footnotes.—ED.)

1. On Bultmann's distinction between collection (*Sammlung*) and redaction (*Redaktion*), see Lührmann 1969:14–15.

lated announcement of the judgment of Israel, which is even extended to all who refuse the proclamation of the disciples. Even if these observations must remain hypothetical in view of the character of this [85] material, available only through inferences from Luke and Matthew about their common source, they nevertheless point to the strong probability of redactional shaping of the tradition.

THE DATE AND COMPOSITION OF Q

One should not date this redaction too early. To begin with, the process of transmission visible behind Q presupposes a certain span of time between the beginnings of the collection and the transmission of Jesus' preaching and its provisional result in the redaction of Q. From the standpoint of tradition history, Q 10:21-22 points to the Greek-speaking Hellenistic community rather than the Aramaic-speaking church. The Son of Man problem, a controversy in recent research, cannot be treated extensively in this work. Even if the sayings of Jesus that concern the Son of Man coming in judgment could be traced in part to Jesus—which, however, does not seem likely to me—the identification of this coming Son of Man with Jesus belongs to the tradition inherited by Q and probably goes back to the Palestinian community.[2] This point is indicated by Q-sayings that speak of Jesus as the earthly Son of Man (Q 7:34; 9:58), for these sayings cannot be traced to the redaction of Q.

Hence this identification does not have the significance for the evaluation of Q that Tödt had assumed.[3] In fact "Son of Man" is not the only christological title in Q,[4] and it is impossible to assert with Tödt's confidence that "Son of Man Christology and Q belong together both in their concepts and in their history of tradition" (Tödt 1965:269). In the redaction of Q the sayings that concern the Son of Man coming in judgment are one means of enforcing its motif of the announcement of judgment, [86] but only one means; they appear along with a saying such as Q 11:49-51, which reflects completely different tradition-historical presuppositions but which serves the same purpose.

Even the opposition between the disciples of Jesus and those of John that shaped the tradition at an earlier stage no longer plays any role in the redaction of Q.[5] The delay of the parousia reflected in various texts likewise indicates an advanced stage in the history of primitive Christianity. What is more, Q, in my opinion, presupposes the mission to the Gen-

---

2. Tödt 1965:138–39; Hahn 1969:36–37; against this view, Bultmann 1951–55:1.30.
3. Tödt 1965:252–53, 254–55, 264–65. For another contrasting view, see Polag 1968:72.
4. Thus Tödt 1965:264. On this matter, see below, p. 69.
5. See Davies 1966:369: "Q was not concerned with polemic against John's followers but with the crisis which he announced to be impending." Against this view, see Streeter 1924:291–92; Bornkamm 1958:758. In this point we obviously have an index of the lateness of Q inasmuch as a longer process of tradition is presupposed. In other strata of tradition, even at a later date, the conflict with the Baptist community still plays a role (e.g., in Luke).

tiles. This is indicated by the story of the "centurion from Capernaum" (Q 7:1-10), by the emphatic contrast of the Gentiles and Israel in the threats characteristic of Q,[6] and especially by the commissioning speech, which closes with one such threat but which begins with a promise to the Gentiles.[7] There is at least a positive attitude toward the Gentiles in Q; thus, in reference to Q 7:1-10 Manson wrote: "The Roman centurion takes his place along with the folk of Tyre and Sidon, the men of Nineveh, and the Queen of Sheba in the company of Gentiles who by repentance or faith or zeal for wisdom put the chosen people to shame."[8] Simply to call this attitude "friendliness toward Gentiles"[9] or even to refer to the OT [87] prophets[10] is not enough. Along with Manson one must say at least of these passages: "all contain a tacit invitation to the Gentiles" (Manson 1935:28 n. 2). Yet Q 7:1-10 and 10:2 may suggest in particular that the community in which Q was transmitted had also expressed this invitation.

Besides the texts mentioned already, the parable of the great supper (Q 14:15-24) should probably also be noted. The mission to the Gentiles is clearly envisaged in the arrangements of Luke and Matthew (Luke 14:22 and Matt 22:7-8);[11] but one must ask whether this is not also the case for the version of Q that both used.[12] At least the sequence of one invitation that is rejected by those who were first invited, followed by a second invitation,[13] is amenable to this interpretation, as indeed Luke and Matthew show, each in its own way (see Hahn 1965:35-36).

To be sure, Steck thinks that "even in Q the guiding concern is the 'revival of Israel,' "[14] and that "there is no question of a mission to the Gentiles operating in parallel with the 'revival of Israel' any more than is the

---

6. Q 10:13-15; 11:31-32; 13:28-29. See Bultmann's presentation (1968:111-18).

7. Lührmann (1969:60) refers to Q 10:2, where he understands the use of the word *harvest*—used in the OT with respect to the eschatological judgment of the nations—to indicate that the Q-community regards its mission as an expression of this harvest and therefore as presupposing a Gentile mission.—ED.

8. Manson 1935:31. Manson's n. 2 should also be mentioned: "It is doubtless a mere coincidence, but nevertheless suggestive, that Q has these four examples of Gentile people contrasted with Israel to the disadvantage of the latter—Tyre and Sidon in the north, Nineveh in the east, Sheba in the south, and Rome in the west—and also the saying (Lk. xiii. 29), . . . which in Matthew is appended to the conversation with the centurion."

9. See Manson 1949:20: "a friendly attitude toward Gentiles"; Tödt 1965:244; Steck 1967:287 n. 2 (quoted below, p. 62).

10. Thus Harnack 1908:233. [Harnack (ibid.) states: "The expression of friendliness toward the Gentiles . . . fits without difficulty into the picture, or rather offers no greater difficulty than earlier utterances of a similar purport found in the Prophets."—ED.]

11. See Jeremias 1972:63-65; Bornkamm 1960:18-19; against this view, see Linnemann 1960:249.

12. That the parable belonged to Q should be assumed to be the case, following Trilling (1960:262), and against Linnemann (1960:247), who takes the two forms to be two independent "variants."

13. Luke's third invitation is secondary when compared to the two invitations in Matthew (and in *Gos. Thom.* 64).

14. Steck 1967:286. The authors Steck cites in his n. 8 do not agree with *this* hypothesis of Steck!

case with the tradition of the Deuteronomistic understanding of history."[15]
He justifies the latter statement with the remark: "Even the positive description of Gentiles in Q (Matt 8:5-13 par., Luke 10:13 par., Matt
12:41-42 par.) does not indicate a Gentile mission; the butt of these statements is not the behavior of these Gentiles but rather the determined obsti-
nacy of the Israelites" (Steck 1967:287 n. 2). Steck is probably right about
the original meaning of these pericopae, which arose in the conflict of the
early Christian mission with Israel.[16] But in my view he overlooks the
principle with which opposition to Israel is expressed in Q. Here it is [88]
no longer a matter of "revival" but only of judgment. Furthermore, one
may ask whether Q is as indelibly stamped with the Deuteronomistic view
of history as Steck supposes.[17] He himself shows on the one hand how this
idea had also been taken over in a modified form by Hellenistic forms of
early Christianity,[18] and on the other that there are enough other ideas in
Q that cannot be derived from this one source. Like Tödt, Steck has identified a particular aspect of the tradition used by Q with Q as a whole.

Finally, in the history of primitive Christianity, especially in the realm
of the Greek-speaking church, a community that did not include Gentiles
is hardly thinkable because, to a considerable degree, Judaism itself engaged
in this mission (see esp. Georgi 1986:83–117). Thus all the evidence sup-
ports the view that Q also presupposes the church's mission to the Gentiles
and, therefore, the presence of Gentiles in the church.

All these observations indicate that the redaction of Q should not be
placed too early but rather in the Hellenistic community of about the 50s
or 60s.[19] Wellhausen assumed that Q (like Mark) originated in Jerusalem
(Wellhausen 1905:88; 1911:78); against this view, Harnack suggested
Galilee.[20] Such local specifications are, however, precarious, since we know
too little about geographically distinctive developments within primitive
Christianity. One might suggest Syria—where Matthew probably also
should be placed—without making it any more specific than that. [89]

The setting of Q proposed here is in contrast to the view that apparently

---

15. Steck 1967:287. [For an outline of the Deuteronomistic understanding of history, see
Jacobson 1982b, repr. here, chap. 6.—ED.]

16. See also Conzelmann 1969:114.

17. Steck 1967:288: "Q itself might be a sayings collection for the instruction of preachers
to Israel from which they could quote their message to Israel, sayings for adherents, and sayings for themselves, but also woes and judgment threats for the obdurate. For me, the connection of this early Palestinian Jewish Christianity with the eschatologically oriented late Jewish
repentance movement representing the sphere of tradition of the Deuteronomistic view of
history—its message, its activity, its conceptual framework, and its inventory of ideas—seems
unavoidable. The tradition of the Deuteronomistic view of history that has been sketched conceptually and historically in the present work may also open up new paths for understanding
Q, to which we can only point here."

18. Steck 1967:265-79 (in reference to Acts 7:52; Mark 12:1-9; 1 Thess 2:15-16).

19. This estimation of Q's date is widely advocated in studies of Q; the only point of disagreement is whether Q is regarded as "early" or "late."

20. Harnack 1908:171; against this view, Bussmann (1929:117-19) suggests both
Jerusalem and Galilee.

goes back to Harnack, for whom Q was a collection of Jesus-traditions in the Palestinian community.[21] The arguments cited above speak against this view. Q certainly contains units of tradition that have their origin in this period. But in this respect Q does not differ from Mark or the special material of the other two Gospels. In these as well as in Q, there are very old traditions lying both alongside and within later constructions. In this regard Q is not a special case.[22]

FORM

The method of the redaction of Q is essentially the same as that used in Mark, Matthew, and Luke. It is especially visible in the association of various originally isolated sayings, or of sayings that had already been gathered into small collections, under definite theological perspectives.[23] But in addition to this point, there is also the probability of the joining of various units of tradition by sayings that were originally formed in the process of redaction (e.g., Q 11:30; 10:12). The most common form taken by these traditional units associated by redaction is the sayings cluster (*Spruchreihe*),[24] in some cases in the form of an extended apophthegm with an introduction giving a brief description of the scene (e.g., Q 7:18-35; 11:14-23).

Since both Luke and Matthew have allocated the contents of Q variously in their [90] Gospels, only one large block can be reconstructed for Q with some certainty: the block that extends from the programmatic speech to Jesus' thanksgiving [Q 10:21-22].[25] As for the rest, the original sequence of the units contained in Q must remain uncertain. But since Matthew, especially in the speeches of his Gospel, conflated Markan and Q-material to a much greater degree than Luke,[26] the original order may be preserved bet-

21. Harnack 1908:226–29; Bultmann 1913:35 [p. 23 in this volume]; Tödt 1965:224 (see also 257); also Bornkamm 1958:758, who argues more cautiously; for an opposing view see esp. Wellhausen 1905:73–89.

22. The four pericopae that Wellhausen (1905:34, 88) explains as translation variants of an Aramaic original are not conclusive enough to warrant the positing of such an original. Still less can one distinguish on *literary grounds* younger and older sources within Q (as Harnack and Bussmann do), though of course a *history of tradition* of the Q-materials can be discerned.

23. These results are adversely affected by the fact that at many places either Luke or Matthew has severed a connection that existed in Q. This sort of activity, however, is restricted to relatively small units, and therefore the results, which are of course hypothetical, do not suffer too much from their tentative character.

24. See in particular Q 12:2-9, where originally isolated sayings can be detached easily through a comparison with the parallel Markan tradition (Mark 4:22 and 8:38).

25. Knox (1957:4–5) goes so far as to assert: "it seems worth asking whether Q as a single document ever contained more than those elements in which Luke and Matthew employ their common material in the same order, beginning with the appearance of John the Baptist and ending with, perhaps, the charge to the disciples which Luke gives as a charge to the Seventy, while Matthew conflates it with Mark's charge to the Twelve." This complex is also essentially identical with what Polag (1966:128) regards as the kernel of Q around which other layers were subsequently added: roughly Luke 6:20-49; 7:1-35; 9:57—10:24; 11:14-54.

26. See Streeter 1924:271. Luke has more doublets than Matthew even if Matthew has

ter in Luke,[27] although this cannot be a hard and fast rule. Since Luke 17:22-24, 26-30, 34-35, 37//Matt 24:24-28, 37-41 and Luke 19:12-27// Matt 25:14-30 are for both Luke and Matthew the last large pericopae that come from Q,[28] one could assume that Q concluded with pericopae having eschatological contents (see Harnack 1908:177–78), which is a typical occurrence in both Jewish and Christian literature.[29]

The forms of tradition employed in Q are common in the Synoptic tradition.[30] Sayings and the sayings compilations predominate to be sure, but alongside these one also finds parables, brief scenes, and miracle stories. It is striking, however, that the other forms are virtually negligible in comparison with the various forms of the sayings tradition: the wisdom saying, the threat, and the legal saying.[31]

[91] Regarding the genre of Q as a whole, James M. Robinson has shown that a genre of λόγοι ("sayings") can be identified, extending from Jewish wisdom literature to late gnostic texts, and that Q has its place in this history (1971b:103, 113). One must, however, object to Robinson's hypothesis, stated here and in another essay (1971a:41–46, 56–59), that the genre of Q is gnosticizing per se.[32] In the first place, that collections such as the paraenetic book of 1 Enoch and the Mishnah tractate 'Abot[33] —which belong to the same genre—can scarcely be considered as "gnosticizing" speaks immediately against this hypothesis. Moreover, the gnostic use of collections of sayings of Jesus,[34] of which Robinson makes much, is first attested only by the heretics against whom Polycarp of Smyrna struggles and not, as Robinson holds, already with the opponents of Paul in 1 Corinthians.[35] A gnosticizing character will have to be demonstrated from

---

some (e.g., Matt 12:38-42 [Q] and 16:1-4 [Mark]).

27. See esp. Wernle 1899:186–87; Wellhausen 1905:67; Bussmann 1929:35; Manson 1935:31; V. Taylor 1959:266–67; Polag 1966:123; against this view, Harnack 1908:180.

28. In Luke, 22:30 (to which Matt 19:28 is parallel) follows this pericope, but it appears in a Markan context.

29. Compare, e.g., the Didache. See on this point Bornkamm 1961:25–28; repr. 1971b:179–82.

30. On the forms, see Harnack 1908:163–72.

31. Miracle stories: only in Q 7:1-10 and Q 11:14; but see also Q 7:22 and Q 10:13; see Bultmann 1968:240–41. Parables: besides the parousia parables (Q 12:39-46 and 19:12-27), 15:3-7; 13:18-21; 7:31-32; 14:15-24. The form of controversy story is wanting in Q; see Bultmann 1968:52. Therefore there are no controversies about the Sabbath (and none of the miracles in Q is a Sabbath healing).

32. Robinson 1971b:104–5, 113; 1971a:43. Also against this view is Polag 1966:129.

33. The common title, Pirke Aboth, is first encountered in the Middle Ages. See Maass 1937:9 n. 1.

34. Koester has demonstrated the existence of such sayings collections in the Apostolic Fathers. [The reference is to Koester 1957.—ED.]

35. Pol. Phil. 7.1: "And whosoever perverts the oracles [λόγια] of the Lord for his own lusts, and says that there is neither resurrection nor judgment,—this man is the first-born of Satan" [ET by Lake 1912–13:1.293].

an investigation of Q, not simply asserted from observations regarding the genre.[36]

Robinson's suggestions remain valuable, however, since he has succeeded in discovering an illuminating description of the genre of Q. It explains the one-sided preference for sayings and groups of sayings even in the expansion of brief scenes, such as in Q 7:18-35 and Q 11:14-23. Of course, the development in Q is not as far advanced as it is in the *Gospel of Thomas*, which, in accord with its incipit [**92**] οἱ λόγοι οἱ [ἀπόκρυφοι οὓς ἐλά] λησεν 'Ἰησοῦς ὁ ζῶν . . . ,[37] merely arranges individual sayings or small groups of sayings with the stereotyped introduction "Jesus says/said"[38] or sometimes with a question asked by the disciples. But Q lacks a prefatory saying such as Thomas has: [ὅστις ἂν τὴν ἑρμηνεί]αν τῶν λόγων τούτ[ων εὑρίσκῃ, θανάτου] οὐ μὴ γεύσηται.[39] A privileged understanding of the sayings of Jesus, possible only for certain pneumatics, does not lie within the scope of Q.[40]

36. Robinson's suggestions in 1971b:113 (see below, p. 70) and 1971a:43 are not sufficient.

37. ("These are the secret sayings that the living Jesus spoke. . . .") Greek text of *Papyrus Oxyrhynchus* 654 according to Fitzmyer's reconstruction, following the Coptic text of the *Gospel of Thomas* (NHC II, 80:10–11). See Fitzmyer 1959:513. While Garitte (1960a:171; repeated in Garitte 1960b:335–49) regards *P.Oxy.* 1, 654 and 655 as retroversions from Coptic, the majority of critics rightly assume that these three papyri and the *Gospel of Thomas* derive from an older Greek text. See Quispel 1958–59:277; Till 1959:449; Guillaumont 1960:333; Cullmann 1960:324, ET 1962:421–22; Haenchen 1961b:157–60 (on Garitte); Schrage 1964a:252–53. Edition of the Oxyrhynchus texts: White 1920. Fitzmyer's reconstruction of the Oxyrhynchus texts on the basis of the Coptic text is taken over (with minor variations) by Aland's *Synopsis* (1985). Another reconstruction is offered by Hofius 1960:21–42, 182–92.

38. This uniformity should be ascribed to redaction even if the sayings themselves are older.

39. "Whoever finds the interpretation of these sayings will not taste death." Text: Fitzmyer 1959:513, following NHC II, 80:12–14.

40. As early as 1930, Bacon (1930:91) referred indirectly to the formal relationship between Q and the newly discovered *Gospel of Thomas* (in the form of *P.Oxy.* 1, 654, 655). The literature on the *Gospel of Thomas* has frequent references to the common character (e.g., Cullmann 1960:330, ET 1962:434–35; North 1962:169–70; Schulz 1964:141–42; Koester 1971a:135–36). Now Robinson has situated this question in a larger context in his abovementioned essay (cf. also Koester 1971a:135–36). Wilson (1958–59:276) correctly points out that the discovery of the *Gospel of Thomas* does not prove the existence of Q; how Bartsch (1959–60:258) can say that the *Gospel of Thomas* is proof for the non-existence of Q is beyond me. Notwithstanding occasional essays, the interpretation of the *Gospel of Thomas* has not been pursued sufficiently from a form-critical standpoint (cf. Koester 1971a:130–32; source criticism has been dominant here too. Quispel (1958–59:289; 1957:189–90) and Till (1959:451) have adopted Puech's "two-source theory" (Puech 1957:160: *Gospel of Thomas* = the *Gospel of the Egyptians* + the *Gospel of the Hebrews*; cf. Cullmann 1960:328, ET 1962:430; Haenchen 1961b:162, 176 against Cullmann's solution). Doublets prove the composite nature of the *Gospel of Thomas*, but to allot the material to various related sources that we know only by name is a questionable matter. Now Koester has proposed an interesting thesis: "The basis of the *Gospel of Thomas* is a sayings collection which is more primitive than the canonical gospels, even though its basic principle is not related to the creed of the passion and resurrection" (Koester 1971b:186). "It must have been a version of Q in which the apocalyptic expectation of the Son of man was missing, and in which Jesus' radicalized eschatology of the kingdom and his revelation of divine wisdom in his own words were dominant motifs" (ibid.). As questionable as I find Koester's attempt to see in the *Gospel of Thomas* a prototype of Q, I do think

THEOLOGY

[93] What then is the scope of Q? The most important redactional motifs are the opposition to Israel[41] and the announcement of judgment. The opposition to Israel is no longer an opposition to its leaders, as is partly the case in the tradition, but is extended in blanket form to Israel as a whole, to "this generation." This extension is made particularly evident by the attachment of the threat made against the whole of Israel (Q 11:49-51) to the speech against the Pharisees, and by the comparison of the request for a sign (Q 11:29-32) with the Markan version (8:11-13). In connection with this point one can again note the surprisingly frequent contrast of the Gentiles with Israel, partly in sayings that come from Jesus and partly in community constructions.[42] Its frequency in Q makes it a characteristic feature for determining the theology of the redaction of Q. The announcement of judgment against this generation creates a decisive opposition between Jesus and the community on the one hand and Israel on the other: for Israel there remains only judgment.

Davies described this opposition:

> Moreover, [94] an examination of all of the material in Q, as far as we can reconstruct it or in so far as it is preserved, reveals that it brings into prominence two things, that the coming of Jesus was a crisis of the old order and the inauguration of a new and that this crisis, as this implies, centres in the figure of Jesus himself. (1966:382)[43]

But here Davies overlooks the fact that for Q this motif is not grounded christologically in this way; besides, the term *crisis* is far too general a description.[44]

Before coming to the question of the Christology of Q, however, I need to make a brief digression. Jesus' proclamation of the imminent βασιλεία τοῦ θεοῦ ("kingdom of God") was taken over in Q just as it was in the Markan tradition and in the special material of Luke and Matthew.[45] Because of the strong emphasis on the announcement of judgment that, as has been shown, is characteristic of the redaction of Q, this proclamation is ab-

---

that new directions for further work on the *Gospel of Thomas* are indicated here (see Koester 1971b:170–87).

41. See Harnack 1908:230: "But the opposition to the present generation in Israel, to the 'evil and adulterous generation,' which would bend the people of God to its will, and the conflict against its spiritual rulers the Pharisees, are nowhere more sharply brought out than in this source." Also Bultmann 1913:36 [p. 26 in this volume].

42. The following are probably community constructions: Q 10:13-15; 11:31-32 (cf. Bultmann 1968:112–13); see also Q 7:1-10. Q 13:28-29 may derive from Jesus himself.

43. Note his argumentation with respect to this assertion. It is not enough simply to add up the various assertions in Q; it is necessary to ask about Q's formative motif.

44. Davies's statement is more applicable to Matthew.

45. In Q: 6:20; 7:28; 10:9; 11:20; 13:18, 20; 13:28; (Q 14:15); 16:16.

sorbed into the apocalyptic expectation of judgment. Even if this expectation of judgment originated with Jesus himself,[46] in Q at least it has been emphasized in a one-sided manner and has become a decisive factor in the interpretation of Jesus' proclamation of the βασιλεία.[47] Therefore one can even speak of a "re-apocalypticizing" of the proclamation of Jesus in Q; of course, the obvious references to the delay of the parousia indicate that this cannot be the only reason for the redaction of Q.[48]

Tödt rightly stressed the fact that the passion kerygma plays no role in Q (1965, esp. 275–77). When Kümmel objects "that in the Palestinian community in which Q must have originated, [95] the passion kerygma repeated by Paul (1 Cor 15:3-5) was formulated at a very early date and that it attests the *redemptive* significance of Jesus' death" (1975:73), the problem is made even more urgent if Q does not, as Tödt and Kümmel suppose, come from the Palestinian church but was rather first compiled in the Hellenistic church. Kümmel's remark—recalling Dibelius's description of Q (1935:233–46), "that apparently Q was organized for the need of the community itself, for whose existence the primitive Christian kerygma was a presupposition"[49]—remains unsatisfactory if one considers how, on the one hand, for Paul and the deutero-Pauline epistles the kerygma was the starting point for theological reflection[50] and therefore a formative motif; and how, on the other, Mark revised his tradition with the kerygma in view (see Bultmann 1968:347–48), even if he did so quite transparently. This feature is completely absent from Q. Tödt's recognition[51]—following Bornkamm and to which Kümmel obviously assents[52]—that, despite the absence of a passion kerygma, Q is very probably determined christologically suggests that the solution is to be sought in another direction.

It is now evident not only in Q but in the Synoptic tradition generally that the passion kerygma is in no way the formative motif, and indeed in Mark it frequently functions as an alien element. One may ask whether, in addition to the various dynamics of individual traditions that become visible in form-critical investigation of their respective *Sitze im Leben*, there are not also completely distinct Christologies that have shaped the Synoptic

---

46. Kümmel (1964) summarizes the state of the question. Yet this seems to me to be an open question. Of course, it is connected with the classification of the sayings concerning the coming Son of Man.

47. See above all Q 11:20 together with Q 11:29-32.

48. At the same time, it shows how little the delay of the parousia was really a problem for early Christianity (see Bornkamm 1968:46).

49. Kümmel 1975:74. Compare ibid.: "In any case, the source Q owes its existence to the need of a Christian community that separated itself from Judaism, to strengthen its faith in the Advent and the awaited fulfillment of the kingdom of God by appeal to the traditional words of the risen Jesus and to provide guidelines for its preaching."

50. In addition, paraenesis is grounded in the kerygma: see Romans 6.

51. Tödt 1965:244-53; Bornkamm 1958:759.

52. Kümmel 1975:73; see also Conzelmann 1969:97.

tradition.[53] Thus for instance, the miracle stories in Mark, in much the same way as [96] the σημεῖα ("signs") of John, offer a Christology[54] that cannot easily be reconciled with the passion kerygma, and that Mark connected with the passion kerygma only by considerable effort through the "Messianic secret."

Tödt sees Q's dominant christological motif in the renewal of the proclamation of Jesus.[55] But this thesis must be made more precise. Like Jesus himself, the disciple must proclaim the imminence of the βασιλεία τοῦ θεοῦ (Q 10:9); but as has been shown above,[56] the proclamation of Jesus has already been given a special interpretation, namely, the announcement of judgment. In the same way the preaching of the disciples means the announcement of judgment for those who refuse it. The announcement of judgment now applies not only to Israel alone but has been extended. For the Christology of Q that extension means that the continuity between Jesus and the community is found in eschatology, not in the kerygma.[57] Jesus is not what is proclaimed; [97] instead, the content of the proclama-

---

53. Even Tödt (1965:234–35, 268) speaks of two distinct spheres of tradition ("Son of Man" and "kerygmatic"); cf. also Georgi 1986:16–74. Wilckens attempts to trace the traditional stratum of the kerygma to the Stephen circle that later emigrated to Antioch (Wilckens 1965–66:335). In the chaos of the Jewish War the two branches of tradition came together (ibid.). Koester demonstrates four distinct forms of early Christian Jesus-tradition: Gospels in the form of sayings collections, as aretalogies, as revelation discourses, and as a Gospel defined by the Credo. Thus he differentiates not only form-critically but also historically among various branches of tradition, not all of which are determined by the kerygma (see his comments on Schniewind: Koester 1971b:165–66). One could also mention the pre-Markan passion tradition as another branch of tradition unmarked by the Credo; see below, n. 57).

54. On this point see Robinson 1971a:51–58; Koester 1971b:187–92.

55. Tödt 1965:232–50. Neither Tödt nor Bornkamm (1958:759) thinks that their assertion that Q does "not yet" presuppose the passion kerygma (Tödt 1965:234 [=1959:215]—to my knowledge, the only place where "noch nicht" ["not yet"] is used)—is a proof of Q's relative antiquity (although Kümmel 1975:73 uses it this way). This formulation is, however, misleading.

56. See pp. 66–67.

57. The concept of "continuity" (or discontinuity), which has played such a large role in the recent debate about the historical Jesus, is burdened by this matter, for this problem could only arise from the Pauline statements or from the tradition of the kerygma, which Paul used in his theology. As long as one agrees with form criticism in seeing in this kerygma the independent interpretive background for all early Christian tradition—distinguished according to various Sitze im Leben—the problem has a general validity. But as soon as one asks historically about various, more-or-less independent traditions, the problem of the "proclamation of Jesus and the proclaimed Christ" may be associated with only a single branch of tradition, that of Paul and his tradition (see also Wilckens, 1965–66:336–37). For example, the apostles' miracles in Acts, just as the promises in the mission speech and of the secondary Markan conclusion, reflect a conception that proceeds from the continuation of the deeds of Jesus in the actions of the disciples: "signs and wonders" were not only performed by Jesus in the past; they happen from now on through the disciples ("in Jesus' name"). The conflict between Paul and his opponents in 2 Corinthians indicates how Paul had to come to a completely different conception of (dis-)continuity on the basis of the kerygma (2 Cor 13:4; see also the peristasis catalog [in 2 Cor 11:23–29]). In contrast to both ideas, Q reveals a third, independent one: continuity exists in the adoption of Jesus' proclamation of judgment. Besides these, still other possibilities exist for showing the continuity between Jesus and the community (Luke! Matthew!).

tion is the coming judgment, in which Jesus as the Son of Man will save his community.[58]

Accordingly, besides υἱός ("son," Q 10:22), one encounters only "Son of Man" and κύριος ("Lord")[59] (esp. in the vocative) as christological titles in Q. Except in Q 7:6, the latter designates the eschatological judge, while the former refers to the Son of Man who is coming for judgment and who has already come. Even if the Christology of Q cannot be comprehended solely in terms of the titles mentioned here, these titles nevertheless provide a clear indication of how determinative eschatology is for Q. By contrast, the disciples never appear as individuals (Peter, John, etc.), not even as οἱ μαθηταί ("the disciples"), but only as "the followers" (ἀκολουθεῖν) (see Harnack 1908:153). This fact may be an indication that for Q the community continues the preaching of Jesus in an unbroken succession, not through the mediation of the authority of the disciples.

One set of sayings that are clearly influenced by late Jewish wisdom[60] turns out to be the latest stratum, and therefore the stratum that is chronologically, although not necessarily tradition-historically, nearest the redaction of Q. That datum may not at first glance [98] be surprising, since the influence of this current on the preaching of Jesus is recognizable elsewhere in the Synoptic tradition.[61] But, the frequency and the special character of these sayings and the patterning of Q as a whole on a genre deriving from sapiential literature indicate that this influence had considerable importance in the transmission of Q.

This point is seen immediately in the way in which Q uses the OT.[62] Apart from the temptation story (Q 4:1-13), which is unique in other respects too,[63] Q has only one quotation from the OT that is identified as such: Q 7:27. The reasons for this may be that controversy and didactic stories, which conduct their arguments by means of quotations, are entirely lacking in Q and that, in addition, even the redaction of Q does not elaborate the account with OT quotations, as is the case with Mark and especially with Matthew.[64] Nonetheless, besides allusions to several biblical texts (e.g., Q 7:22), Q has frequent allusions to entire OT episodes—comparable to other Synoptic pericopae such as Mark 2:25-26 and Luke 4:25-27.[65] These include allusions to Solomon and the queen of the South (Q 11:31), Jonah and the Ninevites (Q 11:32), Noah and the Flood (Q

---

58. Compare also 1 Thess 1:9-10, which is of course based on the kerygma.

59. See Harnack 1908:153. The χριστός ("Christ") title in Matt 11:2 of course belongs to Matthaean redaction.

60. See Q 7:35; 11:49-51 (13:34-35); 10:21-22; 11:31-32.

61. See Bultmann 1968:69–108; Bornkamm 1960:106–9.

62. On the use of the OT in Q, see Tödt 1965:266–69 and Manson 1951-52:319–20.

63. Lührmann elsewhere (1969:56) expresses doubt as to whether the temptation account belongs to Q at all. It is included, however, in Lührmann 1985—ED.

64. Compare also the pre-Markan passion account.

65. See further Jas 2:21-26 (and on this, Dibelius 1976:166–67) or Hebrews 11 and the sapiential survey of history in Wisdom 10 and Sirach 44–50.

17:26-27), Sodom (Q 10:12), and Tyre and Sidon (Q 10:13-14). In Q 11:51 the entire history of Israel (ἀπό . . . ἕως) is embraced.

The way in which the OT is used in Q—which is distinct from allusions to OT figures, as occurs in Q 12:27 or Q 13:28[66]—points to a sapiential interpretation of the historical material in the OT that, as [99] the excursus on Q 17:26-30 showed,[67] has clearly had an influence on the subsequent expansion of Q that Luke used in his Gospel. A paraenetic aim, admonition to watchfulness, is especially clear in Q at this point; other passages contain the typically Q form of the threat, and all of these probably originated in the tradition of the community.

The interest that the redaction of Q had in these threats is seen precisely in the fact that with the help of these threats[68] Q develops its motif of the announcement of judgment. In Q 10:12 and 11:30, such threats are created by redaction. As much as it is already characteristic in the tradition taken over by Q, the way in which Q uses the OT is therefore also a distinctive feature of the redaction of Q, insofar as it confers on Q a characteristic stamp over against other Synoptic collections, and insofar as it is consciously used in the redaction.

The influence of late wisdom in Q is therefore clear. To be sure, Jesus is nowhere identified with Wisdom herself, as Wilckens suggests and as Robinson also indicates.[69] This identification cannot be concluded on the basis of Q 11:49, 7:35, or any other text. The pericope in Q most obviously influenced with sapiential imagery (Q 10:21-22) designates Jesus not as σοφία ("Wisdom") or λόγος ("Word") but as υἱός ("son"), even if the idea of λόγος is in the background. The continuation of this pericope (Matt 11:28-30), which is lacking in Luke but which may derive from Q, recalls quite clearly the speeches of Wisdom. But even this recollection does not make it an explicit identification.

The interest in Q 10:21-22 is not in the first place christological but rather soteriological: the emphasis falls on the conclusion of Q 10:22: καὶ ᾧ ἐὰν βούληται ὁ υἱὸς ἀποκαλύψαι ("and to whomever the Son wishes to reveal him"). [100] Following immediately after a threat against those who reject the preaching of the disciples, and forming the conclusion of a long complex in Q on the theme of discipleship, this text serves to justify the claim of the disciples: one's status at the judgment depends on the response

---

66. See also Q 10:23-24 and 16:16.

67. [Lührmann (1969:75-83) catalogs the allusions to Noah and Lot in Sir 16:5-10; *Jub.* 20:3-6; *T. Naph.* 3:4-5; 2 Macc 2:4-5; Wis 10:4-6; Philo *Vita Mosis* 2.263; and various later texts, observing that this use of historical example is a new development in sapiential tradition.—ED.] Compare Sir 47:22; 2:10 (Baumgartner 1914:189); 16:7-10. Eberharter (1911) shows in long parallel registers how thoroughly Sirach is interlaced with allusions to the OT. Compare also the use of OT stories in the paraenesis of the *Testaments of the Twelve Patriarchs* or *4 Ezra*.

68. The Son of Man sayings are related to these.

69. Wilckens 1971:517; Robinson 1971b:113 (above, p. 58); see also Feuillet 1955:164.

to their preaching, precisely because what was hidden to the wise and understanding has been revealed to them, the babes.

The arrangement of materials in Q means in the first place that the incorporation of Jesus' proclamation of the βασιλεία into the apocalyptic announcement of judgment is rationalized, from a history-of-religions point of view, with motifs deriving from wisdom. Again we see what was already clear from the exegesis of Q 10:21-22: that apocalyptic and wisdom, which, in the development of late Judaism, had already influenced each other, should not be considered as mutually exclusive entities in the history of the Synoptic tradition but must be seen in their interplay. That the association of the two cannot be regarded simply as the coexistence or succession of different strata is shown in Q 10:21-22 and most clearly in Q 11:49-51, where Wisdom is the speaker of a threat.

In Q 10:21-22, therefore, the continuity between Jesus' preaching and that of the community which was seen in eschatology is now grounded christologically—not in the kerygma but in the mediation of salvation by the Son.[70] The exclusive nature of his mediation of salvation presupposes the claim of the community. That this exclusivity is not yet conceived in gnostic terms is indicated by the content of the proclamation. In contrast to the *Gospel of Thomas*, it is not a matter of a ἑρμηνεία ("interpretation") of the sayings of Jesus that preserves one from death but the response to these words that in the judgment is decisive for life and death.[71]

CONCLUSION

Thus, in rough outline one can sketch a redaction that shaped and presented the [101] material of tradition from definite editorial perspectives. It remains an open question whether a single redactor or a larger circle is responsible for this redaction; the redaction probably reflects a distinct community that had transmitted the materials that were collected in Q. One cannot dispute that this redaction already found the essential motifs in the tradition, especially that of the announcement of judgment. Yet the uniformity with which this motif is deployed in diverse pericopae indicates that the redaction consciously employed it in the shaping of the material.

For the problem of the history of the Synoptic tradition, the redaction of Q signifies in the first place a combination of the two disciplines of source criticism and form criticism. While source criticism regarded Q as only one of the two (or possibly four) sources that Luke and Matthew used, form criticism opens a vista on the history of the tradition lying behind this source. Of course, this inquiry does not investigate the history of the individual forms but rather the composition history of discrete blocks of assembled Q-traditions. It was also shown that the analysis of "collection" and

---

70. Of course, this does not function as an answer to the problem of theodicy, as it does in Wisdom of Solomon.

71. On the *Gospel of Thomas*, see above p. 65.

"redaction" can uncover a history of forms inasmuch as new forms, complex literary types, and large-scale forms[72] come into existence through the collocation of originally isolated and form-critically diverse units, which in the case of Q is mainly the expanded apophthegm.

A source-critical approach is not an ahistorical, form-critical investigation oriented only to universally applicable laws of tradition and to a model of the progressive development of tradition from simple to complex—which of course neither Dibelius nor Bultmann had in mind.[73] Instead, the source-critical [102] approach includes historical questions from the very outset, simply because they have to do with the question of the historical priority of Mark and Q over Luke and Matthew. The helplessness and wrong moves of the purely source-critical approach do not dispense one from dealing with the questions that it raises about the setting and intention of the sources, about the relationships between these sources and the treatment of existing sources by later redactors. These questions again come into prominence in redaction criticism, in contrast to a form-critical discipline oriented only to the history of the forms. But redaction criticism is also in conscious continuation of form criticism.[74] This work is an attempt to raise these questions in connection with Q.

With due allowance made for the individuality of the material that was investigated, one can propose a place for this source within the history of primitive Christianity. The collections edited by Mark on the one hand, and the sayings collections to which Koester and Robinson refer, up to and including the *Gospel of Thomas*, on the other, show that Q belongs to a widely circulated genre for the recording of the preaching of Jesus, yet one that kept expanding into other contexts.[75] Its particular orientation to the announcement of judgment and its continued proclamation by the disciples make Q an entity of a special kind within the Synoptic tradition and in the

72. See Koch 1969:23–26. But the concept of a complex literary type (*Rahmengattung*) does not seem to me to indicate clearly enough that *new* forms can actually come into existence through the absorption of smaller forms into larger ones.

73. See Dibelius 1935:287–301; Bultmann 1968:1–7. Dibelius of course inquires only into the *form* of Q (paraenesis) and therefore also about its *Sitz im Leben* (the teacher's admonition of the converted community). He is inclined to see Q only as a "stratum" (*Schicht*) rather than as a "document" (*Schrift*) and thinks that Mark wished only to provide an extract of this "stratum" (Dibelius 1935:233–35; similarly, Wernle 1899:212). By contrast, Bultmann, at least in his chapter on "Collections," inquires into the place of Q in the *history* of the Synoptic tradition (see also Bultmann 1913 [chap. 1 in this volume]). Other matters (e.g., the respective treatments of the passion narrative by Dibelius and Bultmann) illustrate the difference in their approaches. The approach of the present work is closer to that of Bultmann than to that of Dibelius. But I think that the question of the history of primitive Christianity has come more strongly to the fore for NT theology, as various recent approaches show. Of course, this question cannot be silenced in a "theology of history."

74. See Gerhard Iber's remark in the postscript to the 3d ed. of Dibelius (1959:310–12); also Bultmann's description of the "Editing of the Traditional Material" (Bultmann 1968:321–28). See also Iber's remarks on redaction criticism as form criticism in Dibelius 1959:307 n. 2 (commenting on Held 1963).

75. Robinson has proposed this idea following the preliminary work of Koester (1971a:135–43; see also Harnack 1908:187–92).

history of its genre. From the perspective of the history of religions, [103] Q presents a picture that is as typical for primitive Christianity in general as it is for the Synoptic tradition insofar as it cannot be adequately compassed either by "apocalyptic" or by "wisdom." Rather, elements of both currents come into play in the traditional material as well as in the redaction. The Christology of Q is as little influenced by the passion kerygma as must be assumed to be the case with the Synoptic tradition in general. It represents instead a specific type of Christology that is oriented to the continuation of the work of Jesus through the church's taking up of his proclamation, interpreted with the announcement of judgment in view.

Luke and Matthew have joined Mark with Q in varying ways, and thereby have created in various ways the compromise between Q's tradition of Jesus returning in judgment as the Son of Man and Mark's tradition shaped by the passion kerygma. In Luke this compromise is seen in the interpolation of the motif of the suffering Son of Man (17:25), deriving from Mark, into a context taken from Q (Luke 17:22-37).[76] In Matthew the union of Q and Mark leads to a transformation of the genre of "gospel" created by Mark. Of course, Matthew takes over the outline of Mark; but the importance that speeches have in his Gospel, each marked off by stereotyped formulae forming caesurae in the Gospel,[77] and the obligation of the disciples to observe what was commanded by Jesus in the final commissioning (Matt 28:20; cf. also 10:27)[78] show that in Matthew the motif of the continuation of Jesus' message that came from Q has become a foundational motif. The motif of the announcement of judgment is also found in Matthew in a double form, just as in Q: on the one hand, against Israel, especially in the Matthaean interpretation of the three parables in Matt 21:28—22:14;[79] and on the other, this time in contrast to Q, in a Matthaean reformulation that even the church is headed for judgment (see Bornkamm 1963:38-51) In Matthew, in contrast to Q, there is a much stronger christological and salvation-historical reflection, which from a source-critical perspective is the result of the union of Q with Mark and other material. [104] But that the community from which Matthew obtained Q had already reworked Q and thereby created the preconditions for the Matthaean editing of Q will be demonstrated in the following analysis, designated as an appendix.[80]

---

76. See Conzelmann 1960:153 n. 3, who refers to the fact that Luke here makes use of the motif of eschatological suffering.

77. Matt 7:28; 11:1; 13:53; 19:1; 26:1.

78. See Bornkamm 1971a:222–24; and Trilling 1964:39–40.

79. See now Steck 1967:297–304; and Trilling 1964:55–65.

80. Lührmann 1969:105–21: Lührmann argues that Matthaean tradition shows a further Jewish Christian reworking of the Q-tradition.—ED.

5

Observations on the Son of Man
Title in the Speech Source

Its Occurrence in Closing and
Introductory Expressions*

HEINZ SCHÜRMANN

INTRODUCTION

1. An Observation

The starting point for the following arguments is an observable regularity: in the Synoptic Gospels the Son of Man title (about 69 times; setting aside parallels and derivatives, perhaps 35 times)[1] occurs in the speech material.[2] The title occurs just as frequently in the various layers of the tradition as it does in the redactional revision of the speech material. It occurs only in concluding and introductory expressions,[3] albeit in very different forms.

---

* First published as "Beobachtungen zum Menschensohn-Titel in der Redequelle," in R. Pesch and R. Schnackenburg, eds., *Jesus und der Menschensohn: Für Anton Vögtle* (Freiburg im Breisgau, Basel, and Vienna: Herder, 1975) 124–47. The essay appeared in a slightly revised version as pp. 153–82 in *Gottes Reich—Jesu Geschick: Jesu ureigener Tod im Licht seiner Basileia-Verkündigung* (Freiburg im Breisgau, Basel, and Vienna: Herder, 1983). The pagination indicated in brackets corresponds to that of the 1983 reprint. For the purposes of an English translation, Professor Schürmann has kindly provided the editor with a list of terminological adjustments to bring the article into closer correspondence with Schürmann 1991 (see below, note 109). He has also reworked various sections slightly, in particular §4 on Q 11:30. Preliminary translation by Neil Parker; revised by John S. Kloppenborg. (Abbreviations: S = *Sondergut*, special material, unique to one Gospel; Sv = Special verse [unique to one Gospel]; diff. = differs from.)

1. Cf. nevertheless, in addition, Acts 7:56 (in dependence on Luke 22:19) and the approximately twelve occurrences (cf. *v.l.*) in John (add to that 5:27 without the article). Cf. also υἱός ἀνθρώπου—not as title—in Heb 2:6 (following Dan 7:13 LXX) and further Rev 14:14; cf. 1:13.

2. I include apophthegms with speech material. Now and then Son of Man sayings are secondarily attached to pieces of narrative (cf. Mark 9:9, [12] par.; Luke 19:10) or inserted at the end (cf. Mark 14:41 par. Matt). In all other cases the occurrence of the Son of Man title is also proven to be secondary—cf. Mark 2:10 par.; 14:62b par.; Luke 22:48; 24:7; Matt 26:2.

3. The interpretation of the parable of the weeds would be one exception, unless one were permitted to understand the Matthaean depiction—with some justification—as a concluding illustration of the parable. Moreover, with Jeremias (1972:81), one must distinguish two parts.

This tendency in placement can be shown to be the case throughout the Synoptic tradition, [154] but here I can demonstrate (and carefully evaluate) it more exhaustively only in the traditions of the Speech Source.

The thirteen Son of Man sayings (=14 occurrences) in Mark use the title only four times by way of introduction (see Coppens 1981b). In each of the doublets of 8:31; 9:31; and 10:33-34 a saying sequence opens with reference to the suffering Son of Man. The same is true of the account of the last supper in 14:18-21, which has two references to the suffering Son of Man. Elsewhere in Mark, Son of Man statements are added to a dominical word by way of explanation (14:62b), possibly as a word of commentary (cf. 2:28). Son of Man sayings can terminate a series of sayings, debate, or speech composition (cf. 2:28; 8:31, 38; 10:45; 13:26). Finally, they can even be inserted into, or added to, a piece of narrative material. Hence in Markan redaction and tradition, logia, series of sayings, and speech compositions, even pieces and sections of narrative had the tendency to grow by means of concluding (and occasionally introductory) Son of Man sayings. This growth can only raise doubt as to their originality. This doubt grows stronger when one notices that not a few Son of Man logia in Mark (however they may be conditioned in inner-Markan tradition) depend on one another. Of course, I cannot defend this observation here. But the following comparisons are noteworthy in this connection: compare 9:31[4] with 8:31; 10:33, also with 14:21 (bis); 14:41; 9:12 (9); cf. also 10:45b with Mark 14:24; and further, 14:62b with 13:26.[5]

The special Matthaean material does not appear to know the Son of Man title. Yet where Matthew—undoubtedly or presumably—redactionally inserts the Son of Man title himself, he employs it by way of introduction to the earthly Jesus (13:37 [S]) or the Jesus who is proceeding to his passion (16:13 diff. Mark;

There is the allegorical explanation in 13:37-39 and the description of the separation of sinners and righteous ones at the end of time in 13:(40), 41-43 (cf. the parallel in 13:49-50!). Both mention the Son of Man title by way of introduction.

4. For more details cf. Schürmann, 1969:536–38; 1974:21.

5. There remain few Son of Man logia that can be questioned as to whether they have reached Mark from the tradition. Of these, the majority of those which designate the earthly (cf. 2:10; 2:28) or suffering (see 9:31 and its derivatives) Jesus as "Son of Man" require that one not regard them as genuine. The "suffering Son of Man" is a paradoxical *theologomenon* of Markan redaction, perhaps even Markan tradition. Mark 10:45b is certainly dependent on the liturgy of the Lord's Supper, and 13:26 appears to originate from apocalyptic traditions. In 8:38 Mark gives evidence of access to a tradition that also survives in Q (cf. Q 12:8-9; see below, §5). Can these possibly pre-Markan traditions support the assertion that Jesus had spoken of himself as the coming Son of Man? Cf. additionally the findings and helpful remarks of Vögtle below in nn. 17, 52, 59, 64, and 91.

26:2 diff. Mark). In all other passages relating to the coming or judging Son of Man, he uses the title in a variable manner in the development of more extensive units (13:41 [S];[6] 16:28 diff. Mark; 19:28 diff. Luke; cf. 25:31 [S]; 24:30a [Sv] diff. Mark).[7] That should not surprise us, since eschatological outlooks often come in conclusions. [155] It is all the more striking that Matthew— except in 16:28—always mentions the title by way of introduction in the respective individual logia of these concluding formulations. Apparently, Matthew redactionally uses a title that is almost out- dated in his community—mostly in dependence on his Synoptic sources—as a cipher to introduce Jesus' majesty or to christologize apocalyptic texts.

Luke uses the Son of Man title, which his special material does not seem to know any longer, where his Markan and Q sources have it. Now and then he also employs the title redactionally—yet always in dependence on Mark or Q.[8] He adds the coming Son of Man in an introduction in 17:22 (S) and in 18:8b in a conclusion (see below, §9); in 17:25 (S) he inserts the Son of Man who must suffer by way of commenting on a saying (see below, §10);[9] in 19:10 (cf. Mark 2:17b and the reference back to Matt 10:23) he adds the earthly Son of Man and in 21:36 (cf. Mark 13:26) the judging one, in each case as a conclusion. Moreover, in 22:48 and 24:7 Luke inserts, respectively, the earthly and the suffering Son of Man—both passages taken over from Mark 14:41b (?). Luke ev- idently employs the title only as a copyist, in dependence on his sources; his community no longer used it as a title in preaching.

"Our gospels may be regarded as having been committed to writing between 70 and 100 A.D. In this period the title Son of Man had long been obsolete in proclamation and teaching, as is proved for this period and earlier by the collection of Pauline Epistles, which does not know the word."[10]

2. Methodological Requirements

What we can establish in Markan redaction or Markan tradition, and in Matthaean and Lukan redaction, also becomes apparent in the Speech

---

6. See above, n. 3.

7. Theisohn (1975) believes that he is able to demonstrate the influence of the parables of *1 Enoch* for Matt 13:41; 19:28; 25:31.

8. See further details in Schneider 1975:267–82. According to him Luke accentuates in particular the Son of Man's path of suffering, his parousia as Savior, and the soteriological sig- nificance of the One who has come. Everything is integrated into the general conception of the Christ's path (1975:282).

9. In addition, cf. Zmijewski, 1972:286–310, esp. 291–94; Keck 1976, esp. 268–80, 295– 314. Keck also mentions opposing views on p. 276 nn. 95–96. See also Geiger 1973.

10. Schelkle, 1971–78:2.192; cf. Perrin 1967:154–206, esp. 164–65.

Source, though it is to be evaluated differently. Here too we find the coming (or judging) Son of Man[11] or the earthly Son of Man only in concluding and introductory expressions. [156]

In the course of Son of Man research,[12] conclusions drawn from the observations of "regularity" divorced from the necessary individual investigations have led repeatedly to misjudgments.[13] Here are some examples:

> May we, for instance, infer the *ipsissima vox Jesu* from the fact that the Son of Man title is always encountered on the lips of Jesus,[14] or, on the contrary, must we conclude that the Son of Man title is relatively late—Hellenistic—if it is not encountered in any early Christian confessional formula (Teeple 1965, esp. 250)? Again, does the fact that in the Gospels only Jesus speaks about the Son of Man allow the conclusion that he had differentiated between himself and the Son of Man?[15] Can we in fact gain access to "the oldest layer of the Son of Man logia" by disregarding the Son of Man words that have a parallel tradition without the title?[16] Again, it has been observed that the "Son of Man" and the coming βασιλεία in the NT (as in Judaism) are never encountered together in similar units of tradition. May we conclude from this that the Son of Man title,[17] or conversely that the βασιλεία proclamation, is to be denied Jesus? [157] Again, would "the statements concerning the present Son of Man" have "the precedent of authenticity" because they would have "no religion-historical parallels" (Schweizer 1963; Bammel 1964:20)? On the whole may we—

11. The "suffering" Son of Man of the Markan redaction, which is taken over and further disseminated by the Matthaean and Lukan redaction, is not known in the Speech Source. On the "interpretation of the death of Jesus being under the influence of the prophetic tradition and the Son of Man confession," cf. Hoffmann 1972:187–90.

12. See, apart from some contributions in Pesch and Schnackenburg 1975, and the older reports of research mentioned by Hahn 1969:42 n. 1, the following literature: Vögtle 1962 (up to 1961); Colpe 1972, esp. 400–401 (up to 1968); Marshall 1965–66, continued in Marshall 1970; and after that Maddox 1972 (very comprehensive); Coppens 1973.

13. Cf. Kümmel, 1973:79: "there necessarily follows the implication that the question as to the originality and the possible meaning of this on the lips of Jesus [I would add: and in the layers of tradition] can be answered only by an unprejudiced testing of each individual text." In characteristically contrary fashion—arguing from general criteria—is Teeple 1965.

14. Thus with many others, Cullmann 1959:155; Schweizer 1963:57–58; Maddox 1972:160; Goppelt 1981–82:1.180.

15. Bultmann 1951–55:1.29–31 and many following him.

16. Thus the title of the essay by Jeremias 1967; cf. idem, 1971:263–64.

17. Vielhauer 1965a, 1965b; Jeremias (1971:267) names H. B. Sharman and H. A. Guy as predecessors. Cf. already Käsemann 1964:46. Cf. also Conzelmann 1969:136 (expressly). See also the statement of Vögtle 1971b:27: "Lately the hypothesis that Jesus did not speak about the Son of Man at all is advocated ever more emphatically. This also proves to be not objective." (Vögtle adds a note: "Thus, among others, E. Käsemann, P. Vielhauer, H. Conzelmann, E. Haenchen, and finally H. Teeple, 'Origin.'") Even in this case "the belief in the parousia of Christ, the 'Marana-tha' of the original Palestinian community would be securely attested, moored, and established in an act of the revealing God, namely, in the resurrection of Jesus Christ." Cf. Vögtle below, esp. n. 91.

with the majority—proceed from the assumption that only one of the three groups of Son of Man words could be ascribed to Jesus, that the one in each case excludes the others (against this view, Maddox 1968–69)? Again, there are the "eight sayings of Jesus about the coming Son of Man that yield a consistent apocalyptic picture" (Colpe 1972:433) in which "a fourth tradition which is independent of Daniel, 4 Esr. and Enoch" is visible (438). Have at least the seven of these that are found in speeches to the disciples withstood tradition criticism, because "prior to the confession of Lk. 22:69 Jesus announced the Son of Man only in esoteric speech"?[18] It has been observed that once the title is used it is hardly ever lost again in secondary strata—and when it is, the reasons are always obvious;[19] can we draw from this observation the general conclusion that the title is a mark of sovereign "Christ-language"?[20] Can one conclude, from the important observation that the Q-sayings that (in their Lukan versions) speak of the coming Son of Man all use the form of the "eschatological correlative," that they emerged in the *pesher* tradition of Q?[21]

Such conclusions from general regularities must be a warning not to draw any hasty conclusions even from observations that I have just made. Still, one must attach significance to functional regularities because they teach us how to see and sometimes even let us make some assumptions. [158]

My interest here, therefore, is in the concluding and introductory Son of Man sayings of the Speech Source.[22] This is, however, a stratum that grows in the tradition and an amplified composition: At the beginning there were individual logia ("primary sayings" [*Grundworte*]), to which "auxiliary sayings" (*Zusatzworte*) of a different kind were attached. Thus we find "paired

18. Colpe, 1972:440; p. 457: Of them no fewer than six are in the special Lukan source [?]. Here Colpe presents the thesis of A. Schweitzer, that Jesus had spoken about the "Son of Man" as another figure in public but as himself in the presence of the disciples. It should be noted, of course, that Colpe does not employ these general criteria as a standard but relies on tradition criticism.

19. A secondary loss of the title seems to be attested in Matt 5:11 (see below, §1) and 10:32, (33) (see below, §5) diff. Luke, where the title is replaced by the first person. Cf. also Matt 16:21; diff. Mark 8:27; but here the title is only moved ahead from Mark 8:31 to Matt 16:13. Cf. also Matt 9:8 generalizing Matt 9:6. Mark loses the title in 3:28-29 (see below, §6). Luke avoids a doubling in 22:22. Nevertheless, he has hardly omitted it in Luke 22:27 diff. Mark and 22:30 diff. Matt. The antithetical parallelism in Luke 12:9 (see below, §5) does not repeat the title—unlike Mark 8:38 par. Luke 9:26 (cf. Matt 16:27).

20. On the phenomenon cf. Schürmann, 1968a:88. Cf. also Jeremias 1967:169.

21. So Edwards 1969. Edwards refers to the logia listed here as §§4, 5, 8, 9, 10 (twice).

22. Matt 19:28 // Luke 22:29 requires no investigation in the following, since the Son of Man title owes itself to Matthaean redaction. This is the case whether the Speech Source had been reproduced in both Gospels or only in Matthew. Cf. Matt 25:31 (see above, n. 7) and Schürmann 1957:37-54. Bammel (1970) believes he is able to find "the end of Q" in Luke 22:29-30. Also Luke 17:22, (25) cannot be ascribed to the Speech Source; cf. below, §§9 and 10.

sayings." Some of these pairs—often with additional auxiliary sayings—come together into "saying groups" (*Spruch-Gruppen*). From two or more of these are formed "structured compositions"—mostly for kerygmatic purposes. Eventually "dominical discourses" (*Reden Jesu*) arise from these, each having its own community *Sitz im Leben*.[23] The Speech Source was assembled from these. The first two and the last two stages of development in each case should presumably be closely associated (see the third section below, under §§2 and 3). We still lack material criteria[24] but beyond that also formal characteristics by which to delineate these four stages[25] (which in any case will always be only partially feasible).[26] Therefore a difficulty arises for our investigation: if we ask about the significance **[159]** of the Son of Man title in the Speech Source not only synchronically—inevitably an obscure question—and if our concern is not only a reasonable arrangement of the interpretive possibilities of meaning but also the effort to locate them diachronically in the four stages of tradition and redaction mentioned above; and if, further, we follow a functional interest and try to arrive at the *Sitz im Leben* of the Son of Man sayings, we must impose some restrictions. Our attention shall focus in a particular way on the question as to where the Son of Man sayings exercise their primary function. Are they are intended primarily to comment on a preceding or subsequent individual logion, or to complement it in some way? Must we attribute a commenting or complementing function to them in the final redaction?[27] Put differ-

23. On the question cf. Schulz 1964:138: "The thematizing of these groups of logia, . . . i.e., the pooling of them into systematic speech units, is largely the doing of the Q-redactor." Hoffmann (1972:3–4 n. 10) agrees with this judgment. Here I would prefer to judge more cautiously—at least more discriminatingly; see below, nn. 24 and 25.

24. So rightly Hoffmann 1975:113. In Schulz 1972:57–175, 176–489 much remains problematic in the distinction between the "kerygma of the oldest Q-community of the Palestinian-Syrian border area" and "the later Q-community of Syria." Hoffmann (1972) perhaps allows redaction to become too obscured in the process of tradition. Lührmann (1969) *ex professo* is concerned with this redaction (although he has not said the last word on this topic). The resigned skepticism of Hoffmann (1972) appears to me unfounded: "I would regard it as an unproductive and, from a methodological perspective, not sufficiently secure enterprise to wish to delineate the individual redactional stages of Q." In individual cases, at least, this delineation is quite possible and necessary. For more details see, in addition, Schürmann 1982.

25. Observations on "introductory" and "closing expressions," but above all on "commentary sayings" (which deserved a more thorough investigation), could have helped further here and elsewhere. For a more exhaustive treatment see Schürmann 1982 as well as the efforts of Wanke (1980, 1981). See also the results of Edwards 1969. It would also require a scrupulous removal of the Matthaean and Lukan layers in order to recognize the final redaction (see n. 27) of Q—a redaction-critical and tradition-historical elicitation of the "discourses" assembled in this "Speech Source."

26. Worthwhile literary-critical findings on the redaction of Q can be found in Polag 1966; 1977:3–29.

27. By "final redaction" I mean the stage of development of the Speech Source that, according to my working hypothesis, both the evangelists Luke and Matthew had before them in a more-or-less identical Greek form. Here I cannot agree with the judgment in the valuable work of Hoffmann (1972:3): Q "identifies itself with it [the tradition] indeed in such a direct way that we can infer as strong a temporal as a local and ideal proximity to the point of departure of the tradition." Cf. also the abridged version of Hoffmann's work (1970); cf. Hoffmann 1969, esp. "Jesus der Menschensohn" (143–47).

ently, did the Son of Man sayings appear at the first or second stages of tradition in the logia source mentioned above, or not until the third or fourth,
or only at the final redactional stage? (In what follows, assertions about the
above-mentioned intermediate stages will always claim only hypothetical
value.) Naturally this question is not identical with the next question: Does
the Son of Man title that exists in the pre-redactional Q-traditions still retain its basic importance in the final redaction of the Speech Source and for
its overall thought?[28] Yet perhaps our diachronic and functional framing of
the question can still be of some small help for the more synchronic subject
matter. [160]

In the following I briefly examine individually the ten[29] Son of Man
logia of the Speech Source in order then to attempt an overall assessment.

THE TRADITION-HISTORICAL LOCATION
OF THE SON OF MAN SAYINGS
IN THE TRADITION OR THE REDACTION
OF THE SPEECH SOURCE

1. Q 6:22

The original trilogy of Q 6:20b-21 has grown secondarily by the addition
of Q 6:22-23—probably before 6:24-26 was added (cf. Schürmann
1969:339–41; 1982). In a certain respect Q 6:22-23 is an auxiliary saying
(Zusatzwort)[30] that reapplies the beatitudes for the time of the church to the
disciples: they are characterized not only as "poor" but additionally as
"persecuted."

The composition of Q 6:20-21, 22-23 exhibits numerous traces of having been redactionally joined together with 6:27-28, 32-33, 35 (Schürmann
1969:346–47, 358). The Son of Man title is not encountered elsewhere in
the composition of Q 6:20b-23 (24-26), 27-38 (39-49) (cf. only vv. 40,
46).[31] Nonetheless it probably should be ascribed to the Speech Source.[32]
Thus we may certainly attribute the title to a (secondary) composition in
[161] Q 6:20b-21, 22-23, which was previously transmitted in isolation. Q

28. On this point see below, in the evaluation.
29. Here I understand Q 17:26-30 as a logion (see below, §10) and will also include Matt
10:23 (S) (cf. below, §7).
30. So Schulz 1972:452–57, and the almost universal opinion.
31. The "Lord, Lord" address in Q 6:46 does not likely have the "Lord of the judgment"
in view and thus neither is the coming Son of Man in view. Indeed in Q 6:47-49 he does not
make his appearance as judge! The address [Lord, Lord] refers more generally to the confession
of Jesus—against Hoffmann 1972:309.
32. Luke would not have added the title (see above, n. 19). One may postulate it for the
Q-tradition since Matthew as a rule deletes it (Matt diff. Mark 8:31; cf. also Matt diff. Luke
12:8b). No doubt Luke has now and then inserted Son of Man logia (see above) in dependence
on his Markan and Q Vorlagen. But he never inserts the title by itself.

6:22-23 was attached to 6:20b, and then 6:27-35 made reference to 6:22-23 secondarily.

The question as to whether a logion that could originally have been transmitted independently underlies Q 6:22-23 does not have to be settled here.[33] No doubt the supplementation in Q 6:22-23 has acquired colors that tangibly reflect a post-Easter situation.[34] For that reason even the designation of Son of Man (diff. Matt 5:11), which here—placed in the mouth of the pre-Easter Jesus—has the earthly Jesus in view,[35] cannot be guaranteed as *ipsissima vox Jesu*. The title underlines how dangerous it is for his disciples to follow the one who will one day come as world Judge.[36]

2. Q 7:33-34

Q 7:33-34 is an "auxiliary saying" that secondarily applies the metaphor of the playing children in Q 7:31-32 to the Baptist and Jesus.[37] Perhaps the metaphor was originally connected to the invitation and the call to repentance of Jesus alone.[38] The concluding verse in Q 7:35 still allows for the prospect of conversion. The titular use of "Son of Man" for the earthly Jesus[39] who is coming again at the parousia and judgment is certainly secondary, though perhaps Palestinian.[40]

But the Son of Man logion—along with Q 7:35—does not merely comment on the foregoing metaphor. At the same time it concludes [162] the entire section on the Baptist in Q 7:18-35.[41] Yet it is not formulated for the entire section but occurs as a result of the preceding metaphor. Moreover, because the title is not encountered elsewhere in 7:18-35 (cf. only vv. 19-20, 27),[42] one may posit that it existed in the unit Q 7:31-32, 33-35 as it was originally transmitted in isolation. This view is confirmed by the observation that Q 7:31-35 could not be joined thematically with the speech

33. As an individual logion Q 6:22-23 may have originally had "(Jewish) Christian preachers in view"—so Steck, 1967:259 n. 4; cf. v. 23c.

34. On the pre-Lukan tradition history of Luke 6:22-23, which is sketched here, cf. Schürmann 1969:332–36 for more details. In addition (and to some extent disagreeing) see, in particular, Steck 1967, esp. 20–27, 257–60, 283.

35. See the authors for and against this view in Schulz 1972:455 n. 399.

36. Cf. Hoffmann 1972:148, who does not "differentiate between the coming Son of Man and the Son of Man active on earth."

37. This is a widely held opinon. See, in detail (with references to commentators for and against), Schulz 1972:380–86 and Lührmann 1969:29–31. The contrary position is taken by Schweizer 1963:56–84, esp. 72–73; Jeremias 1971:261–62; Mussner 1959.

38. On the tradition history cf. Schürmann 1969:425–26 for more details.

39. So with Hoffmann 1972:147 and Schulz 1972:382–83.

40. See Tödt 1965:117–18, 138; Hahn 1969:42; Lührmann 1969:85 (above, p. 60); Schürmann 1969:428–29. According to Bultmann 1968:165, Hellenistic; according to Schulz 1972:66–68, 382, Hellenistic Jewish Christian.

41. On Matt 11:2-5 [*sic*] // Luke 7:18-23 cf. Vögtle 1971d.

42. The notion that the composition in Q 7:18-35 "as a whole is governed by the leitmotif of confessing the Son of Man" (Hoffmann 1972:230–31, cf. also 180, 231–33) seems to be something read into the text.

about the Baptist without the reference to the Baptist in 7:33-34. It is
therefore relatively old.

3. Q 9:57-58

The trilogy of Q 9:57-58, 59-60, 61-62 (S) sets forth by way of introduction in a "foreword" (Q 9:58) the homeless life-style of the Son of Man as
the fate in store for the disciple who is prepared to follow him. Q 9:57-58
indicates that a reenactment of the homeless life of Jesus is fundamentally
demanded of Jesus' disciples—and early Christian itinerant missionaries. In
the Q-tradition, an earlier form of Q 9:59-60 was formerly transmitted
with an earlier form of Q/Luke 9:61-62 (S) as a "paired saying."[43] Having
recognized this link, one can understand Q 9:57-58 as an introduction to
this unit, which has been secondarily placed ahead of it[44] and which at the
same time generalizes and motivates the demands in Q 9:60, 62. If, therefore, one perceives in the earthly Jesus, introduced in Q 9:58, the majesty
of the coming Son of Man, the difficult demands in vv. 60, 62 receive their
emphasis and motivation. Thus one may assume that Q 9:57-58 already
prefaced the "paired saying" (Q 9:59-60, 61-62) before the stage [163] of
tradition at which Q 9:57-62 was connected with the commissioning scene
of Q 10:1-12 (13-16, 17, 20).

It is likely that an early composition like Q 9:57-62, which may have
collected the (more or less combined) individual traditions, could have designated the earthly Jesus with the "Son of Man" title prior to the redaction
of the speech composition in Q 10 and the entire Speech Source. It could
already have seen in him the Coming One and the world Judge (cf.
Hoffmann 1972:149–50, against Tödt 1965:122). In an attempt to salvage
the saying as authentic,[45] one should not assume that the title here took the
place of an original "humankind" (der Mensch) and that there is a "translation mistake."[46] Even the supposition that the title has here taken the place
of an original "I" in the mouth of Jesus robs the personal declaration of

43. Here I cannot prove this point in further detail. See, nevertheless, the suggestions in
Schürmann 1968b:121; cf. also Hengel 1981:3–4; Hahn 1969:119 n. 99 [for the Lukan version of Q]. Taking a different position are Lührmann (1969:58 n. 5) and most others. The assumption of such a unit of tradition in Luke 9:59-60, 61-62 certainly does not mean that 9:61
must be just as original as 9:59-60. Cf. in addition Schürmann 1982:142–46, along with its
doubt as to whether service of the βασιλεία, specifically in vv. 60b, 62, was already
pre-Lukan.

44. Cf. also Schulz 1972:436: Q 9:57-58, 59-60 was "likely a tradition-historical unit from
the beginning."

45. Moreover, Q 9:58 is frequently given—albeit with different perspectives on the Son of
Man title—a chance of having been a previously isolated tradition. Schulz (1972:436 n. 240)
names E. Klostermann, R. Bultmann, and H. D. Betz. According to Schweizer (1963:72) it
could even be a question of "a historical scene." Cf. also Grässer 1973:51–52; Hoffmann
1972:91–92 n. 46: "There are no objections against the originality of Matt 8:20, apart from
those based on the Son of Man designation."

46. Cf. the authors noted in Schulz 1972:438 n. 260. Hoffmann (1972:90–91) rejects the
thesis of a translation mistake.

much of its weight and takes away its power to motivate the demands for discipleship. In any event, someone is speaking here whose majesty is evident from the Son of Man title, and it is from this basis that the argument gets its force. The demands of vv. 60, 62 require an appeal of this kind as their basis.

Perhaps this situation of the homeless itinerant Jesus was the occasion for Luke to place 9:57-62 before the commissioning scene of 10:1-16. Here we do not have to examine whether and to what extent the context Luke 9:57-62; 10:1-12 (13-16, 17, 20), 21-24 was shaped by Luke or by the redaction of the Speech Source or whether it already existed in an earlier stage of the Speech Source. It is sufficient to observe that the issue in Q 9:57-58 is not commissioning but sharing the homeless life-style of Jesus and a corporate imitation of his itinerancy. Q 9:57-58 was placed at the beginning in order to accentuate 9:59-62, not 10:1-16. The commissioning speech received its "foreword" (Vor-Wort) from a composition that already existed in 9:57-62. The Son of Man title was not introduced during the final redaction of Q. One can be quite sure of this conclusion, since the title is not encountered again in the context of the Lukan commissioning scene.[47] [164]

4. Q 11:30

The enigmatic saying about the sign of Jonah[48] in Q 11:29 is also found without the reference to Jonah[49] in Mark 8:11-12 (par. Matt 16:[1-2], 4, where it is augmented from Matt 12:39). In the course of transmisson, an interpretive saying (Q 11:30) has been added,[50] explaining the puzzling saying in 11:29: as the marvelous deliverance of Jonah was a sign establishing Jonah's credibility for Nineveh, so also will the Easter exaltation of the Son of Man be a sign from heaven (for all the world). He is the "light set upon a lampstand" (Q 11:33).[51] It is evidently an instance of a secondary addition.[52]

---

47. Hoffmann (1972:182) offers the following explanation: Here "the Jesus who sends out his messengers" would be "designated as Son of Man. That means, the authority of Jesus" would be "seen to derive from his dignity as Son of Man (cf. Luke 10:21-22 as an interpretation of Luke 10:2-16)." For details cf. 1972:102-42. I cannot agree with this view.

48. Cf. in addition esp. Vögtle 1971c, and more recent literature in Bultmann 1971:45 (supplement to Bultmann 1968:118 nn. 1, 2).

49. The "sign that is Jonah" (epexegetically) has originated in the redaction that added Q 11:30 as commentary.

50. I cannot pursue here the problem of the material content any further.

51. These last two sentences mark a significant shift from the 1975 and 1982 versions of the essay: "As Jonah was a sign of judgment for Nineveh, so also will the coming Son of Man bring judgment to Israel. (Matt 12:40 is then secondarily related to the fate of Jonah and that of Jesus.)" There, he added the note: "Matt 12:40 does not represent the original Q-version." Cf. the reminiscence in Matt 12:45c and also Vögtle 1971c:119–27.—ED.

52. Q 11:30 is scarcely conceivable as an isolated logion. Cf. also Vögtle 1971a:308 n. 43. Vögtle considers the possibility, indeed the likelihood, that apart from Mark 8:38 par.; Q 12:8-9 (see below, §5) even the underlying Son of Man word was secondary. "Thus both inter-

Q 11:30 was probably added by way of interpretation before 11:29-30 was combined with Q 11:31-32. For in Q 11:30, the coming Son of Man is (ἔσται)[53] the "sign." But in Q 11:32 Jesus, like Jonah, is only a preacher of judgment (and is not in this respect a "sign"). Further: while Jonah's preaching led Nineveh to repentance, the one who is "more than Jonah"— Jesus—was not successful in calling Israel to conversion.[54] Q 11:30 has been secondarily added to Q 11:29 before 11:31-32 was inserted between the primary saying (11:29-30) and the supplemental saying, Q 11:33 (34-35). Therefore, [165] Q 11:29 scarcely served 11:31-32 (cf. v. 32: Jonah) as its introduction at an earlier stage, prior to the insertion of v. 30.[55]

The new unit, 11:29-30 (31-32),[56] having also grown prior to the final redaction of Q through the addition of Q 11:33-36, was appended to the Beelzebul speech (Q 11:14-26). (The variant in Mark 3:[20-21], 22-27 did not yet include the Son of Man saying.) Thus Q 11:30 does not merely form an addition to the preceding logion; as a constituent part of the composition of Q 11:29-32, with its reference to the κυριότης ("lordship"; cf. Q 6:46) of the "Son of Man" (11:30) being "more" than Solomon and Jonah (11:31, 32), it also accentuates—right at the end—the entire Q-version of the Beelzebul speech. The suggestion that the interpolation of Q 11:30 must have occurred only during the redaction of the Speech Source (see n. 55) cannot be proven, since threatening speeches to Israel can also be found along with the judgment in the early layers of tradition.[57] Obviously Q 11:30 genuinely interpreted the unintelligible logion in Q 11:29. Q 11:29-32 (33-36) as a whole, then, enhanced the Beelzebul speech in 11:14-26 by means of a threat of judgment.

5. Q 12:8

"An essential result of recent discussion is an insight that suggests itself to the observer, namely, the settling of the Son of Man problem depends quite

---

pretive sayings that were formulated as Son of Man words would be secondary, and the answer of Jesus, as is indeed likely, would be confined to Matt 12:39 // Luke 11:29."

53. With the majority I understand ἔσται temporally, not gnomically—as δοθήσεται in v. 29.

54. The 1982 version of the essay reads at this point: "To be sure, if Q 11:30 had been secondarily inserted between Q 11:29 and 11:31-32, this would probably have resulted in the clearer introduction into the Son of Man title—'more than Jonah'—of the idea of the earthly Jesus who called Israel to conversion, in agreement with Q 11:32. (Presumably the verse, even at this stage, is meant to be understood as it is in its present Lukan context)."—ED.

55. Against Lührmann 1969:34-43, 99 and Hoffmann 1972:99, 181 n. 92, 186, who see the final redaction of Q at work here.

56. The reverse order in Matt 12:41, 42 allows the two Jonah sayings to follow one another directly. On the question of greater originality, opinions differ; cf. Lührmann, 1969:38 n. 1.

57. Lührmann (1969:84-85; above, pp. 59-60) is willing to ascribe the "idea of judgment against Israel" to the Q-redaction only "hypothetically." Cf. also 1969:34-36, 43-45, 93, and elsewhere. He notes that this motif was already present in the tradition (1969:101; above, p. 71).

heavily on the understanding of the double saying in Q 12:8-9."[58] To the extent that one might regard the Son of Man title that refers to the earthly and the suffering Jesus [166] as inauthentic, and imagine only the coming Son of Man on the lips of Jesus, Q 12:8 would thus assume decisive importance. For here Jesus does not seem to identify himself with the coming Son of Man.[59] In this context, I cannot treat in detail the content of the speech or the question as to whether and in which sense the saying can be ascribed to Jesus. According to Q 12:8,[60] the Son of Man, as distinguished *verbaliter*[61] from the Jesus who is speaking, professes himself in the judgment of the world to those who confess Jesus. In Q 12:9, however, those who deny Jesus on earth are thereupon denied (passive!).[62] The variant in Mark 8:38 (par. Luke 9:26 // Matt 16:27b) contains only the negative half of the double saying of Q, but there it uses expressly—and no doubt originally—the Son of Man title.

In the Speech Source the requirement of confession (Q 12:8-9) concludes the paired saying on the theme of freedom from fear and anxiety (Q 12:4-5, 6-7), which itself ends by promising a reward. Thus it is attached for the sake of Q 12:4-5, 6-7. For its part, the sayings pair in Q 12:4-5, 6-7 follows the call to proclaim in Q 12:2-3. Hence the saying in Q 12:8-9 points back—beyond the motive of fear in Q 12:4-5, 6-7—right to the beginning, as it were. Therefore it is indirectly also the conclusion of the saying group in Q 12:2-3, 4-7. Q 12:8-9, however, is not directly appended to 12:4-5, 6-7 on account of Q 12:2-3. [167] Rather it has become the closing expression of the whole composition in 12:(1), 2-7 only accidentally.[63]

An early addition allows one to recognize the further addition of Q 12:10, 11-12, which must have occurred on account of 12:8-9 (see below). It would also allow one to explain the different kind of arrangement by Mark, who probably had not seen in their Q-context the logia that are dis-

58. So Haufe 1966:140. Cf. Lührmann 1969:40-41 n. 6: The decision as to whether at least some Son of Man sayings could be traced back to Jesus himself "must fall within the scope of the interpretation of Mark 8:38 and Luke 12:8-9 // Matt 10:23-24."

59. Vögtle (1974:177) considers the likelihood that Luke 12:8-9 par. Mark 8:38 is secondary (see above, n. 52): "On no account can the forms of understanding Jesus as Son of Man mentioned above claim for themselves a historical certainty. As a very widely held opinion would admit, Jesus could have spoken about the future Son of Man in purely objective fashion. Indeed, the apocalyptic conception and expectation of the Son of Man could not have been transferred to the parousia of Christ until the post-Easter period." Cf. the same point also above in n. 17 and below in nn. 64 and 91.

60. The variant in Mark 8:38 par. Luke 9:26 proves that the emphatic "I" of Matt 10:32-33 is not original. It also establishes the fact that Matthew as a rule replaces the title with an "I." See above, n. 19. It is true, however, that Matthew can also insert the title—no doubt everywhere by himself. Cf. 16:13 [cf. Mark 8:31], 28; 24:30a; 13:37, 41; 25:31; 26:2). Cf. Schneider 1975:273; cf. also Higgins 1975.

61. Vielhauer (1965b:106-7) might have discerned rightly that we do not have here two persons in the post-Easter period but two epochs of activity by the same person. Cf. also Conzelmann 1969:135 and Schulz 1972:72.

62. See Schulz 1972:69: "Luke wanted to avoid a clash of the forgivable blasphemy of the Son of Man with the following logion."

63. Hoffmann (1972:306) insists that Q 12:8-9 hearkens expressly back to Q 12:2.

tributed throughout Mark 3, 4, 8, and 13. Thus the Son of Man title here is used in an early layer of tradition to which the tradition of the Speech Source and Mark—probably independently of each other—had access. For all that, the logion is certainly still not proved to be a genuine dominical saying.[64]

6. Q 12:10

The Markan variant in 3:28-29 in itself allows one to recognize Q 12:10 as a unit once transmitted in isolation.[65] But the designation of the Jesus of his earthly days as the "Son of Man"[66] in Q 12:10 probably attests to [168] later linguistic usage.[67] The further growth of the amplified saying group 12:(1), 2-7, 8-9 with the addition of the logion Q 12:10 once again contains a Son of Man word as a closing expression. (Matthew combines the logion with the variant in Mark 3:28-29 and incorporates it into the Markan sequence.) The primary function of this auxiliary saying (Q 12:10) is evidently to (correct and) supplement Q 12:8-9. To reject Jesus (who will be the coming Judge of the world)[68] and his proclamation in the days before Easter can, indeed, still be forgiven—according to the corrector. Refusal, however, of the Spirit-borne post-Easter proclamation or of the testimony of the Spirit of Q 12:11-12 (assuming that it was earlier connected with Q 12:10) can no longer be forgiven.

More than Q 12:8-9 alone, however, the new saying (12:10) now also concludes the amplified saying group in Q 12:(1), 2-7, 8-9. But then a new

64. The exegesis since Vielhauer appears to incline more and more to the view that the logion is not intelligible in the mouth of Jesus, because here "in the Son of Man confession there is already a retrospect question about the significance of the historical Jesus. This is no longer a 'naive' expression of the authority of the historical Jesus but is a conscious formulation of the identity and difference between Jesus and the Son of Man" (so Hoffmann 1972:155–56). Hoffmann mentions other exegetes for (Hahn, Tödt, Marxsen) and against (Käsemann, Conzelmann, Lührmann) (1972:155–56). Vögtle is also critical of this view; see nn. 17, 52, 59, 91 here. But the assumption of a post-Easter origin of this logion also renders improbable the widely held thesis (which is essentially based on Luke 12:8-9) that Jesus had indeed spoken about the coming Son of Man but did not identify himself with him. See above, n. 15.

65. This conclusion, therefore, does not support the view that "originally . . . the saying" belongs "to Jesus' defence against the charge of being in league with the devil" and must be explained from this context: against Tödt, 1965:118. The Markan version is not the more original as many have thought since Wellhausen 1911. Cf. also Bultmann 1968:131; 1971:52–53 (containing a detailed review of research). Against this position are Tödt 1965:312–18; Schulz 1972:246–50 (247 n. 485 for exegetes for and against); and the majority of the more recent exegetes. In addition, on the theme of the logion see Lövestam 1968; Thyen 1970:253–59; Colpe 1970.

66. In Mark 3:28-29 Jesus talks about the "sons of men" and not about the "Son of Man." This reference appears to be a secondary assimilation to the Markan context (cf. Mark 3:22, 30) and Markan Christology.

67. Cf. Schulz 1972:249: it "might . . . belong in the more recent Hellenistic–Jewish Christian tradition of Q." But this is not so certain; see above.

68. Cf. Hoffmann 1972:150–52 against Tödt 1965:119, where also one finds further details on the interpretation of this difficult saying.

conclusion, Q 12:11-12 (which Matthew conflates with its Markan variant in Mark 13:11), is added to this. (Alternatively one might view Q 12:8-9 as a primary saying with 12:10 as an auxiliary saying, and suppose that this pair, along with the logion Q 12:11-12 added as a conclusion [*Nach-Wort*], was added en bloc to the saying group Q 12:[1], 2-7.) But it is hard to discern the redactional intention that deliberately concluded the saying composition in Q 12:(1), 2-7, 8-9 with Q 12:10 without assuming that in Q, 12:10 (11-12?) was not referring to Luke 12:2-3 but to its parallel (Matt 10:26-27). Thus in the introduction and the conclusion, two different periods of proclamation would have been designated. But this assumption remains burdened with elements of uncertainty. More likely, the addition of Q 12:10 itself is not due to the editorial designs of the final redaction of Q. [**169**]

7. Matt 10:23 (S)

If the suggestion that has been made elsewhere[69] is correct, that Matthew found Matt 10:23 in the Speech Source functioning as a commentary and supplement to Q 12:11-12, one should also consider this logion as a conclusion. It was appended to the judgment logion in 12:11-12—probably already in an earlier stage of tradition (cf. the variant in Mark 13:9, 11 with 13:10)—and now serves to supplement it. Matthew 10:23 "is a word of consolation . . . that takes up the assuring promise of the coming of the Son of Man, originating wholly in Palestinian Christendom as an expression of the confident end-expectation of the first generation" (Vögtle 1971a:331). If this is true, then it is unlikely that it was appended only at the final redaction of the Speech Source. In keeping with its primary function, Q/Matt 10:23 indeed supplements Q 12:11-12. To this extent Q 12:11-12 + Q/Matt 10:23 quite aptly and accidentally concludes the entire saying composition in Q 12:(1), 2-10 with a view of the saving Son of Man.

8. Q 12:40

Q 12:40 is a redactional conclusion that in the first instance specifically interprets the metaphor in Q 12:38, 39 on the basis of the coming Son of Man and, at the same time, concludes the saying composition in Q/Luke 12:35-39,[70] which Matthew must have also read in some other form.[71] The discrepancy between the metaphor, which portrays a calamitous event, and

---

69. Schürmann 1968b:150–56; and 156 for the literary addendum. Cf. already Knox 1957:51. Tödt (1965:48), "to simplify matters," lists Matt 10:23 "among the . . . sayings of Q." He does this "especially since tradition-historical and material connections are clearly manifest." (Cf. also ibid., 56–57, 60, and elsewhere). Cf. also Polag 1966:98–100; further Giblin 1968; Künzi 1977, esp. 158–59, 162.

70. A variant exists in Mark 13:33-37 (cf. Luke 21:34-36) as Luke has recognized (cf. Luke 12:41 with Mark 13:37).

71. Compare φυλακή in Matt 24:43 with Luke 12:37 and ἐγρηγόρησεν with Luke 12:37.

its application to the [170] coming Son of Man probably points to a secondary expansion.[72] It is indeed less likely that Q 12:39-40 had earlier served as the introduction for Q 12:42-46 (47-48). Perhaps the composition in Q 12:35-40 had continued to grow secondarily in the Q-tradition through the addition of Q 12:(41), 42-46 (47-48). If so, the Son of Man saying would have earlier functioned as a conclusion—a conclusion that thus would have been added prior to the redaction that added Q 12:42-46 (47-48).

9. Q 17:24

In Q 17:24 the Son of Man is found in the "so" half of this correlative statement.[73] Comparison with Matthew shows that there was a pre-Lukan combination of Q 17:24 with 17:23 (cf. v. 21)[74] (Zmijewski 1972:346). Yet this certainly does not mean that this combination is original; simply compare the variant in Mark 13:21-22.[75] The logion in Q 17:24, which was probably never transmitted in isolation,[76] undergirds the warning in 17:23 (just as the logion in Mark 13:22 buttresses the warning in Mark 13:21).

The description of the parousia of the Son of Man has found its way into early tradition in the unit Q 17:23-24. This development suggested the secondary addition of a further Son of Man saying (Q 17:26-30) (see below)—prior to the Lukan [171] insertion of Luke 17:25.[77] In turn, this addition occasioned still further pre-Lukan or Lukan additions (see below).

10. Q 17:26-27, 28-30

The comparison in Q 17:24 is illustrated and expanded by two incidents from the OT, one from the days of Noah (Q 17:26-27), the other from the days of Lot (Q 17:28-30; cf. Matt 24:39b). The apodosis of the comparison (Q 17:24b) containing the Son of Man statement is repeated in Q 17:26b, 30, in each case in a somewhat different form.[78] Neither of these two re-

72. Cf. Jeremias 1972:48-51. Cf. the metaphor of the thief applied to Jesus again in Rev 3:3; 16:15, and applied to the "day" in 1 Thess 5:1-11; 2 Pet 3:10.

73. On Luke 17:(20-21), 22-37 see, besides the literature above in n. 9, Schnackenburg 1970 (and the literature mentioned there).

74. Luke 17:22 is likely a Lukan formulation that adds by way of introduction the idea of the Son of Man, who is longed for by his own as their savior—a characteristically Lukan idea (cf. 21:28). Through this addition he worked in 17:24, 26-30, as the majority of scholars hold (cf. Schulz 1972:278 n. 90). The same influence probably occasioned the expectation of the Son of Man in the Lukan addition in 18:8b.

75. Luke 17:23 is clearly not taken over from Mark 13:21-22 par. Matt 24:23-24, as the Q-version in Matt 24:26 shows (against Lührmann 1969:72). The parallel in Mark 13:21, 22 makes it unlikely that one could find an earlier unit in Q 17:24, 37b (against Tödt 1965:48-49; Lührmann 1969:72; Schulz 1972:278-81).

76. But v. 24 had some equivalent, as the variant in Mark 13:22 suggests.

77. Luke 17:25 is a Son of Man logion even if the Son of Man title is not repeated. But it too originates in Lukan redaction and is influenced by Mark 8:31a par. Luke 9:22: thus the majority of exegetes (cf. Schulz 1972:278 n. 91). On the Lukan character of 17:22, 25, see Zmijewski 1972:417-20.

78. In Luke 17:26 (diff. Matt) the plural "the days of the Son of Man" (otherwise in Luke

lated examples really illustrates the apocalyptic parousia of the Son of Man in Q 17:24—at least in Luke.[79] On the contrary, they describe it as a judgment on secularized humanity.[80] This discrepancy with 17:23-24 indicates a secondary addition. At an earlier stage Q 17:30 may have concluded the composition in Q 17:23-24, 26-30. Then, at either a pre-Lukan or a Lukan stage, it would have grown further by the addition of 17:31, (32), 33, 34-35, 37; 18:1-8. One might note that the Son of Man title appears with increasing frequency and emphasis (Q 17:[22], 24, 26, 30) in the discourse that in all likelihood concluded the Speech Source.[81] The same holds true of vv. 26-27 in the eschatological discourse of Mark 13:5-29 (cf. also Luke 21:28, 36 diff. Mark). But the fact that the title is emphasized still does not prove that an emphatic use of the title belongs to the final redaction.[82]

[172]

TRADITION-HISTORICAL EVALUATION

The foregoing survey of the ten Son of Man sayings of the Speech Source has shown that these—in varying manner—occur mostly as "conclusions" and occasionally as "introductions." This state of affairs calls for a functional explanation and a diachronic evaluation.

As long as the larger compositional units of Q that can be reconstructed from Matthew and Luke and their layers of tradition have not been educed with certainty,[83] one can venture only preliminary judgments as to the classification of Son of Man sayings into the second-stage "saying groups" and the third-stage "structured compositions" or "dominical discourses" (the fourth compositional stage). But one can be more certain about having shown that throughout Q, Son of Man sayings, as auxiliary sayings, rest upon (other) individual logia, providing a commentary on them (the first compositional stage), and that Son of Man sayings cannot in any case be credited to the final redaction with any security.

17:24, 30 par. Matt) could be Lukan as it is in Luke 17:22.

79. The repetition of the Son of Man logion in Matt 24:37, 39b indeed reveals that Matthew has abbreviated it. Cf. Schnackenburg 1970:229; differently Bultmann 1968:117; Schulz 1972:278; Lührmann 1969:75–83. Zmijewski (1972:452-57) leaves his judgment unsettled.

80. In Luke 17:31-32, 33, 34 the faithful are exhorted to make an effort to escape this judgment of the Son of Man.

81. Cf. Lührmann (1969:75), who follows Harnack 1908:177–78, 179.

82. According to Tödt 1965:271, the "sayings concerning the coming Son of Man"—with four exceptions (!)—are supposed to be "placed together in a subject-thematic category." But Q 17 does not permit one to discern any redactional intention on the part of the Q-redaction or the Q-tradition that is pertinent to this category. These exceptions (in six or seven instances!) already alert one to this fact.

83. See above, in the introduction (under §2); further, Schürmann 1982.

1. The Son of Man Title in Auxiliary Sayings

The foregoing survey of the Son of Man sayings in the Speech Source indicates that without exception they are joined to preceding[84] or following[85] individual logia, serving to comment on, (re)interpret, or supplement these *individual logia*. In the majority of these cases one can assume that the addition of these Son of Man sayings will have occurred prior to their being taken up into a completed composition,[86] though to prove this would, of course, require a more exhaustive investigation than I could offer here. What inferences does this twofold observation permit? [**173**]

(*a*) One might suggest that in the addition of Son of Man logia to individual dominical sayings, the interests of preaching—in the broad sense of commentary, (re)interpretation, or supplementation—are made plain. Son of Man sayings—probably all of them—had their *Sitz im Leben* in the explanatory, hortatory preaching (of early Christian prophets?). In most instances, words of admonition were accentuated with a reference to the Son of Man coming and acting in the judgment.[87] But demands and promises are underscored by reference to the majesty of the earthly[88] or exalted[89] "Son of Man." From that perspective, the widely held opinion that what we have here are independent, prophetic revelatory sayings, purporting to be words "of the Lord,"[90] becomes quite uncertain.

(*b*) Were these added sayings *secondary, auxiliary formulations*? Or were they individual sayings, originally transmitted independently—possibly even genuine sayings of Jesus? This question would certainly require a more thorough investigation of individual cases.[91] Unless other arguments

---

84. Cf. Q 6:22-23 (§1); 7:33-34 (§2); 11:30 (§4); 12:8 (§5); 12:10 (§6); 12:40 (§8); 17:24 (§9); 17:26b, 30 (§10); Q/Matt 10:23 (§7).

85. Q 9:57-58 (§3).

86. This conjecture or probability applies to all ten logia, as was noted when each was investigated. In many instances, the Son of Man logia fit into a composition of sayings only when connected with the antecedent saying for which it was intended. So (perhaps) Q 6:(20-21?), 22-23 (27-28, 32-33, 35) (§1); cf. 7:31-35 with 7:18-23, 24-27 (-35?) (§2); 9:57-58 (59-62) (§3); 11:29-30 (31-32) (§4); 12:(2-7), 8-9, 10 (§§ 5-6); 12:11-12 + Q/Matt 10:23 (?) (§7); 12:(35-38), 39-40 (§8); 17:23-24 with 17:26-30 (§§ 9-10).

87. Cf. Q 12:8 (§5); 12:40 (§8); 17:24 (§9); 17:26b, 30 (§10); Q/Matt 10:23 (§7).

88. Cf. Q 6:22-23 (§1); 7:33-34 (§2); 9:57-58 (§3); 12:10 (§6).

89. Q 11:30 (§4).

90. Thus frequently, since Bultmann 1968:127–28 (who appeals to H. Gunkel and H. von Soden). The thesis was developed in distinctive fashion by Käsemann 1969c, esp. 77–81; 1969a; 1969b; Schulz 1972:482, and elsewhere. Cf. in addition Colpe 1972:438: "First it contradicts all else that we know about primitive Chr[istian] prophecy that anonymous leaders of these churches should prophesy directly as Jesus (rather than speaking in the name of Jesus or developing or remodelling actual sayings of Jesus, as later)." For other arguments against Bultmann, see Neugebauer 1962 and the emphatic and well-documented treatments in Delling 1970, esp. 170–72. Also Hill 1973–74. See "Concerning the form and history of prophetic words" and "The origin of the prophetic-speech genre" in Bultmann 1971a:51–52. Cf. now also Müller 1975 and Schürmann 1982:129 n. 45.

91. Cf. above, n. 12. In the foregoing I could not pursue this question in greater detail. Yet I have previously mentioned suspicious facts that bespeak secondary formation. On the question cf. above, nn. 17, 52, 59, 64. Vögtle (1983:19) rightly stresses: "Even if Jesus did not un-

supervene, the designation of the sayings as interpretive[92] [174] permits one to make no more than a presumption in favor of the view that one may be dealing with secondary formulations or the secondary insertion of the Son of Man title into existing sayings.[93]

2. The Son of Man Title in Conclusions and Introductions of Groupings of Sayings

Both primary sayings [*Grundworte*] and logia that have been augmented by "auxiliary sayings" [*Zusatzworte*], functioning as either conclusions or introductions, find themselves integrated into "saying groups." This process would frequently have occurred at an early stage (before the saying groups developed into "structured compositions" or "speeches"). Son of Man logia can either conclude[94] or introduce[95] such paired sayings or saying groups. In six instances there is a suspicion that they earlier functioned as conclusions[96] to paired sayings that were later added to saying groups. In all ten cases, however, the primary function of these logia is to interpret their respective primary saying, not the composition as a whole. The question is not whether the Son of Man title was inserted in order to define redactionally a preceding or subsequent individual logion. What is at issue is whether the title as such was consciously used to define a comprehensive composition of sayings.

(*a*) From a thematic standpoint the coming Son of Man stands properly within an eschatological framework. Now since such an outlook quite appropriately [175] concludes saying compositions, the title thus sometimes finds its way into the *concluding formulations* almost by itself. On these occasions, at any rate, the Son of Man title as such was not used redactionally to accentuate the saying composition by way of conclusion. Yet there probably would have existed saying pairs or saying groups that were already

---

derstand and announce himself as the coming Son of Man/Judge, he claimed his present activity as something that mediated salvation," and "Jesus' claim of having been sent . . . could not be brought into line with any contemporary conception of a bearer of salvation."

92. For the most part the Son of Man title not only exercises its function (n. 37) within the respective Son of Man sayings themselves; it usually also accentuates—in this or similar fashion—the logion onto which the Son of Man logion in question builds "as a supplement." Cf. on the one hand Q 11:30 with 11:29 (§4); 12:8-9 with 12:2-7 (§5); Q/Matt 10:23 with Q 12:11-12 (§7); 12:39-40 with 12:41-48 (§8); 17:23-24 with 17:20-21 (§9); 17:26-30 with 17:23-24 (§10). Cf. on the other hand 6:22-23 with 6:20b-21 (§1); 7:33-34 with 7:31-32 (§2); 9:57-58 with 9:60, 62 (§3); 12:10 with 12:8-9 (§6).

93. It is doubtful whether the Son of Man title has anywhere secondarily intruded into existing logia. At best one can raise this question in Q 6:22-23; 7:34(?); 9:57-58; 12:8-9; 12:10. In the majority of cases it is set more or less securely and sensibly within its respective sentence, so that if one were to strike out the title, the Son of Man logia would all be vacated.

94. Cf. Q/Matt 10:23 (§7).

95. Cf. Q 6:(20b-21), 22-23 (§1); 9:57-58 (§3); 17:23-24 (§9).

96. Cf. Q 7:33-34 (§2); 11:30 (§4); 12:8-9 (§5); 12:10 (§6); 12:40 (§8); 17:26, 30 (§10).

eschatologically oriented by Son of Man logia. Occasionally, perhaps, these could have been consciously placed at the end of saying compositions.[97]

(*b*) Son of Man logia occur in the introductions of saying compositions only three or four times. Here the Son of Man title does not appear to function within the redactional intention of the more extensive composition.[98] There the matter rests. The self-designation 'Son of Man' is a characteristic of the early transmission of logia and of commentaries on logia.

3. The Son of Man Title in "Structured Compositions" and "Dominical Discourses"

One could suppose a redactional purpose from the outset if one saw that all ten Son of Man logia in Q introduce or conclude "structured compositions" or "speeches," many of which are framed as apophthegms. Since the majority of these compositions have their proper setting in the life of the community, one must first of all, from the standpoint of method, suppose a redactional intention for their composition. This intention, of course, would precede the compilation of these speeches into the Speech Source and their final redaction (although the two stages of redaction must not be considered without some relationship to one another). [176]

(*a*) These "speeches" *conclude* appropriately on an eschatological note.[99] For that reason they marshal "paired sayings" or "saying groups" that have eschatological expressions at the end and that, accordingly, often mention the "Son of Man." Thus the title has found its way into closing formations of "structured compositions" and "speeches" almost on its own. As such it bears no particular redactional emphasis in that context.

(*b*) The Son of Man logia that *introduce* groupings of sayings[100] have likewise come to stand as "foreword" for primary sayings. They attach themselves occasionally almost like a "prelude." Or they have come to stand in the introduction to more complete speech compositions, without the Son of Man title being repeated later in these speeches or used in such a way that it appears to be integral to them in some other way.

The preceding investigations have been able to demonstrate that each of the ten Son of Man logia has a supplementing or correcting function with respect to the saying with which it is directly connected. It is only in the company of their respective antecedents that they have—more or less accidentally—"found their way" into concluding or introductory sections

97. This placement could be deliberate in Q 11:30 (§4); 12:8-9 (§5); 12:10 (§6); 12:40 (§8); Q/Matt 10:23 (§7).

98. Thus it is found as a kind of "prelude" in Q 6:20b-23 (24-26) for 6:27-49 (§1); in 9:57-62 for 10:1-20 [21-24] (§3); in 12:39-40 for 12:(35-38), 39-46(-48) (§8); and perhaps in 17:23 (and continuing in 17:26-30) for the Q extent of the Lukan expansion in 17:20—18:10 (cf. the Lukan redaction in vv. 22 [25] [§9] and 18:10 [§10]).

99. Cf. Q 7:(18-30), 31-35 (§2); 11:(14-26), 29-32, (33-36?) (§4); 12:(1-7), 8-9, 10 (-12 + Q/Matt 10:23?; see above) (§§5, 6, 7); 12:(13-34, 35-38), 39-40 (§8).

100. See above, n. 98.

of structured compositions. Hence it is impossible to show that there was a deliberate redactional intention to bring the Son of Man title into play in the conclusions or introductions of such compositions.

4. The Son of Man Title in the Final Redaction

The *final redaction of* Q, belonging probably to a Hellenistic sphere, no longer inserted the Son of Man title on its own, so far as we can tell, but merely transmitted it. This practice is in keeping with that of Paul, who avoids the title, as well as that of the special Lukan and Matthaean material. Perhaps it even accords with the practice of Mark and John, who in each case reinterpreted the title and made it subservient to their respective Christologies (which, of course, I cannot discuss here). In another way it is also in keeping with the redactional practices of Luke and Matthew, who use the title merely scribally, as a cipher, as an expression of the [177] "language of Christ" (cf. Schürmann 1968a), or in the service of christological heightening. The Son of Man title, unintelligible as it was to Hellenists, vanished quite early from the living tradition of community preaching, even though the acquaintance of the evangelists with the Son of Man title proves that it was, after all—as a given—still usable (see above, in the introduction, §1).

Therefore, if the final redaction of the Speech Source probably no longer used the Son of Man title of its own accord[101] but merely transmitted it,[102] should one nevertheless not still view the title within the context of the redactional intention of the Speech Source,[103] within the context of

---

101. Is there a definite intention on the part of the *final redaction of the Speech Source* to make a specific statement by means of the Son of Man title? (Such an intention can be demonstrated for all four evangelists—each in quite a different manner, of course. See the suggestions above, in the introduction under §1.) To be sure, we could have considered this possibility on one condition only: the final redaction would have to have intentionally placed the "eschatological speech" of Q 17, which deals essentially with the coming of the Son of Man in judgment, at the end of the Speech Source (see above, §10). In that case, however, beyond the function of eschatological coming and judging, the Son of Man designation of Q 17:24, 26, 30 remains quite colorless.

102. Thus also Hoffmann 1972:99: "The exclusivity with which Tödt claimed the Son of Man Christology for Q [see above] stands in need of . . . modification and precision. One cannot restrict the identification of Jesus and the Son of Man to the redaction of Q (in the narrower sense of Lührmann); it already belongs to the antecedent tradition." Yet what is the relationship of tradition and redaction to one another? Cf. above, nn. 23–25.

103. Certainly one can, with Hoffmann (1972:98–101), ask whether the definitive Q-redaction identifies itself with the Son of Man statements of its tradition. For a Hellenistic redaction and for Hellenistic hearers this is perhaps not so certain. It is not as certain as it is in Matthaean and Lukan redaction on the one hand, and in the Markan redaction on the other, where one can study it. See in the introduction above (under §1). Hoffmann regards the identification of Jesus with the Son of Man as "constitutive" for the Christology of the Logia Source (1972:82 and passim). But he then softens this clear statement considerably: "This thesis does not mean that the identification of Jesus with the Son of Man is the work of the Q-redaction. It means rather that the redactors of the Logia Collection have still been determined by this identification. This identification may even have taken place during an early phase of the history of Christianity" (1972:82 n. 2; cf. also n. 100 above). But even this state-

its Christology?[104] More readily than exponents of form criticism would be willing to admit, one must realize that exegesis exists only within the ambivalence between the *skopus* of the individual traditions that [178] contribute to the *skopus* of the overall redaction, on the one hand, and the *skopus* of the overall redaction that incorporates the *skopoi* of the individual traditions and gives each its emphasis, on the other (Schürmann 1969:v). Even if I cannot in the final analysis settle this question here, I should nevertheless not fail to mention two possible counterarguments:

(*a*) The Q-traditions that are taken up in the final redaction employ the title in each case quite irregularly, with the result that no uniform redactional tendency exhibits itself in any place or in any way. In the logia of the Speech Source that have been transmitted, the *coming* "Son of Man" assumes—intentionally or unintentionally—two functions. First, he transcends messianic expectations (expressly so in Q 17:24, but elsewhere as well). Second, he personalizes apocalyptic events (Q 12:33-34; 17:26). The Son of Man can be depicted in some places as more than a Judge (Q 12:40; 17:30), or in others as more than Savior (Q 11:30; 12:8; Q/Matt 10:23). His decision as Judge depends on the posture that a person has with respect to Jesus and his word (Q 12:8-9). This is the message that can be gained from the context of essentially all these passages. The *earthly* Jesus, however, is designated the "Son of Man" as a title of majesty in order to impart vividness and urgency to the demand for imitation (Q 9:57-58), to underscore the reward for perseverance during persecution (Q 6:22-23), to set forth the wretchedness of "the people of this generation" (Q 7:33-34), and to label blasphemy of the Spirit as the worst sin (Q 12:10). One's posture with respect to Jesus and his word, therefore, receives its eschatological significance by means of the Son of Man title.

No doubt, then, one can extract a certain general understanding from the Son of Man sayings of the Speech Source. This is especially true if one reads them in their more specific contexts. Even more strongly evidenced, however, is the fact that the traditions assembled in Q paint the coming Son of Man/world Judge in various bright colors. In consideration of his dignity as Son of Man, the Jesus of his earthly days is portrayed with ever more majesty. In this his sovereign office, however, his functions are again described in various ways. Indeed, one can hardly expect it to be otherwise in a collection of originally scattered traditions. A conscious redactional intention does not manifest itself.

---

ment would have to be presented more convincingly; see below, n. 106.

104. Consequently Polag (1977:185–86) and Lührmann (1969:40 n. 6, 85–86; above, pp. 60–61) are right when they differentiate rigorously between tradition (or the collection) and the redaction of Q and attribute the Son of Man title to the Palestinian community, but assign the redactional activity that no longer uses the Son of Man title of its own accord to the Hellenistic community. My observations confirm the correctness and the necessity of this differentiation.

[**179**] (*b*) But does the Son of Man title not, after all, acquire its function through *proclamation*?[105] Is it not in fact constitutive of it; is it not the fundamental basis of the proclamation of the word, as Tödt and (in a somewhat different way) Hoffmann suppose?[106] As far as the final redaction of the Speech Source is concerned, one can make such a claim only by overinterpreting the function of this title and by stretching its function to the whole of each speech composition that Son of Man logia either conclude or introduce, and to its other christological titles.[107] Or, one would have to give overarching significance to Q 12:8 in the final redaction (along with Tödt and others), or, finally, invoke Q 10:21-22 and read Jesus' majesty as the Son of Man into this statement about the Son (following Hoffmann 1972, esp. 102–42, and others). In fact, "this [last] reference is a valuable one, but it is not entirely satisfactory because the Son title is, after all, something different from the Son of Man title" (Gnilka 1970:119).

To conclude, the matter will have to rest here: the Son of Man sayings of the Speech Source expand on individual logia to which they are appended, functioning as auxiliary sayings, (re)interpreting, commenting, and correcting. As such they belong to a very early stage of tradition that transmitted isolated individual logia and smaller compositions. This finding has two different implications. On the one hand, the Son of Man title does not belong to the oldest stratum of the sayings tradition but must be assigned to a secondary, interpretive layer.[108] On the other hand, it means that Son of Man Christology is probably no longer the [**180**] basic and dominant Christology of the final redaction of the Speech Source. By that time, the Speech Source knew a number of titles for Christ and had various ways to express and present the majesty of the earthly Jesus (Stanton 1973). For its

105. Hoffmann (1972:100–101) emphasizes for good reason against Lührmann that what is at issue in Q is the "highlighting of Jesus' proclamation that Q repeats" (p. 101; cf. also below, n. 106). But is the Son of Man title constitutive for this message as Q repeats it? The later stage of tradition (i.e., of the speech compositions) and the final redaction are characteristically filtered and accentuated through the *Sitz im Leben* of the Q-communities. Here the message of Jesus received its practical and definitive coloring.

106. Cf. Hoffmann 1972:100–101: "It is not enough to assess the Son of Man expression merely as a traditional moment in the indictment. On the contrary, for the Q-group the belief in Jesus the Son of Man appears to ground and even condition the form of this proclamation: their preaching was precisely a repetition of Jesus' preaching."

107. Against this interpretation see above, nn. 31, 42, 47, 55, 63; differently Hoffmann 1972, esp. 152–58.

108. Although Schulz completely misrepresents the oldest logia tradition as the utterances of prophets (see above, n. 90), the view of Polag (1977) and Schulz (1972:481–83) commends itself, that the titular Son of Man Christology is not at home in the oldest logia tradition but rather in a subsequent, theologically interpreted layer (which, however, no doubt must still be Palestinian). The assumption here is that there had never been a nontitular use of "Son of Man." This conclusion also agrees approximately with Hoffmann's results (1972, esp. 182–87), according to which a prophet Christology used in the service of Sophia may have been secondarily superimposed in Q by the Son of Man conception. (One may surely ask, however, whether this result is sufficiently established by means of Q 7:34-35; cf. 9:58 on the one hand, and by means of 11:30 and 13:35 on the other. Conversely, are the wisdom traditions not instead superimposed on the Son of Man statements?)

Christology, the Speech Source appears not to be specifically committed to one or other title, and instead tries to express the majesty of Jesus with the help of sayings of Jesus that have been given narrative frames.

ADDENDUM

Colpe begins his informative survey of the main issues in contemporary Son of Man research with these words:

> The Son of Man problem remains vexing. Otherwise four generations of researchers would not have already broken their teeth on it. It has elicited paper after paper. Every volume, sometimes indeed every fascicle, of every biblical journal contains new contributions. The majority of them give the impression that in the aspect of the problem with which they are concerned, one must begin completely afresh. (Colpe 1981:353)

This state of affairs excuses me from including here the literature that has appeared since 1974. Nevertheless I must mention here—aside from the above-mentioned survey by Colpe—several stimulating works. These especially aid the Son of Man problem (and summarize copious literature): Berger (1976), and above all Kearns (1978, 1980), [181] Coppens (1981a; on Q, esp. 105–7, 155–86; there is copious bibliographical data here and in the religion- and tradition-historical essays on the Son of Man problem by Coppens 1961, 1973, 1976, 1979, 1983).

In the foregoing essay I did not wish to give the impression of beginning completely afresh in regard to the aspect of the problem that I tackled. But a methodological perspective, which does not seem insignificant, should certainly be expressed when it concerns the NT tradition history of this christological title, as well as the issue of the oldest Christology and Jesus' messianic consciousness. I am aware that a monograph would have to be written if the ten Son of Man logia of the Speech Source that I tackled are to be located tradition-historically with any degree of reliability.

In this essay what is at issue is essentially the above-mentioned methodological problem for works on the history of the Synoptic tradition. For the oldest layer of the Synoptic tradition J. Wanke has now made a contribution (1980). In this article he gives advance notice of his comprehensive work (Wanke 1981). He here highlights only "words of commentary" among the various forms of additions. In so doing he articulates the concept more precisely and more narrowly than I did above. The method tested in the present essay was used again in Schürmann 1982.

The last work of the late J. Coppens (1981a) contains a "Note sur l'article de H. Schürmann" [1981a:183–86], concerning which the editors of the posthumous volume provide the following information: "The analysis of the article of H. Schürmann, preserved on a separate sheet, seems to indicate that he was preparing himself to do the same" (1981a:xii).

Coppens himself begins his own analysis by saying, "To my knowledge H. Schürmann is the only author who tried to situate the logia of Q in the successive developments of this document on the basis of the criterion of the literary function that each [of the logia] had in it [Q]" (1981a:184). Here, I would certainly prefer to speak of a [**182**] "tradition-historical orientation." For attempts such as these in particular—and for the last stage of redaction—there are already predecessors. All systematic "attempts at arranging in layers" certainly remain hypothetical as long as we cannot say anything with any degree of certainty about the traditional and redactional layers of Q. (For further discussion, see Schürmann 1982).[109]

---

109. The original 1975 essay unhappily still called Q a *Redequelle* ("speech [sing.] source"). The tradition-historical approach developed here was further refined in Schürmann 1982. [While Schürmann now prefers *Redenquelle* (literally, "Speeches source"), this term is consistently translated as "speech source," since in English "speeches source" is awkward and one would normally suppose that a "speech source" would contain more than a single discourse. In the original version of this essay, Schürmann distinguished only three compositional phases prior to the final compilation of Q: "At the beginning there were individual sayings, to which 'commentary sayings' (*Kommentarworte*) were attached. These soon came together into saying groups (*Spruchgruppen*), connected by catchwords or by common theme. At the end of the process one finds 'speech compositions' (*Redekompositionen*), each of which had its own *Sitz im Leben* in the community. From these the Speech Source (*Redenquelle*) was compiled" (1975:128). In this newest reprinting and translation of the essay, Schürmann now distinguishes four stages prior to the final redaction (p. 79 above). This view corresponds to the position taken in his contribution to the *Festschrift* for Gerhard Schneider: "Beneath the layer of the final redaction of Q one can find (1) 'dominical discourses' (the fourth compositional form [= 4th CF]); (2) among and within these are 'structured compositions' (3d CF), and then (3) 'saying groups' (2d CF) and, finally, (4) existing within these as the basic building blocks, 'paired sayings' (1st CF), which have as their core a 'primary saying' (*Grundwort*) and an 'auxiliary saying' (*Zusatzwort*)" (Schürmann 1991:330).—Ed.]

6

The Literary Unity of Q

ARLAND D. JACOBSON

[**365**] The last two decades have witnessed a dramatic resurgence in Q research.[1] During the same period, however, an increasing number of scholars have questioned the two-document hypothesis or, sometimes, Q only.[2] These widely divergent trends have continued with almost no meaningful conversation between the scholars involved. Defenders of the Griesbach hypothesis, the major current alternative to the two-document hypothesis, have not reckoned with current Q research, attacking instead the classic presentations of the two-document hypothesis of Streeter and others. Q scholars, on the other hand, have made little effort to defend the two-document hypothesis which they presuppose.

In this article, I propose to reexamine some important aspects of the Synoptic problem and to suggest some new reasons why the Q hypothesis is worthy of continued use.

THE LITERARY UNITY OF Q

[**371**] The hypothesis of a written document (Q) used independently by Matthew and Luke was posited because it was a useful way of dealing with the Synoptic problem. The literary evidence was held to require it, and specifically to require a document rather than disconnected oral or written material, though some spoke of Q merely as an amorphous layer of material.[3]

From Arland D. Jacobson, "The Literary Unity of Q," *JBL* 101 (1982) 365, 371–89.

1. For some discussions of this research see Devisch 1972; Worden 1975; Neirynck and Van Segbroeck 1980.
2. See, e.g., Farmer 1976 (a slightly revised version of the 1964 edition, which is cited in this article). See also Dungan 1970. Stoldt (1980) rejects Markan priority as well as Q, but also rejects Matthaean priority.
3. Dibelius (1935:235), for example, preferred to think of Q as a "layer" of tradition.

But if this double-tradition material came from a single document, then it would be reasonable to expect the material to give some evidence of literary unity. If such literary unity could be found, it would support the two-document hypothesis and, of course, the Q hypothesis. At the same time, it would discredit the Griesbach hypothesis. For on the Griesbach hypothesis, "Q" is simply that body of material which Luke copied from Matthew but which Mark copied from neither; such an accidental body of material could hardly be expected to display any unity. However, if, on the Griesbach hypothesis, one still found it necessary to posit some body of sayings material used independently by Matthew and Luke,[4] then the discovery of literary unity in the double tradition would encourage the view that some of it at least came from a single written document.

One of the obstacles to the acceptance of the Q hypothesis has, in fact, been the objection that little or no unity could be found in the material. The force of this objection, however, was greatly diminished by the fact that Q was regarded simply as a collection of sayings.

Harnack investigated the vocabulary, grammar, style, and content of Q and, while noting a number of characteristics peculiar to Q, concluded that one could not demonstrate the unity of Q on the basis of its vocabulary or style (Harnack 1908:146–72). Nevertheless, Harnack noted, when compared with the synoptics, the content of Q *"appears to be undoubtedly more homogeneous than any of the three"* (Harnack 1908:167; Harnack's emphasis). [372]

In recent Q research, the old view, propounded by Streeter, that Q was simply a catechetical supplement to the Gospels (Streeter 1924:292), is being increasingly abandoned. The term *catechesis* is inappropriate to Q, as W. D. Davies demonstrated.[5] Beginning with Heinz Eduard Tödt (1965), it has become increasingly clear that Q embodies a kerygma independent of the passion kerygma. Other scholars, while using different approaches and coming to varying conclusions, have nevertheless contributed to the emerging picture of Q as a coherent document with its own theological point of view.[6]

Two things are to be noted about this recent Q research. First, it has, for the most part, simply presupposed the existence of Q. Thus it has neither addressed recent attacks on the Q hypothesis nor has it sought to describe the relevance of its findings to the Synoptic problem. Second, the inability

---

4. Several studies have indicated that in the double tradition, the Lukan version of a saying is often more primitive than the Matthaean (Talbert and McKnight 1972). Farmer acknowledges this point (1975:45–46) and argues that in such cases, Luke relied on "other source material—not another *source*"—rather than on Matthew. He concedes further that "on the Griesbach hypothesis, it is necessary to postulate such collections not only to explain a great part of the text of Matthew, but also to explain much of the text of Luke" (1975:46).—ED.

5. W. D. Davies 1966:366–80. James M. Robinson (1971b) worked out a new definition of the gattung of Q.

6. See Lührmann 1969; P. Meyer 1967; Edwards 1971, 1976; Hoffmann 1972; Schulz 1972; Polag 1977; Jacobson 1978; Laufen 1980.

of recent research to reach a consensus concerning the theology of Q, despite agreement on many particulars, raises the question of whether there might be some coherent perspective which could embrace the various tendencies and themes that have been found in Q. In all these matters, the question of the literary unity of Q is crucial. This article seeks to make a contribution, thus, both to the solution of the Synoptic problem and to the problem in Q research of locating the dominant perspective in Q.

The concept of literary unity used here is borrowed from secular literary criticism, where it may be defined as: "The concept that a literary work shall have in it some organizing principle in relation to which all its parts are related so that, viewed in the light of this principle, the work is an organic whole" (Thrall and Hibbard 1962:500). Since in Q we are dealing with traditional sayings material rather than free composition by an author, we cannot expect a high degree of literary unity.[7] Nevertheless, the idea of literary unity is useful because it **[373]** directs attention to a unity of conception which may stand behind quite varied aspects of a document, including its gattung, its vocabulary and word usage, its themes, its smaller forms, and its redactional traits.

In the following, I shall first call attention to certain features of Q which are distinctive, especially over against Mark, in terms of the form as well as the content of the material. Then I shall ask if some "organizing principle" can render comprehensible the characteristics that are noted.

1. A Form-Critical Survey of Q

We shall be looking here for forms distinctive of Q and/or distinctive qualities in these forms, especially qualities attributable to redactional activity. What is distinctive of Q can often be seen by comparing the Q-material with Mark.[8]

---

7. This investigation will presuppose that material I have shown elsewhere to be very late additions to Q is eliminated from consideration. This material is not extensive. It includes the temptation account (Q 4:1-13), a portion of Jesus' speech to John (Q 7:18-23), and the so-called Johannine pericope (Q 10:21-22). See Jacobson 1978:36–46, 71–76, 93–94, 140–45.

8. I assume the literary independence of Mark and Q as well as their use of some shared traditions. For the study of the theology of Q, it is advisable to include only those possibly shared traditions where there is significant evidence of Q and where there is enough recoverable Q-material so that one can sense that this material presents a point of view different from Mark's. I would include among these especially Mark 1:1-8 par.; Mark 3:19b-30 par.; Mark 6:6b-13 par.; Mark 8:11-13 par.; and Mark 4:30-32 (cf. Q 13:18-21). On the distinctive point of view preserved in this Q-material, see Jacobson 1978, and below under §2.

There has been a good deal of recent research on this problem. See Laufen 1980; Luz 1975; Devisch 1974; Schenk 1979; Vassiliadis 1975. For Lührmann's use of Mark in studying the redaction of Q, see Lührmann 1969:20–21. E. Schillebeeckx depends upon the distinction between Mark and Q in his attempt to examine the emergence of Christology: Schillebeeckx 1979:100–102, 146–54, 183–94, 219–29, 233–43, 264–69, 274–76, 282–91, 320–24, 403–23, 429–32, 472ff., 533–55, 550ff. Schillebeeckx is heavily indebted to Siegfried Schulz's work on Q.

1. Forms Common in Q but Rare in Mark

(a) Macarisms. There are at least seven macarisms scattered throughout the Q-material.[9] By contrast, Mark has only two (Mark 11:9-10); one of these is from the OT, the other is a formulation based upon it. Also, Q consistently uses *makarios* (except Q 13:35 = Ps 117:26 LXX); Mark uses *eulogeō*. What is striking, then, it the relative abundance of macarisms in Q and their scarcity in Mark.

At least one macarism in Q is identifiable as a later creation, namely Q 6:22-23, but here we can observe two stages of **[374]** composition.[10] The first concerns the suffering of the righteous on behalf of the Son of Man; the second stage (Q 6:23c) interprets the persecution encountered as merely one more instance of Israel's persistent opposition to the prophets. In the first stage (Q 6:22-23b), a traditional macarism (cf. *Gos. Thom.* 68; 1 Pet 4:14) is taken up and interpreted in light of the Son of Man. The second stage puts those blessed not in the tradition of martyrs but of prophets, and introduces the Deuteronomistic tradition of the violent fate of the prophets (see Steck 1967:257-60). Thus, where redaction can be most easily observed, namely in relation to an old collection of macarisms, the tendency at work at the latest stage derives from the Deuteronomistic tradition and emphasizes that the addressees, the Q-community, stand in direct continuity with the prophets of old who also experienced Israel's impenitence in the form of hostility to them and their message.

(b) Woes. There seem to have been at least nine woes in Q, seven of which had already been gathered into a sayings composition.[11] By contrast, Mark has no woes at all.

Again, redactional activity is observable in Q, namely at the end of the collection of woes. The older woes accuse Jewish leaders of hypocrisy; those woes reflect inner-Jewish debate (Jacobson 1978:187). To those woes have been added an expanded woe (Q 11:47-48) and a threat (Q 11:49-51) which accuse Israel of always persecuting the prophets; the threat says that "this generation" will now experience God's wrath. Thus, where redactional activity is observable we again encounter the Deuteronomistic tradition. Here, however, it is linked with the idea of Wisdom as sender of the prophets. This association of a particular form of the Wisdom tradition with the Deuteronomistic tradition is, as we shall see, found elsewhere in Q and is unique in the gospel tradition.

---

9. Q 6:20, 21, 22-23; 7:23; 10:23; 12:43; possibly also Luke 11:28.

10. See Steck 1967:52-55.

11. The woes are in Q 10:13 (bis); 11:39 (// Matt 23:25), 42, 43, 44, 46, 47, 52, and possibly 17:1 (on this last, see Bultmann 1968:144-45). On the collection of woes, see Bultmann 1968:113-14; Lührmann 1969:43-48. For the original Q-sequence of the woes, see Jacobson 1978:183-85.

(c) The Eschatological Correlative. The eschatological correlative, a form identified by Richard A. Edwards (1969), occurs four times in Q,[12] never in Mark. As with the macarisms and woes, the eschatological correlatives tend to be clustered together (three of the four occur in Q 17:22-37). It is **[375]** clear that the eschatological correlative is a prophetic form of speech.[13] It belongs to the tradition rather than the redaction of Q.[14]

(d) Prophetic Threats (Drohworte, "Minatory Sayings"). Q has a disproportionate number of prophetic threats. Bultmann discussed fifteen such sayings or clusters of sayings. Of the fifteen, twelve (or thirteen, if Luke 6:24-26 were assigned to Q) occur in Q. Mark has two such sayings, both also known to Q. But the prophetic threats in Mark (Mark 8:38; 12:38-40) are really only warnings, while in Q most of the sayings announce judgment in view of impenitence or of failure to respond to a divine appeal.[15] Especially revealing is a comparison of Mark 12:38-40 with Q 11:37-52. Mark has mere warnings, but in Q we have prophetic woes.

Common in the prophetic threats in Q is the use of invidious comparisons,[16] and of explicit reference to a call and its rejection.[17] Rhetorical questions are also common.[18]

It is relevant at this point to note that a comparison of word usage related to the prophetic announcement of judgment reveals a sharp contrast between Mark and Q. Words related to judgment are common in Q but completely missing from Mark.[19] Even more striking are the frequent references **[376]** to the "day" (*hēmera*) of judgment.[20] Mark knows of the "days" of tribulation and the "day" of the parousia but he speaks of the "day" of

12. Q 11:30; 17:24, 26, 29, 30.

13. Cf. D. Schmidt 1977. Schmidt claims to have found a LXX prophetic form which stands behind both the "sentences of holy law" (Käsemann) and the eschatological correlative. His evidence calls into question Edwards's view that the eschatological correlative was created by the Q-community. However, his evidence is drawn only from the OT, excluding the Apocrypha (but see, e.g., Bar 4:24, 33). His assumption of direct use of the LXX ignores the underlying correlatives in the Hebrew text (e.g., *ka'ašer . . . ken . . .* in Jer 31:28; 32:42; 42:18; 5:19; Isa 20:3-4; 55:10-11; Ezek 12:11) and the possible continuation of such prophetic usage in late Jewish writings. But if Schmidt's view is correct, then the apocalyptic Son of Man sayings in Luke 17:24, 26, 28, 30 presuppose a prophetic tradition which used the LXX.

14. In the small sayings composition in Q 11:29-32, the latest stage is to be found in Q 11:31-32 which, as we shall see, reflects the Wisdom and Deuteronomistic traditions. The eschatological correlative in Q 11:30 belongs to an earlier stage of the redaction of Q. On this, see Jacobson 1978:166-71.

15. Q 3:7-9; 6:46; 10:13-15; 11:31-32; 11:(39), 42-44, 46-47, 52, 49-51; 12:8-9, 54-56; 13:26-27, 28-29, 34-35; 17:26-27, 34-35. Q 11:47-51 takes the form of a prophecy of disaster; see Steck 1967:51-53 and cf. March 1974:159-62.

16. Q 10:13-15; 11:31-32; 12:54-56; 13:28-29.

17. Q 10:13-15; 11:31-32; 11:49-51; 12:8-9; 13:34-35.

18. Q 3:7-9; 6:46; 10:13-15; 12:54-56.

19. *Krinō*—Q, 3 times; (Mark, 0) (Q 6:37-38 [bis]; 22:30); *krisis*—Q, 4/6; Mark 0 (Q 10:14; 11:31, 32, 42; cf. Matt 10:15; 11:24 [cf. Luke 10:12]); *kritēs*—Q, 3; Mark 0 (Q 11:19; 12:58 [bis]).

20. Q 6:46 and 13:26-27 (Matt 7:22); 17:24, 26, 27, 30; 10:14 (Matt 11:22); 12:40; 10:12 (Matt 10:15); 12:46; 6:22-23; cf. 12:39.

judgment only once (13:32). It may be noted that in Q the "day" is often associated with the Son of Man; that is not characteristic of Mark's use of Son of Man. Further, the pejorative epithet, "this generation," while known in Mark (8:12, 38; 9:19; 13:30), is used with greater uniformity in Q.[21]

2. Forms Common in Mark but Rare in Q

(a) Conflict Stories.   There are eleven conflict stories in Mark but only one in Q, namely the Beelzebul controversy (Q 11:14-23). This one story is traditional since Mark has a variant of it (Mark 3:22-30). Neither the Q-version nor its Markan variant is typical of the conflict stories. For example, it does not involve a disputed point in Jewish law.[22] We will examine this story in greater detail later. However, we may note that, characteristically, the other conflict stories were put in the service of Christology, both in Mark and in the pre-Markan tradition.[23]

(b) Miracle Stories.   The rarity of miracle stories in Q has often been noted.[24] There are two such stories: Q 7:1-10 and 11:14. The latter serves as a setting for the Beelzebul controversy and thus is used in a way similar to a use of miracles in the Fourth Gospel, namely to introduce discourses.

The healing of the centurion's servant or child (Q 7:1-10) is not a typical miracle story. Indeed, Bultmann discusses it in an addendum to his section on apophthegms (1968:38–39). The earliest form of this story is probably to be seen in the pre-Johannine tradition behind John 4:46-54. Comparing this earlier form to the version in Q brings to light two important features of the Q-redaction. First, the stress in Q shifts from the miracle itself to Jesus' word.[25] Second, the Q-version has been edited to reflect a theme found [377] elsewhere in Q, namely the positive response of Gentiles which puts Israel to shame (Q 7:9).[26]

It should also be noted that throughout Q, miracles are associated with the kingdom of God (Q 11:20; 10:8-9; cf. 10:23-24); and in Q the proper response to miracle is repentance (Q 10:13-15; cf. 10:5-11, esp. 10:8-9). By

21. The genitive *tēs geneas tautēs* occurs in Q 7:31; 11:31; 11:32; 11:51. This phrase reflects Deuteronomistic usage; see Jacobson 1978:121–24 n. 181.

22. See Hultgren 1979:100–106.

23. See esp. Luz 1975:368–70. Hultgren, who stresses apologetic as the motive for the pre-Markan collection of conflict stories in Mark 2:1—3:6, also notes that they "would have provided ... an answer to the question ... of why Jesus was put to death" (1979:177). For a comparison of Q and Markan traditions concerning Jesus and the Law, see Schillebeeckx 1979:33–43.

24. Mark has eighteen miracle stories in addition to summaries and, toward the end of the Gospel, a series of instances of miraculous foreknowledge.

25. See Robinson 1971a:56–58; also Blank 1969.

26. Note Q 7:9; cf. 10:13-15; 11:29-32 and see Lührmann 1969:37, 63. "Israel" here is a religious self-designation; cf. K. Kuhn 1965:359–65.

contrast, in Mark and in the pre-Markan tradition this eschatological context gives way to christological motifs.[27]

(c) Parables, Similitudes, Comparisons.

(c) *Parables, Similitudes, Comparisons.* The use of metaphor and comparison is certainly not rare in Q but certain qualities seem to be distinctive of Q parabolic language over against that of Mark. The element of comparison is more common in Q than in Mark.[28] Unlike the Markan parables, the Q parables often contain comparisons of two (or more) situations or people.[29] Also, the introductory formulas are different in Mark and Q.[30]

The difference between the Markan and Q parables may also be seen in the fact that the parables in Q often have a clearly eschatological setting.[31] Many of the Q parables are really part of a prophetic call for a response in view of an imminent decisive moment.[32] Striking in this regard is a group of parabolic sayings which begin with *tis ex hymōn* ("who among you") and which appeal to everyday experience.[33] Such sayings are absent from Mark. [378] Further, "who among you . . . ?" is not a typical introduction to a parable; it reflects prophetic usage.[34]

Thus if a general tendency can be observed in the Q parabolic material, it would be that in Q this material is used in the context of prophetic preaching.

Where redactional activity is observable in Q, a tendency may perhaps be noted to allegorize, though not for christological purposes.[35] Two parables have been attached to longer sayings compositions (Q 7:31-35 and 11:24-26); they serve the purpose of announcing judgment upon "this generation."[36]

27. See Luz 1975:355, 360–67. Bultmann attributed the relative scarcity of miracle stories in Q not to the general lack of narrative in Q but to the view of Jesus in Q as "eschatological preacher of repentance and salvation, the teacher of wisdom and the law" (1968:241).

28. See Edwards 1976:71–79. Several expressions of comparison are common in Q but absent from Mark: *pleion* (Q 11:31, 32; 12:23; cf. 7:26); *posō mallon* (Q 11:13; 12:24; 12:28); *anektos* (Q 10:12, 14). The word *parabolē* does not seem to occur in Q.

29. Cf. Satake 1978. McDonald (1979:85) rightly notes the use of such contrast parables for "the prophetic call for decision."

30. The Q-parables are often introduced with the verb *homoioō* or with *homoios estin*; see Q 7:32; 13:18-19, 21; 6:48, 49; cf. also 6:47; 13:20; 7:31. Such an introduction occurs only once in Mark—in the one parable it has in common with Q (Mark 4:30-32); more commonly, *hōs* is used by Mark (4:26-29; 4:31; 13:34).

31. Luz also calls attention to the loss of eschatological context in the parables in Mark (1975:357).

32. See Q 3:9; 3:17; 6:47-49; 12:39-40, 42-46, 57-59; 13:25-29; 14:16-24; 19:12-13, 25-26. On the use of parables by the prophets, cf. Westermann 1967:201–2.

33. Q 12:25; 11:11; 15:4 (diff. Matt 18:12); Matt 12:11 (diff. Luke 14:5); cf. 11:33.

34. See Greeven 1952 [repr. as Greeven 1982]. Cf. Schulz 1972:63; Jeremias 1972:103. The expression is found in Isa 42:23; 50:10 (both with *tis en hymin*) and Hag 2:3 (*tis ex hymōn*). The use of *homoioō* in the interrogative may also be prophetic; see Isa 40:18; 46:5; Lam 2:13; Ezek 31:2, 18; cf. Q 7:31; 13:18-19, 21.

35. See Q 7:31-35; 19:12-27; 14:16-24; 13:18-19 (in the last, note the explicit reference to a "tree" in v. 19 and cf. Crossan 1973:98–99).

36. On Q 7:31-35, see Jacobson 1978:84–91, 96–97; on Q 11:24-26, see ibid., 171–80, 194.

3. Results of the Form-Critical Survey

This form-critical survey of Q has not covered all the types of material in Q, but several things seem clear. First, the fact that forms dominant in Mark (miracle stories, conflict stories) are rare in Q and that other forms which are common in Q (macarisms, woes, eschatological correlatives, prophetic threats) are rare in Mark suggests that Mark and Q must represent independent traditions. Second, the prophetic character of the Q-material is evident not only in the use of prophetic forms but in those characteristics which distinguish the parables in Q from those in Mark.[37] Third, the survey suggests a considerable measure of literary unity in Q simply in terms of form and general content.

Finally, in those places where redactional activity could be observed most clearly, the latest levels showed the influence of the Deuteronomistic and/or Wisdom traditions; these redactional additions served to condemn Israel for her impenitence and resistance to God's messengers.

2. Traditions Shared by Mark and Q

There are several instances where traditions are shared by Mark and Q. By comparing them, we can often sense more clearly what is distinctive of [379] Q. We are not concerned here with short sayings but with longer sayings compositions where redactional tendencies are more easily observable.

1. The Mission Discourse (Mark 6:6b-13; Q 10:2-16; cf. also Luke 9:1-6). The Markan version is brief, telling only of the sending out two by two of the Twelve, of the restricted provisions (no bread, no bag, and so on), and of their authorization to cast out demons. Later the disciples report back to Jesus (Mark 6:30).

The Q-version differs from Mark's at many points. Present in Q but absent from Mark are the following:

an introductory saying about the abundant harvest,
a sending statement ("I send you . . ."),
the warning that the "laborers" will be like lambs in the midst of wolves,
the peace greeting,
the saying about the laborer worthy of his wages/food,
the proclamation that the kingdom is near,
the proclamation of judgment against those rejecting the "laborers,"
the woes against the Galilean cities, and
the concluding messenger saying (Q 10:16).

---

37. After a brief survey of the Q-material, W. D. Davies (1966:382–86) noted that Q is pervaded by a sense of eschatological crisis. A similar point is made by H. C. Kee (1977:84–117). Earlier, T. W. Manson (1949:16) observed that Q "begins and ends with the thought of coming judgment"—which suggests intentional shaping of the material (cf. Schulz 1972:26).

In contrast to Mark, who omits any reference to the kingdom, Q makes it clear that in the "laborers" the kingdom draws near to Israel, and that this means judgment, so that those in Israel who reject the "laborers" reject God and bring wrath upon themselves.[38] What we have in Q, therefore, is not really a mission at all but rather an errand of judgment. The results seem presupposed from the outset, for the discourse opens with a saying describing the laborers as lambs in the midst of wolves. Here the image of God's lamb, Israel, in the midst of hostile gentile wolves has been sarcastically inverted (Hoffmann 1972:294–95). The appended prophetic threat (Q 10:13-15),[39] which says that Gentiles would have responded better than Israel, assumes the failure of the call for Israel to return to Yahweh.[40]

The tradition shared by Mark and Q must have related an account of a sending of messengers to call Israel to repentance and, should that fail, to [380] announce judgment upon Israel.[41] The Markan redaction adds some Christianizing details.[42] But more importantly, the Markan redaction uses the account to illustrate the fact that the disciples, whose activity parallels that of Jesus, will be rejected just as Jesus was (cf. Mark 6:1-6a; see Grässer 1969–70:11, 21–22). This same motif is pursued in Mark 6:14-29 where the Baptist becomes the "forerunner of Jesus' passion."[43] Thus the Markan redaction has adapted the mission account to the passion kerygma, while the Q-redaction was concerned to speak of Israel's impenitence and of the fateful consequences of her refusal to heed those sent to her.

2. John the Baptist (Mark 1:1-11; 6:17-29; 9:9-13; Q 3:7-9, 16-17; 7:24-28; 16:16; 7:31-35; also Luke 3:1-6 // Matt 3:1-6).

The differences between Q and Mark are fundamental. The basic difference is that in

---

38. The image of the harvest in Q 10:2 establishes the context for understanding the function of the "laborers." Harvest is a common metaphor for judgment (e.g., Joel 3:13; Isa 27:12; Hos 6:11; Mark 4:26-29; John 4:35; Rev 14:14-20). The laborers are harvest workers sent out by the "lord of the harvest," who is probably the same figure who appears in Q 3:17 (i.e., Yahweh). Cf. Q 11:23 and see Hoffmann 1972:289–92. The remarkable feature here is that the laborers are not angels (as in Matt 13:41; cf. Rev 14:19) but humans, and that the eschatological judgment takes place already in the "mission" of the laborers.

39. The double saying in Q 10:13-15 is clearly not a continuation of the instruction in Q 10:3-12; it has been added to serve as a comment on the sending discourse.

40. For a more detailed discussion of the whole discourse, see Jacobson 1978:133–40; cf. P. Meyer 1970; 1967:7, 28, 75–78, 86.

41. For an analysis of the tradition, see Hahn 1965:41–46. The original character of the account can be glimpsed in Mark 6:11 (cf. Q 10:10-11), the announcement of judgment, which fits poorly into the picture the redaction seeks to create. Mark can interpret this only as the usual call to repent; indeed, he seems to think that the Twelve preached Jesus (cf. 6:14). The two-by-two sending may also be primitive: if judgment is to be announced (Mark 6:11), two witnesses would be required (Deut 17:6; 19:15).

42. The "laborers" become the Twelve. Reflection of early Christian missionary practices may be seen in the more realistic, if austere, requirements in Mark 6:8-9, in the reference to staying at a house (Mark 6:10), and anointing the sick with oil (6:13). The authority over demons may also be redactional (6:7; cf. 3:14). Cf. Hoffmann (1972:237–43), who shows how Mark's version has been adapted to the early Hellenistic Christian mission.

43. Knigge 1968:68–69. Cf. esp. Marxsen 1969:38–40; Wink 1968:1–17.

Q John appears as a prophet in his own right but in Mark he has been subordinated to Jesus (Marxsen 1969:33).

In the first common material, Q spoke of two baptisms, John's baptism of water in preparation for the coming judgment, and the baptism of wind (*pneuma*) and fire by Yahweh—the judgment itself (Jacobson 1978:32–35). This two-baptism scheme also appears in Mark but it has been reformulated so as to contrast the inferior water baptism of John to the superior Spirit baptism (bestowed by the risen Lord).[44] Likewise, Q and Mark both cite Mal 3:1 with reference to John. But in Q, the context is different, and the meaning is that John was the forerunner of Yahweh's judgment; Mark uses the passage to declare John the forerunner of Jesus. The subordination of John to Jesus may go back to the pre-Markan tradition (Luz 1975:353–54, 360).

Thus neither in Mark nor in the pre-Markan tradition was John a prophet in his own right. But in Q, John is independent, a preacher of [381] repentance before the imminent judgment of Yahweh.[45] Especially in Q 7:31-35, Q places both John and Jesus in a common front against "this generation" which rejects both (Jacobson 1978:84–91).

3. The Beelzebul Controversy (Mark 3:19b-27; Q 11:14-20).

In the Markan redaction, a charge that Jesus is possessed by Beelzebul, the *archōn* of the demons, is shifted to a new context: the accusation by Jesus' family and others that he is a demoniac. In this way, Mark prepares the way for the identification of Jesus as bearer of the Spirit (Mark 3:30) (Luz 1975:360).

The Q-version differs at a number of points. The setting is different: a brief miracle story instead of the accusations by Jesus' relatives and the scribes. Also the Q-version lacks the parable of the divided house as well as the parable of the strong man bound and the concluding saying about blaspheming the Holy Spirit. On the other hand, there are several new elements in the Q-version—a rhetorical question about other Jewish exorcists, the saying linking exorcisms with the kingdom, and a concluding parable about the seven unclean spirits which return to reside where only one had lived before.

The basic difference is that in Q attention is focused on the kingdom rather than on Jesus. Exorcism is linked directly to the kingdom (Q 11:20). But the context does not permit this saying to refer exclusively to Jesus' exorcisms. Rather, the coming of the kingdom is the presupposition for all exorcisms.[46] That alone makes comprehensible why the other Jewish exor-

---

44. Cf. Hoffmann (1972:21), who notes that Mark shifts from two baptisms to two persons; see further 1972:19–22.

45. See Jacobson 1978:76–84. A late addition to Q (7:28) seeks to subordinate John to Jesus.

46. Noack 1948:70–72. Though he denies that the connection of Luke 11:19 and Luke 11:20 is original, Bultmann (1968:14) observes that their connection logically requires the

cists (the "sons" of Jesus' opponents, Q 11:19) will stand in judgment upon their fathers, the Jewish leaders.

In Mark, Jesus overcomes the opposition by showing that their accusations are foolish; indeed, he is not possessed by an unclean spirit but by the Holy Spirit. In Q, however, the issue is the kingdom, not Jesus himself.[47] The parable appended to the Q-version (Q 11:24-26) implies that "this generation" has provided a hospitable dwelling for unclean spirits.[48] Thus the Q-version concludes with a harsh condemnation of the Jewish leaders. [382]

4. The Sign to This Generation (Mark 8:12b; Q 11:29-32).

An originally isolated saying (Q 11:29) has been developed in Q into a brief sayings composition. In the pre-Markan tradition, the saying was probably already attached to the feeding miracle.[49]

The Markan redaction serves a christological purpose. Jesus shows his superiority over the Pharisees (who, for Mark, are "this generation") by overcoming their attempt to test him and by refusing to manifest himself to them as a divine being.[50]

In Q, the saying has undergone at least two stages of expansion (see Jacobson 1978:166–71). The original saying (Q 11:29) contains an exceptive clause: no sign except the "sign of Jonah." This enigmatic saying has prompted an explanation in Q 11:30: "For as Jonah became a sign to the men of Nineveh, so will the Son of Man be to this generation."[51] Here "sign" is not understood as a prodigious miracle but, in the prophetic sense, as a warning concerning the future. And "Son of Man" is not the apocalyptic figure but simply Jesus.[52]

The second stage in the development of the composition is the addition in Q 11:31-32 of a double saying.[53] This addition expands on the judgment

---

view that the exorcisms of the Jewish exorcists also demonstrate the coming of the kingdom.

47. Q 11:23 does not introduce a more exclusivistic view of Jesus but rather repeats what is said elsewhere in Q, that to reject Jesus (or John or the "laborers") is to reject God. See further Jacobson 1978:165–66.

48. For the interpretation of this parable, see Jacobson 1978:171–79.

49. Cf. Mark 8:1-10, 11-13 to John 6:1-13, 30. On this, see Haenchen 1966:285–87; also Schulz 1972:254 n. 537 and 255–56.

50. For this interpretation, see Luz 1975:353 n. 1. Edwards (1971:76) notes that Mark's *peirazontes* (testing) is redactional and that it serves a christological purpose; see Mark 8:11.

51. Lührmann (1969:40–42), however, sees Q 11:30 as the last addition to the composition—as a saying created to link Q 11:29 to Q 11:31-32, both of which he takes to be originally independent sayings.

52. The use of a future verb in Q 11:30 does not require that the Son of Man there be an apocalyptic figure; on this see Jacobson 1978:168; Vielhauer 1965b:111–12; and Schulz 1972:256.

53. The double saying is a product of the Q-community. The structure of the saying and the use of Gentile examples to shame Israel both reflect a scheme of "primitive Christian polemic" (Fridrichsen 1972:75; Bultmann 1968:13; cf. Q 10:13-15). Q 11:31-32 and 10:13-15 both stand close to the Deuteronomistic call to repentance (cf. Steck 1967:286). Wisdom influence is evident, both in the unexpected inclusion of the example of the *sophia* of Solomon

of "this generation." For indeed the Ninevites did repent, but "this generation" rejected Jesus. Therefore, these Gentiles—the men of Nineveh who
repented at the *kerygma* of Jonah and the queen of Sheba who responded to
the *sophia* of Solomon—will arise in the judgment to condemn Israel. One
should note here a phenomenon attested elsewhere in the redaction of Q,
namely the close association of Wisdom and prophetic preaching (e.g., Q
11:49!) and, with that, the condemnation of Israel for her impenitence.
[**383**]

5. Results of Comparing Mark and Q.

In comparing the use of Mark
and Q of shared tradition, certain themes and interests kept recurring. Mark
adapted the tradition to his Christology and to the passion kerygma. In Q,
we noted a recurring stress on the impenitence of Israel or "this generation," on judgment, and on the fateful consequences of rejecting God's
messengers. These themes were evident within the sayings compositions as
well as in additions at the end of the compositions (Q 10:13-15 added to
10:2-12; Q 7:31-35 to 7:24-28 + 16:16; Q 11:24-26 to 11:14-20, 23; Q
11:31-32 to 11:29-30). Particularly striking were certain traits peculiar to
Q: the eschatological significance of rejecting not only Jesus but others as
well (John the Baptist—Q 7:31-35; "laborers"—Q 10:2-16; other Jewish
exorcists—Q 11:19) and the use of various examples to shame Israel (Q
10:13-15; 11:31-32; 11:19).[54]

3. The Source of the Literary Unity of Q

The study thus far strongly suggests that Q stands within a prophetic tradition. Indeed, it is clear from the redactional addition in Q 6:23c that the
community sees itself as successors to the persecuted prophets of the past.
They understood themselves as messengers[55] sent to call Israel to repentance in view of the imminent kingdom of God, but experiencing rejection
(Q 10:10-12, 13-15). Particularly important to note are two passages (Q
11:49-51; 13:34-35) which seem to give programmatic expression to the

---

and in the peculiar type of OT interpretation found here (and elsewhere in Q; see Lührmann
1969:75-83, 98-99; above, pp. 69-70).

54. Similar themes dominate other sayings compositions in Q which have no parallels in
Mark. (a) *The Sermon on the Mount/Plain.* I have argued elsewhere (1978:49-66) that the Sermon, which had attained its basic shape prior to the redaction of Q, was edited in such a way
as to introduce, from Q 6:39 on, a polemic against the Jewish leaders. This editing of the Sermon was buttressed by Q 7:1-10 which was clearly attached to the end of the Sermon in Q;
there a Gentile's readiness to believe puts Israel to shame. (b) *The woes* (Q 11:39-52). Here the
concern to denounce the Jewish leaders and to announce judgment is obvious, and was
strengthened through the attached threat in Q 11:49-51. (c) *The Q Apocalypse* (Q 17:23-37).
Here too the concern about the impending judgment is obvious, but this material is addressed
to the community, not to Israel, and there is no reproach of Jewish leaders. We shall see later
that this block of material, dominated by apocalyptic Son of Man sayings, represents a chunk
of older material.

55. Note, e.g., the prophetic sending formulas in Q 10:3; also Q 7:27; 11:49; cf. 13:34.

tendencies we have seen to be at work in much of the Q-material. Both passages are frequently recognized as additions to Q (Lührmann 1969:97; above, p. 69), primarily because both present Wisdom as sender of the prophets.[56] O. H. Steck has shown that both passages stand within the [384] Deuteronomistic tradition (1967:26–58, 222–39), while influence was noted earlier in other passages as well (Q 6:23c; 10:13-15; 11:31-32). The suggestion is at hand that it is the Deuteronomistic tradition which provides the theological framework for the redaction of Q, and thus is the source of its literary unity. Because of the importance of that tradition to the question of the literary unity of Q, we must now examine it in some detail. We shall be particularly concerned with one aspect of the Deuteronomistic tradition, namely the statements about the prophets which occur in reviews of Israel's history and thus are part of what Steck calls the "Deuteronomistic sketch of history."[57]

In the Deuteronomistic tradition, Israel's history is pictured as a history of disobedience. God in his forbearance sent warning to the people through the prophets, yet they rejected and even killed the prophets. Therefore God's wrath was—or will be—experienced. References to the prophets are a recurring but not a constant element in the Deuteronomistic tradition; the rejection of the prophets is cited as simply one indication of the stiffneckedness of the people. Certain distortions of history are conventional: the prophets appear almost exclusively in the role of preachers of repentance; far more prophets are killed than actually were; there is a tendency to expand the list of prophets (cf. Q 11:49-51 which begins with Abel!). It is noteworthy that the guilt of the fathers is said to remain even up to the present (Ezra 9:7; Neh 1:6; Ps 79:8; cf. Q 11:49-51). The primary concern of the tradition is the call for Israel to return to Yahweh.[58]

Steck identifies seven elements characteristic of the Deuteronomistic tradition in its later, expanded form.

---

56. The speaker in Q 13:34-35 is not Jesus but Wisdom; cf. Bultmann 1968:114–15; Steck 1967:230–32; P. Meyer 1967:22–28; Schulz 1972:349–50 n. 194; R. Meyer 1970: 50–51). Jesus cannot be the speaker because the speaker is the one who sent the OT prophets. Since Wisdom is explicitly named as sender of the OT prophets in Q 11:49, one must assume the same for Q 13:34-35.

57. The Deuteronomistic sketch of history can be seen especially in the penitential prayers such as Ezra 9:6-15; Neh 1:5-11; 9:5-37; Tob 3:1-6; Dan 9:4b-19; Bar 1:15—3:8 and in the confessions of sin (Lam 3:42-47; cf. Ps 106:6-46). See Steck 1967:110-37. However, the Deuteronomistic view of history is also to be found in a tradition of preaching, including Jeremiah, source C (7:25-34; 25:4-14; 29:17-20; 35:15-17; 44:2-14); 1 Kgs 8:46-53; Deut 4:25-31; 28:45-68 + 30:1-10; Zech 1:2-6; 7:4-14; 2 Chr 30:6-9; 29:5-11; 15:1-7; Tob 13:3-6; T. Levi 10:2-5; 14; 15:1-4; 16:1-5; T. Jud. 23:1-5; T. Iss. 6:1-4; T. Zeb. 9:5-9; T. Dan 5:4-9; T. Naph. 4:1-5; T. Asher 7:2-7; 1 Enoch 93:1-10 + 91:12-17; 85–90; 91–104; Jub. 1:7-26; Bar 3:9—4:4; 4:5—5:9; CD 20:28-30; 1:3-13a; 4QDibHam I,8—VII,2; Pss. Sol. 9; 2:9; 8:2; 17:17; 4 Ezra 14:27-35; 3:4-25, 27; 7:129-130; Ps.-Philo, Bib. Ant. 2; 2 Apoc. Bar. 1:1-5; 4:1-6; 31:1—32:7; 44:1—46:7; 77:1-17; 78—87.

58. For the role of repentance in the Deuteronomic history, see Wolff 1982; also Brueggemann 1968.

(a) The whole history of Israel is pictured as one of persistent disobedience. Cf. Q 6:23c; 11:47-51; 13:34-35; 14:16-24.

(b) Therefore Yahweh again and again sent prophets to call Israel to return, to repent. Cf. Q 11:47-51; 13:34-35; 14:16-24. **[385]**

(c) Israel always rejected these prophets, often even killing them. Cf. Q 6:23c; 11:47-51; 13:34-35; 14:16-24. In Q, Israel's impenitence is expressed not only by accusations of complicity in the death of the prophets (e.g., Q 11:49-51) and by continued opposition to the prophets (Q 6:23c; 14:16-24; cf. 7:31-35; 10:2-16; 9:58) but also by other accusations (see 11:39-52; 3:7-9; 6:39-46; 7:24-27, 31-35; 11:24-26; 12:54-56). The use of Gentile (and other) examples to shame Israel also exposes her impenitence (Q 3:7-9; 10:13-15; 11:31-32; 11:19). The epithet, "this generation," is used to characterize Israel as impenitent.

(d) Therefore Yahweh punished, or will punish, Israel. In the earliest Deuteronomistic tradition, the catastrophes of 722 and 587 B.C.E. are cited. In the later form of the tradition, the *Unheilsstatus* of Israel is said to continue (e.g., *Jub.* 1:7-26 Jub. 1:7-26). Cf. Q 11:47-51; 13:34-35.

(e) But now a new call for repentance is issued. Cf. Q 3:7-9, 16-17; 6:20-49; 10:2-12; 7:31-35; 11:29-32; 11:39-52, and so on. In Q, even miracles are understood in the context of repentance (cf. 10:13; 11:14-20; 10:5-12; and cf. 11:20; par. to 10:9).

(f^1) If Israel repents, Yahweh will restore her, gathering those scattered among the nations.

(f^2) And he will bring judgment upon Israel's enemies. In Q, the numerous statements about the kingdom of God and the Son of Man take the place of element f^1 (Steck 1967:286 n. 6). Also, in place of promises to Israel (though cf. Q 13:34-35), Q offers a redefinition of Israel (Q 3:7-9; 13:28-29; cf. 22:28-30; 14:16-24; 13:19; 11:19; 11:31-32; 10:13-15; 16:16; 7:35). The use of a threat of rejection of those who reject the call to return is attested often in Q (e.g., 10:10-12; 10:13-15; 10:16; 12:10) and is attested as part of the f^1 element in pre-Christian Deuteronomistic preaching (Steck 1967:217–18). Also a part of element f is the eschatological separation of the righteous from the sinners, which is found in Q as well.[59]

In its oldest form, the Deuteronomistic tradition was at home in Levitical circles. Later, the tradition was borne by the Hasidic movement which, in the first half of the second century B.C.E., united several groups to form a common front against Hellenization and the deteriorating reli-

---

59. Steck 1967:187, 286 n. 5. Steck cites Q 17:34-35, to which may be added Q 3:7-9; 3:17; 13:23-24, 25, 27; 13:28-29; 10:13-15.

gious conditions, especially in the priesthood and the urban population. As Steck notes, "the *Levitical tradition of the Deuteronomistic sketch of history was that conception which enabled a theological grasp of contemporary events in the context of the concern for the conversion of Israel*" (1967:206; his emphasis). In the formation of this renewal movement we can see the mingling of several traditions: Levitical-deuteronomistic, eschatological, and Wisdom (see, e.g., Bar 1:15—5:9; *Testaments of the Twelve Patriarchs*).[60] [386]

During the period from 150 to 100 B.C.E., the Hasidic movement broke up into several groups. From this point on, Steck contends, the Deuteronomistic tradition became the common property of a number of groups and it is difficult to isolate any one as primary bearer of that tradition.[61]

That Q stands within the Deuteronomistic tradition seems evident. The elements of the Deuteronomistic view of history are widely attested in Q. The basic concern—to call Israel to repent—underlies both Q and the earlier Deuteronomistic tradition. One may conclude, therefore, that the Deuteronomistic view of history which comes to clear expression in Q 11:47-51 and 13:34-35 represents the theological framework undergirding a large part of the Q-material.

Once it is understood that the Deuteronomistic tradition provides the theological framework for Q, several peculiar features of Q become explicable. First, the absence of a passion narrative in Q becomes understandable because, in the Deuteronomistic tradition, Jesus' death was understood not as a salvific act but as evidence of Israel's continuing impenitence. Second, Q is peculiar in giving independent status to John the Baptist. Rather than being the forerunner of Jesus, John is presented in Q as a prophet (Q 7:26) who functions as a forerunner of Yahweh by issuing a call to repentance (Q 3:7-9, 16-17).[62] Remarkably, John and Jesus are even placed in [387] tan-

60. See Steck 1967:205–8. The terms *prophets* and *wise* could both be used to designate people who called for obedience to Torah; see Steck 1967:208 nn. 4, 5. It is important to note that the mingling of traditions (Wisdom, Deuteronomistic, eschatological) occurred within a specific context. Others have observed the interrelation in Q of, e.g., Wisdom, prophecy, and eschatology; thus Edwards 1976. Cf. Zeller 1975 and Grundmann 1977. But it is precisely in the Hasidic movement that we find the context for the intermingling of traditions. To be sure, the Hasidic movement had, by the time of Jesus, broken up into a number of parties, so one would need to specify further which branch of the later Hasidic movement stands closest to Q. One must dissent from H. C. Kee's suggestion (1977:83) that "The closest historical analogy we have for the itinerant charismatic preachers pictured in Q (Luke 10:1-20 [*sic*]) is that of the prophetic-revolutionary leaders whom Josephus describes." The understanding of the role and fate of the prophets in Q differs sharply from these savior prophets as well as from the "prophet like Moses" (Deut 18:15; on this see Steck 1967:240).

61. See Steck 1967:209–12. Steck (212) assumes that, in addition to the Qumran community, there was a complex renewal movement evidenced in texts such as *Psalms of Solomon, Assumption of Moses*, Ps-Philo, *Biblical Antiquities*, 4 Ezra, and 2 *Apocalypse of Baruch*. The movement had scribal leaders (p. 212) designated the "wise" (212 n. 5) and perhaps—though this is not directly attested—"prophets" (212 n. 6); the term *messenger* (or "apostle," cf. 3 Kdgms 14:6 LXX) may have been used (214–15; cf. Q 11:49).

62. The reference to "sandals" in Q 3:16 does not require a human figure instead of Yahweh, for the sandals should be understood as belonging to John himself, not to the figure to

dem (Q 7:31-35; Robinson 1975:5-6). This treatment of John is possible because, in the context of the Deuteronomistic tradition, John and Jesus are both seen as sent to call Israel to repentance.[63] Third, Wisdom plays an important role in Q. Jesus is implicitly a messenger of Wisdom (Q 7:31-35; 11:47-51; 13:34-35; 11:29-32) but he functions more as prophet than as wise man. Q is formally a collection of wise sayings but it includes a large amount of prophetic material. These phenomena are comprehensible in terms of the Deuteronomistic tradition, where a Wisdom component was long at home, and especially in terms of the Hasidic movement where the Deuteronomistic and Wisdom traditions had merged.[64] However, the notion of Wisdom as sender of prophets as part of the Deuteronomistic tradition is not attested in pre-Christian tradition or elsewhere in early Christian traditions, even though the Deuteronomistic tradition was adapted by Christians very early.[65] The peculiarity of the role of Wisdom in Q—its association with prophets and prophetic material—derives from the identification of Wisdom and Torah (cf. Sirach 24; Bar 3:9—4:1; *1 Enoch* 42). When Torah is Wisdom and the prophets are seen primarily as calling people to return to Yahweh and hence to Torah, then the prophets can be regarded as the "wise" and Wisdom as the sender of the prophets.[66]

Thus the organizing principle which gives literary unity to Q and provides coherence to its various characteristics is to be found in an understanding of Israel and the mission to her of John and Jesus, an understanding shaped by the Deuteronomistic and Wisdom traditions as

---

come. See Bretscher 1967. The meaning is that John is not worthy to wear his sandals in the presence of the Coming One (cf. Exod 3:5). However, since the whole fragment, "but he who is mightier . . . untie," interrupts the contrast between the two baptisms, it may be a later addition; see Jacobson 1978:32–35.

63. Schillebeeckx (1979:126-36) correctly emphasizes that John stands within the Deuteronomistic and Hasidic traditions, and that he represents not apocalyptic but a renascence of ancient Israelite prophecy.

64. Steck (1967) notes that the Deuteronomistic view of history is not linked to Wisdom in Sirach (147) but they are joined shortly thereafter in Tobit (147–49) and then in *Testaments of the Twelve Patriarchs* (150 n. 1; 151 n. 5), the Ten Week Apocalypse (*1 Enoch* 93:1-10 + 91:12-17; see p. 154 n. 4), 4 Ezra (177–80), Ps.-Philo, *Biblical Antiquities* (176), and esp. Bar 3:9—4:4 (164–65 n. 5). Also see Prov 1:20-33 (205 n. 2, 222, 225 nn. 1, 3, 232).

65. It is also attested in the pre-Markan traditions (Mark 12:1b-9; see Steck 1967:269-73) and the pre-Pauline tradition (1 Thess 2:15-16; cf. Steck 1967:274-79); see also Acts 7:52 (Steck 1967:265-69).

66. The role of Wisdom in Q is not directly related to the role of Wisdom in such christological hymns as Col 1:15-20. The *Sitz* of the latter is liturgical and focuses upon the cosmic role of Wisdom. In Q, Wisdom is not co-creatrix nor (aside from Q 10:21-22) revealer. Q does not identify Jesus with Wisdom, against F. Christ (1970). Aside from Q 10:21-22, Wisdom in Q is not hidden but public; she speaks through prophets in the places people gather (cf. Prov 1:20-21). However, one may see a connection between Q and those heretical traditions which saw Jesus as the last of a chain of divine envoys; see Robinson 1975; 1962, esp. 82–86. Jesus appears as a member of the chain of envoys in the Koran where, furthermore, Deuteronomistic themes continue to reverberate (Sura 2:87; 5:70-71; 6:34; cf. Steck 1967:97–99).

they were mediated by the [**388**] Hasidic movement. Indeed, one may perhaps say that in Q we see the soil of the Hasidic movement still clinging to
the roots of earliest Christianity.

SOME QUALIFICATIONS

The claim advanced here concerning the literary unity of Q must be qualified in several respects.

First, the nature of the claim must be clarified. It is not being claimed
that in identifying the source of the literary unity in Q we have explicated
the theology of Q. Put otherwise, the Deuteronomistic and Wisdom perspective is not the *content* of the Q-proclamation but simply the vehicle for
its expression. The Deuteronomistic tradition seems to have provided a
framework within which to reflect theologically upon the disappointments
of the Jesus movement among their fellow Jews. The integration of the
figure of Wisdom into the Deuteronomistic sketch of history served to
draw John and Jesus into Israel's *Heilsgeschichte* as the last in a series of
Wisdom's envoys.

Second, the comprehensiveness of the claim must be qualified. For although large portions of Q are comprehensible in terms of the
Deuteronomistic-Wisdom perspective, some portions are not. Roughly the
first half or two-thirds of Q (following the Lukan sequence) is dominated
by the Deuteronomistic and Wisdom traditions (see Jacobson 1978). Beginning at Q 12:2, one comes upon a section of Q in which apocalyptic
paraenesis dominates and where traces of the Deuteronomistic-Wisdom
perspective are infrequent (though see Q 13:34-35; 14:16-24). All of the
apocalyptic Son of Man sayings occur in this latter portion of Q (Q 12:8,
10; 12:40; 17:23-24; 17:26-27, 30). In contrast to most of the material in
the first part of Q, the material in the latter part is usually addressed to the
community itself. It deals with typical apocalyptic concerns: exhortation to
remain faithful during persecution (Q 12:2-9), the promise of God's care
(Q 12:11-12; 12:22-31), calls to be watchful (Q 12:35-46), exhortations
concerning radical discipleship and faithfulness (Q 12:49-53; 14:26-27;
17:5-6), calls to righteousness in view of the coming judgment (Q 12:57-
59; 13:23-24, 25-29; 16:16-18), and warnings about the end time to come
(Q 17:23-37). Such apocalyptic paraenesis is by no means alien to the
Deuteronomistic tradition. Nevertheless, the material in this second portion
of Q (the material interspersed from Q 12:2 to 22:30) must be regarded as
representing an older block of material (with exceptions such as Q
13:34-35).

The relationship between the Deuteronomistic-Wisdom material and
the apocalyptic Son of Man material is decisive here. In at least two instances, it seems quite clear that the Deuteronomistic-Wisdom perspective
has been imposed upon an older Son of Man layer, namely Q 6:22-23a,b +
6:23c [**389**] and Q 11:29-30 + 11:31-32. Further, in the Deuteronomistic-

Wisdom material "Son of Man" is simply a designation for Jesus. This is very clear in Q 7:34 but also in Q 11:31-32 and Q 9:58. Thus an apocalyptic Son of Man theology is not characteristic of the Deuteronomistic redaction but is prior to it. From this we may conclude that the whole block of apocalyptic paraenesis, buttressed as it is by the imminent expectation of the Son of Man, must underlie a later layer of Deuteronomistic-Wisdom material.[67]

What therefore emerges is the beginning of a tradition history of Q. The Deuteronomistic-Wisdom perspective represents a shift away from the earlier view focused on the imminent expectation of the Son of Man. This shift probably reflects a shift in the community's understanding of itself over against Israel. In the block of apocalyptic paraenesis, the community sees itself as the righteous minority, the community of the elect within Israel who must remain faithful and watchful during difficult times, while the majority are portrayed as heedless of the gravity of the hour. But in the material subjected to redaction from the Deuteronomistic-Wisdom perspective, we find an intensification of polemic. "This generation" is not only heedless, it shows its solidarity with past impenitent generations by violently opposing the prophets. Indeed, Israel is being redefined and those who now call themselves Israel will be replaced by others.[68]

One can only speculate as to what caused this shift and thus what motivated the Deuteronomistic-Wisdom redaction of Q. However, the introduction of the motif of the violent death of prophets suggests that one factor may have been persecution (cf. 1 Thess 2:14-16). Another factor was probably the success of the mission to the Gentiles. We frequently hear in the Deuteronomistic-Wisdom layer of Q of Gentiles (or others) whose faith puts Israel to shame (Q 7:1-10; 10:13-15; 11:31-32; 11:19; cf. 13:28-29) (cf. P. Meyer 1970). One may note that the Deuteronomistic perspective is used in other early Christian sources precisely in dealing with the problem of the relation of the Gentiles to Israel.[69]

67. In my dissertation, I try to unravel several layers of redaction; that stage of redaction of Q when the material was subjected to redaction under the influence of the Deuteronomistic-Wisdom tradition I have called the "compositional stage" of the redaction of Q. It seems to have been the most extensive of the redactional stages. [A thoroughly revised and much expanded version of Jacobson's dissertation is due to appear soon from Polebridge Press.—ED.]

68. The emphasis upon judgment is now so strong that it is no longer clear whether there is any hope of Israel's awakening. Cf. Lührmann 1969:47 n. 6. Lührmann holds, contrary to Steck, that the proclamation of judgment in Q does not have in view the conversion of Israel. According to Lührmann, for Israel "there yet remains only judgment" (47).

69. See Acts 7 (esp. v. 52); Romans 9–11 (esp. 11:3); Mark 12:1b-9; *Barn.* 5:11; and esp. 5 Ezra (=2 Esdras) 1–2 (and cf. Stanton 1977).

7

Redactional Processes and Changing Settings in the Q-Material

THE STATE OF THE QUESTION[1]

If Q can be assumed to be a literary entity,[2] it can be approached either tradition-historically or redaction-critically. Several recent studies of Q have appeared almost simultaneously and completely independently of one another; for this reason, unfortunately, they could at best refer to each other in passing. They also are not always congruent from a terminological point of view.

1. Dieter Lührmann is an exponent of a strict redaction-critical approach. He endeavors to discern the intention operative in the compilation of the Q-tradition. For Lührmann, "redaction" is to be distinguished from mere "collection," which follows its own transmissional rules.[3] "Community formulations" should be taken into account "only insofar as they derive from the redaction itself or go back to the most recent stratum of the tradition preceding the redaction" (1969:22). While Lührmann reckons with only a few redactional formulations,[4] the most recent attempt at the reconstruction of Q by Wolfgang Schenk ascribes substantially more pericopae to

---

Translated from Dieter Zeller, "Redaktionsprozesse und wechselnder 'Sitz im Leben' beim Q-Material," pp. 395–409 in Joël Delobel, ed., *Logia: Les Paroles de Jésus—The Sayings of Jesus: Mémorial Joseph Coppens*, BETL 59 (Leuven: Uitgeverij Peeters and Leuven Univ. Press, 1982). Zeller refers to Q-texts sometimes by their Matthaean location, sometimes by Lukan versification. All have been converted into "Q" (i.e., Lukan) versification.

1. See the overview in Schulz 1972:11–44; Devisch 1972; Worden 1975; and Neirynck 1982.
2. See more recently, Vassiliadis 1978.
3. See Lührmann 1969:19, 84–85. [See chap. 4 above, pp. 59–60—ED].
4. Lührmann 1969:89 n. 4 (above, p. 63) gives only two sayings as examples [Q 10:12; 11:30].

"Q's own final redactional stratum" (1981:14). Here, however, tradition-historical features (e.g., wisdom Christology) often serve as criteria.

2. The tradition-historical approach is epitomized above all in the work of Siegfried Schulz.[5] For Schulz, Q-redaction is grasped exclusively in the composition and selection of the Q-material.[6] In general he disputes that there are redactional formulations,[7] and he differentiates the Q-material by geographical provenance and by age.[8] Q is of interest above all as the kerygma of a particular community.[9]

3. Paul Hoffmann's *Studien zur Theologie der Logienquelle* [Studies in the theology of Q] stands in the middle. He infers the theology of Q from the sayings compositions collected and [396] transmitted by the "Q-group." In this he allows himself to be guided by redaction-critical questions, but he begins from the assumption that Q-redaction is generally identified with the tradition.[10] Against Hoffmann, however, one must object that he makes the process of transmission that leads to the final redaction all too brief.[11]

4. In addition to these pioneering, but in many respects one-sided, endeavors there are noteworthy attempts to associate redaction and tradition criticism more closely. One such study is Athanasius Polag's investigation, which was unfortunately published after some delay, and even then only in part.[12] He distinguishes a "main collection" (*Hauptsammlung*), which used smaller, previously existing sayings clusters (*Spruchreihen*), from a later redaction (1977:8). The value of Polag's suggestive explanations is diminished, however, by the fact that he includes much Lukan *Sondergut* ("special material").[13]

5. Heinz Schürmann appears to have in mind a related notion of the gradual growth of the Speech Source (*Redenquelle*) and worked out this idea with the Son of Man sayings. "At the beginning there were individual logia, to which 'commentary sayings' (*Kommentarworte*)[14] were attached.

---

5. [Schulz 1972.] For individual themes in Q, see the earlier studies of Tödt 1965 and Steck 1967.

6. Schulz 1972:39. This assumption, in any event, is nowhere worked out. See the contradictory statements in Schulz 1972:192.

7. Schulz 1972:38, criticizing Lührmann.

8. For a critique, see the review by Hoffmann 1975:104–15.

9. Similarly, Edwards 1976.

10. Only infrequently does Q-redaction actually produce sayings: thus—accepting Lührmann's suggestion—Q 11:51 Hoffmann (1972:168); 11:30 (p. 181 n. 92); 10:12 (pp. 288–90). Hoffmann does not sharply differentiate these from instances where a saying was "formed in the Q-tradition": thus, Q 3:16bc (p. 25); 6:22-23 (p. 182); 13:35b (p. 177); 7:27, 28b (p. 218) 7:33-35 (p. 227).

11. Thus Schulz 1972:36 and Polag 1977:9.

12. See Polag 1977, 1979. [Polag's Trier dissertation was completed in 1969 under the title *Die Christologie der Logienquelle*, "The Christology of Q".—ED.]

13. This criticism also applies to the Mainz dissertation of Katz (1973).

14. Schürmann's student, Joachim Wanke (1980:211), understands these to be previously isolated sayings that were transmitted independently or were capable of independent transmission. By contrast, Schürmann now has developed the notion so that even "newly formed explanations" (*erläuternde Neubildungen*) are included. In his 1982 essay, he speaks of primary sayings (*Grundworte*) and auxiliary sayings (*Zusatzworte*). [In the updated version of Schürmann

These soon came together into saying groups (*Spruchgruppen*), connected by catchwords or by common theme. At the end of the process we find 'speech compositions' (*Redekompositionen*), each of which had its own *Sitz im Leben* in the community. The Speech Source was assembled from these" (1975:128 [slightly modified on p. 79 in this volume]). Thus in spite of Hoffmann's skepticism, scholarship has tended in the direction of establishing various redactional phases of the sayings material.

METHODOLOGICAL REFLECTIONS

The question now is whether there are solid criteria for establishing redaction or even for redactional stages in Q. The present essay contributes in particular *text-linguistic*[15] considerations to this project. **[397]**

1. First of all I must clarify the notion of "redaction." The terminological oscillation between tradition and redaction or even references to "redactional layers" in some of the works mentioned above betrays an uncertainty. By "redaction" I mean a purposeful interaction with an existing, transmissible text—not necessarily written, but nevertheless "complete"—in its finished (in some circumstances, revised) form.[16] Hence redaction is always relative to each literary stage of a text and to its literary-critical delineation (although in the case of Q, not even the result of the redaction is available to us). For this reason one can also speak of the redaction of the written component collections that preceded the finished form of Q insofar as these came into existence as the result of intentional editing. Correspondingly, redactional creation of text must result from conscious interactions with tradition. This means that the new text is not independent but must have had its starting point in what was already there;[17] and, naturally, it should be in accord with the tendency of redaction as it is seen elsewhere.

2. For a collection of sayings that are at most only partially supplied with settings that frame them, there are right from the outset certain limits to redaction. One can see redaction:[18]

1975, translated for this volume (above, p. 79), Schürmann has substituted even more recent terminology, including "paired sayings" (*Spruch-Paare*), "structured compositions" (*struktierte Kompositionen*), and "dominical discourses" (*Reden Jesu*).—ED.]

15. See Dressler 1972; Kallmeyer, Klein, Meyer-Hermann, Netzer, and Siebert 1974; Plett 1975; Berger 1977:§§2–3.

16. Here I am following Barth and Steck 1978:51. A different view is offered by Fohrer, Hoffmann, Huber, Markert, and Wanke 1973:136–37. Their definition, according to which redaction includes "all recognizable literary revisions subsequent to the final writing down," could not, for example, be used in the analysis of a Markan miracle story.

17. This principle applies to the appending of sayings. For example, it is improbable that Q redaction would have connected Q 11:31-32 with v. 29 if the latter had not already contained the catchword *Jonah*. The exceptive clauses in 11:29c and 11:30 are thus not the work of Q-redaction (against Lührmann 1969:41–42). See below, "Case Studies," §2c on Q 10:2.

18. Bultmann's account of formulations by analogy and explanatory expansions (1968:84–94) and his explanation of the editing of the sayings material (1968:322–37) are rendered here

a. in the *interpretive expansion* of a unit. Here, however, it is difficult to prove that such an expansion did not already come from an earlier oral stage.

For example, the repeated threat in Q 11:51b seems to have been needed because of the added explanation in 11:51a. Does v. 51 then belong to Q redaction?[19] If v. 51a is a Christian addition, however, why is the death of Jesus not selected as the terminus ad quem?

b. in the *juxtaposition* of units. Here redaction creates a certain "coherence" in the sayings. There are various means at its disposal: [**398**]

  i. *Semantic. Either* recurring lexemes are used, normally in catchword composition. This use does not necessarily have a mnemonic function, thus betraying oral tradition.

  For example, Matt 4:1 may have been attached to the preceding pericope by the catchword *spirit.* The two light sayings (Matt 5:15; 6:22-23) in Q 11:33-36 were probably already associated in oral transmission. Elsewhere (1977b:191 n. 233), I have conjectured that in Q these sayings stood before the sayings cluster Q 12:2-12, which begins with the same catchwords: φῶς, σκότος or σκοτία (Q 11:35; 12:3), and σῶμα (Q 11:34 and perhaps 11:36; 12:4). εἰς κρύπτην [Luke 11:33] may be a Lukan reminiscence of κρυπτόν (12:2). Luke's interpolation of the speech against the Pharisees has a ready explanation: the demand for a sign in 11:16, 29 has its parallel in the "great omission" (Mark 8:11, where the Pharisees are the subject). At this point, therefore, Luke worked in other elements with an anti-Pharisaic thrust (Luke 11:37-38 = Mark 7:1-2, 5; Luke 12:1 = Mark 8:15) and used them to frame the Q-speech against the Pharisees and teachers of the Law.

  Or redaction looks beneath the surface of the text for common themes. Today one could speak of a continuous table of isotopes that is constituted from a mass of semantic signs.

  For example, the sayings cluster in Q 12:2-12 is interlaced with the duality of human action or action in the human forum and action of God or before God.

  ii. *Syntactical-grammatical.* Of special importance here are anaphoric and cataphoric elements that relate the material to the preceding or following speech elements. Coherence is further established by the use of conjunctions and particles (such as ἄρα in Q 12:42).[20]

  iii. *Formal.* Common grammatical structure can originate from

---

in a somewhat more technical idiom.

19. Thus Lührmann 1969:47; Hoffmann 1972:168.

20. N. Turner (1968–69) listed coordinating particles but often his examples are attested in only *one* evangelist, e.g., Matthew's οὖν ["therefore"].

commonality in form. Units of similar form are often juxtaposed, as happens, for example, in Q 9:57-60 and in 13:18-21.
Insofar as the redactor himself has composed the additional
units, it is a case of a "formation by analogy."

iv. *Pragmatic.* General introductions constitute all the sayings in the
same communication act. The introduction to the speech can itself be a piece of discourse—such as (ἀμὴν) λέγω ὑμῖν,[21] a so-
called performative hyper-statement (Dressler 1972:94)—or it
might be narrative.
The introduction that can be inferred from Matt 3:7a // Luke
3:7a has the Baptist addressing those coming for baptism in Q
3:7b-9, 16-17. This address probably occurs in anticipation of
3:16, since the role of vv. 7b-9 is first of all to encourage the
repentance for which baptism is the initial sign. It is now difficult to know whether there were any narrative conclusions in
Q [399] since, for example, the agreement in content between
Matt 7:28a and Luke 7:1a is probably coincidental.
A pragmatic unity may be conferred on disparate pieces of tradition not only by the description of the communication situation but also by the typical relation of author and recipient.
Formerly, one spoke of identical *Sitze im Leben.* Shifting *Sitze im
Leben* can be conditioned by a higher plane of redaction. There-
fore, I will devote particular attention to this phenomenon.

3. In the case of doublets, comparison with the Markan version of a saying provides an additional means for determining Q's redactional augmen-
tation, if this turns out to be more original.[22]

REDACTIONAL STAGES IN Q

Each stage of redaction can be defined in accordance with its scope, by the
degree of coherence that it brings about. Here I propose a model of possible
levels at which sayings aggregate at increasing orders of magnitude.

1. Appending of "Commentary Sayings"

In this case, individual sayings that are transmissible on their own are appended for the purposes of providing a commentary (see Wanke 1980:211–
12). Of special interest are instances in which the appended saying stands in
tension with the preceding one, as is the case with the relationship of Q
12:10 to 12:8-9. Confessing Jesus, which is all-important [in 12:8-9], seems
suddenly relativized by the even more important act of speaking against the
Holy Spirit. It is not only the catchword *Son of Man* but material considera-

---

21. Obviously, when the formula appears within a saying, it may belong to Q-tradition. It
has a linking function in Q 7:27 (see below, "Case Studies," §1d).
22. On the relationship of Mark to Q see Laufen 1980.

tions as well that account for the association.[23] By itself, v. 10, which is directed primarily at outsiders, falls outside the *Sitz im Leben* of 12:2-9, which is a composition admonishing the disciples. But by continuing on with vv. 11-12, the situation of confession is reestablished and what originally was foreign to the unit is integrated. Did the explanation in v. 10 therefore happen at an earlier stage (thus Schürmann 1975:137)?

2. The Formation of Thematic Sayings Complexes

(*a*) The phrase μὴ μεριμνήσητε ["do not be anxious"] in Q 12:11 probably also supplied the catchword used to bind together the entire unit on the theme of "freedom from anxiety" (Q 12:22b-31). It is introduced by a performative hyper-statement, διὰ τοῦτο λέγω ὑμῖν ["therefore I tell you"].[24] you"].[24] [400] The anaphoric διὰ τοῦτο anchors this act of speaking in the preceding one (see Zeller 1977b:83 n. 213). Hence we have here a redactional clasp joining two sayings complexes.

(*b*) The composition in 12:22b-31 itself displays the obvious signs of redaction (Zeller 1977b:86–87). The question in Q 12:25, which did not originally belong here, has been interpolated. At the same time, 12:26 was composed in order to return to the topic of 12:23-24. Thus redaction has created the elements of thematic arrangement.[25]

(*c*) Since the sapiential admonition already has a summary in 12:29 and a concluding justification in v. 30b, vv. 30a and 31 should probably be ascribed to a further redaction.[26] It transcends the negative appeal in vv. 22b-23, 29 through a positive requirement and a promise. Is the redactor who made this addition also the author of v. 22b?[27] In any event, the complexity of the editing indicates that the material was already in written form.

(*d*) In the concluding verses, the increase of anaphoric pronouns also points to redactional retouching (τούτων earlier in v. 27, then πάντα ταῦτα in v. 30a, τούτων in v. 30b, αὐτοῦ, ταῦτα in v. 31a; the referent for these is v. 29). In concise, pregnant prophetic or sapiential sayings, such forms are

23. See most recently Wanke 1980:223–24.

24. The formula is used redactionally only to a limited extent (Mark 11:24; Matt 12:31; 21:43; cf. also *Gos. Thom.* 21). In 11:19, Q-redaction is certainly responsible for the comparable phrase, διὰ τοῦτο καὶ ἡ σοφία τοῦ θεοῦ εἶπεν ["therefore the Wisdom of God said"]. It incorporates the saying of Wisdom as a prophetic threat against the conduct described in v. 47. See Steck 1967:52; Lührmann 1969:46. The formula, however, in no way diminishes its character as a quotation.

25. One can observe a similar procedure in Q 12:4-7: the prohibition in 12:7b, which resonates thematically with 12:4-5, is connected with the interpolation of 12:7a. See Zeller 1977b:95–96.

26. In spite of Merklein's protest (1981:179), I prefer to retain this association, which is in the first place justified through linguistic arguments. I have subsequently confirmed this point by means of *Ep. Arist.* 140–41: The Gentiles strive for food, drink, and clothing; but Israel is occupied with the rule of God. That is the non-eschatological variation of the contrast posed in Q 12:30a, 31.

27. The prophetic emphasis that is common to the two parts of the text, in spite of their functional differences, might point in this direction (see Merklein 1981:177–78).

suspiciously redactional. Hence Schenk (1981:76) justifiably thinks that in Q 11:42c the hand of an editor (Q redaction?) is at work. The cataphoric imperative in Q 12:39 may also be redactional (1981:94). In Q 3:16c αὐτός has the position of the original subject, which was displaced when the saying about the stronger one was interjected. In addition, the ἐκεῖνος and the οὕτως of Q 12:43 may have arisen from a reworking of vv. 42b-44. **[401]** In 12:30-31 the point of reference remains within the unit; it is only the introductory formula in 12:22b that directs attention beyond.

3. Juxtaposition of Macro-Texts

(a) As we saw with the example of Q 12:2-12, 22-31—this chain of sayings can probably be extended even more by including at least 12:33-34—thematically coherent complexes[28] were joined into large paraenetic units by means of catchwords at the beginning and end. One might also consider whether the catchword διορύσσειν ["dig"] in Q 12:33 [// Matt 6:20] has provoked the association of 12:39-40 after it (thus Schweizer 1973:102).

(b) A paraenetic unit of just this sort is found in the first discourse of Jesus, Q 6:20-49. One can debate whether it was the final redaction of this unit that placed the beatitudes where they are. Despite its differing literary form, the final beatitude provides the ostensible setting for the admonitions that follow concerning behavior with respect to the opponents. One can be more certain about the conclusion. Appended to a group of sapiential sayings that concern ways of speaking with one's brothers and sisters (6:37-38, 41-45), there is a prophetic reprimand that has to do with the relationship of the audience to the Lord who is speaking (6:46). The same is the case in the concluding parable (6:47-49). Hence in these materials there is already a reflection on the kind of result that the admonition of Jesus contained in Q should produce. This discussion, conducted on a pragmatic meta-level—together with the change of literary form—seems to me to point unavoidably to the final redaction of Q.

This hypothesis can be corroborated if Schenk's observation, that the introductory formulae in the concluding parable originate with Q-redaction, turns out to be correct.[29] This performative hyper-statement would then betray the same hand from a stylistic point of view. Add to this the tradition-historical suggestion that the metaphorical material of the saying—following Jewish analogies (see Strack and Billerbeck 1922:469–70)—originally illustrated the observance of the Law and was transferred by Christians to the topic of acting in accordance with the commandment of Jesus.[30]

28. On the paraenetic sayings complexes, see Zeller 1977b:191–92.
29. Schenk 1981:35. They should be reconstructed with reference to Q 7:31-32; 13:18,
20. Schulz (1972:312) conjectures an interrogative formulation, and with good reason.
30. See in general Denaux 1982.

4. Arrangement of the Macro-Texts

The final redaction may be discerned where there is a significant sequence of larger units. For example, one can find reasons why [402] the apophthegm in Q 7:1-10 follows the first discourse of Jesus (see Lührmann 1969:58) and why it comes before the Baptist's question, where Jesus' miracles are presupposed. Similarly, it appears significant that the apophthegms on discipleship in 9:57-60 have their place prior to the commissioning speech. For disciples must first be called—at least by way of illustration—before they can be sent out.

Hence there is a hierarchy of editorial phases whereby with an increasing range of influence and increasing levels of complexity, the probability likewise increases that they were concretized in written form and that, consequently, one is dealing with redaction.

CASE STUDIES

After having laid out the criteria for possible redaction and constructing a picture of the approximate gradations in Q-redaction, we should test this sketch in a preliminary way on several texts, without having to go into all the questions of detail.

1. Q 7:18-28, 31-35 (Jesus and the Baptist)

(a) The apophthegm in 7:18-23 stands out as the first sub-unit. In the introductory question, the use of ὁ ἐρχόμενος ["the Coming One"] is striking. What is meant by this phrase appears to be part of the background knowledge presupposed by both the addressees and the readers. Since ὁ ἐρχόμενος is not a usual messianic title, a redactional reference back to Q 3:16 [// Matt 3:11] is proposed,[31] even though the relational phrase ὀπίσω μου ["after me"] is missing. The article would then have an anaphoric force. It would be a case of a "referential form" (Kallmeyer, Klein, Meyer-Hermann, Netzer, and Siebert 1974:230–32).

Nevertheless, it is not necessary in my view to assume that redaction deliberately created a retrospective formulation. The phrase ὁ ἐρχόμενος is intentionally left open and hence the response, which is interspersed with allusions to prophetic texts, is satisfactory. The "Coming One" is therefore the one who brings salvation promised by the Scriptures.[32]

(b) Q 7:24 uses a narrative transition that on the one hand introduces the

31. See Hoffmann 1972:199. Since in 3:16 the one who baptizes with the Spirit is expected, the phrase "the Coming One" does not simply refer to the Son of Man. See my remarks in Zeller 1975:69–70.

32. It is probably the Messiah who is intended—ultimately Stanton (1973) agrees—even though the quotations that allude to Jesus' wonders and joyful message do not originally have this identification specially in view. Since no OT quotations refer to a wonder-working and preaching messiah, the description in v. 22 must remain general and the notion of what is being sought must remain vague.

speech of Jesus that follows and on the other refers back to the [**403**] preceding episode by means of a genitive absolute (hence redaction in Greek!) and—following Matthew—a pronoun [τούτων]. Thus the topic is announced: "Concerning John." This feature is also necessary, because the person who is the subject of the discourse in vv. 24-27 is not expressly stated. This is obviously a redactional formulation that connects the response to John to a discourse about the Baptist. The introductory formula will now control the speech all the way to v. 35.

(c) Ostensibly, οὗτός ἐστιν in v. 27 might be understood deicticly, as referring to the situation. But the predicate appears more often as an explanatory formula;[33] here, too, the reference is to the figure of the Baptist mentioned in vv. 24-26. In view of this use of anaphora, v. 27 may have been secondarily attached to the discourse in vv. 24-26, which was already complete in itself.[34] The verse now grasps the significance of the Baptist in the fact that he is identified scripturally as the precursor of the Messiah, and thus in this sense he is also subordinated to Jesus.

(d) Verse 28 as a whole may be a commentary saying on v. 27 that relativizes the importance of the Baptist vis-à-vis the disciples of Jesus. In view of the repeated λέγω ὑμῖν, it is scarcely likely that it was originally attached to v. 26.[35] The performative formula signals an addition.

(e) These two interpretive sentences that were appended to vv. 24-26 were not, however, inserted here by the redaction responsible for the assembling of the whole Baptist complex. For this redaction also introduced the parable in vv. 31-35—possibly with a retrospective comment corresponding to 7:29-30—under the purview of the introductory formula in 7:24a. Rather than denigrating John, it places him on the side of Jesus and over against "this generation." The explanation in vv. 33-34 is certainly secondary,[36] but it is not the product of Q-redaction, since v. 33 contains the catchword *John* that enables Q-redaction to incorporate the parable.[37]

The final redactional phase, accordingly, can be seen in the addition of v. 24a and the attaching of the parable—and probably also in the introductory formula of the parable (see above, p. 122). Thus the segment about the Baptist, which originally functioned in the polemic against the disciples of the Baptist (7:18-23, 28), obtained a new focus in the polemic against "this generation." In the end it served the self-justification of the "children of Wisdom" who did not take offense at Jesus. [**404**]

---

33. Compare the redactional use in Matt 3:3; 7:12; 14:2 and—in agreement with Mark—in 13:19-20, 22-23.

34. Compare the "more than" sayings of Q 11:31-32 with 7:26.

35. Along with Schulz (1972:230–31) and, more recently, Wanke (1980:215–16), I now hold it likely that the verse is an original unity.

36. Verses 33-34 are, however, not a commentary saying since they are not independently transmissible (against Schürmann 1975:131 and Wanke 1980:216). The tradents interpreting Jesus' parable will have recognized themselves in "the children of Wisdom."

37. Against Schenk 1981:46, but in agreement with Schürmann 1975:131–32.

2. Q 10:2-16, 21-22 (Instructions for the Missionaries and Jesus' Thanksgiving)

(*a*) Redaction criticism not only postulates an introduction to the speech but also has difficulty with the tension between 10:2 and 10:3. The metaphor of the harvest and the command to pray for missionaries are not directed to those who in v. 3 are sent out but to Christians who are, as it were, gathered for prayer before a commissioning (cf. Acts 13:1-3). In this verse an ecclesial *Sitz im Leben* is visible, while the rules in vv. 3-12 were probably the concern of the messengers of Jesus alone.[38] It is conceivable that the proverb in v. 7b, which uses the same metaphor ἐργάτης ["worker"], was attached at the same stage as v. 2.

(*b*) Comparison with Mark gives rise to the suggestion that v. 3 was also added later, perhaps for the reason that, owing to the presence of the frontispiece of v. 2, it was impossible to have any reference to the commissioning in a narrative introduction as there is in Mark.

(*c*) The actual instructions in vv. 4-7, 8a, 9-11a are probably also the result of some growth. But this growth probably occurred at the oral stage in which it is easier to arrive at the striking *hysteron-proteron* of support in the house mission in the city. Verse 12, which does not appear in Mark, is probably secondary, but it is not the product of Q-redaction,[39] since it has occasioned the connection of vv. 13-15 with its similar-sounding threat in v. 14 (thus, convincingly, Schulz 1972:409).

(*d*) The woes in vv. 13-15 disrupt the catchword connection of Luke 10:10 with Matt 10:40 (δέχεσθαι, "welcome") and originally had a different *Sitz im Leben*.[40] If they are interpolated here, it is probably for the sake of the tradents of the instructions in vv. 3-12 who, like Jesus, were rejected by the Galilean cities. The woes serve to stiffen their resolve by appealing to a saying of Jesus.[41] The current arrangement of materials allows one to think of the wonder-working of the messengers (thus Schenk 1981:56). That the sanctions (in vv. 12 and 13-15) are identical underscores indirectly the authority of the messengers. Verse 16, absent from Mark, also explains that God himself is the authority standing behind Jesus. [**405**]

(*e*) The entire composition, however, is not aimed at the judgment of the unbelieving cities of Israel. For it is apparently followed by a prayer of Jesus (Q 10:21-22), located at the same time of the commissioning by means of

---

38. Schürmann has also noted that in v. 2 God is the sender, but in v. 3 it is Jesus. See Schürmann 1968b:143 n. 24.

39. Against Lührmann 1969:60, 62; Laufen 1980:275.

40. The woes represent a different literary form and have the cities as their addressees. While vv. 13-14 have in mind the miracles of Jesus, v. 15 is, according to Schürmann, an "added saying" (*Zusatzwort*) that treats the prominence of Capernaum with an allusion to the Scriptures. The two units may have been connected in the oral tradition.

41. Lührmann (1969:64) says rightly: "The proclamation of the disciples thus has the same weight as that of Jesus, for the attitude one takes to it is decisive for the outcome of the judgment."

the narrative introduction with an anaphoric temporal reference.[42] In view of this retrospective introduction, the content of the ταῦτα ["these things"] is to be filled in from what precedes it. The critical problem is the rejection of the message of the imminent reign of God, which is attributed to the Father's concealing activity. Now the νήπιοι ["simple"], to whom the mystery is revealed, are no longer just the messengers themselves but all those who have received their proclamation.

In 10:22, which from a tradition-historical point of view is later, what is hidden is no longer the simple message of the reign of God. Here, knowledge of the Father is mediated by the Son; and it is not simply a matter of knowing the Father but also of recognizing the dignity of the Son. The post-Easter setting shines through. Since the verse is coordinated so closely to 10:21 with the catchwords πατήρ ["father"] and ἀποκαλύψαι ["reveal"], a redactor may have constructed a christological explication here; in any event, he employed language that already bore a clear impress, as one can infer from the history-of-religions parallels and the didactic tone of 10:22bc.[43]

Both Q 10:2 and 10:21-22 direct attention to the present experience of the Christian community. Here, the sending of Jesus' envoys reaches its goal in the revelation of the Father disclosed by the Son. Considering the rejection that the message has experienced at the hands of the official circles of Judaism, the revelatory event must be promised to outsiders in an apocalyptic manner. The rules for envoys retain their currency, however, because the community should continue to produce missionaries from its midst (10:2).[44]

3. Q 11:14-15, 17-23, 24-26 (Controversy about Exorcism)

(a) This discourse, unified by the theme of exorcism that is articulated in various lexemes, has a narrative introduction. Although Mark has only the reproach in Mark 3:22, one should not treat the miracle story in Q 11:14 as secondary,[45] since the use of a miracle to occasion a controversy is a well-established form, and the inability of the demon to speak is a concrete detail that plays no further role in the story. Of course, the insinuation in 11:15b is generalizing; it was obviously a widely known accusation. [406]

(b) Since the answer is given in the form of a metaphorical saying and its application, vv. 19 and 20 must be regarded as successive additions, whether or not Mark has omitted them. Nevertheless, the possibility remains that from the point of view of tradition history, 11:19 is parallel to vv. 17-18 as

---

42. See Sabbe's treatment of this saying (Sabbe 1982).
43. Wanke (1980:220) again thinks that 10:22 is a commentary saying.
44. It is not evident that the verse is directed in any special way to leaders of the community (against Polag 1977:14).
45. Thus Fuchs 1979:35-37. Rightly, Bultmann 1968:13-14; Laufen 1980:132.

a response to the widely circulating accusation, and a response in which Jesus goes on the counterattack.[46]

As far as Q 11:20 is concerned, I would like to abandon my earlier view that the verse was first formed as the positive counterpart to the rhetorical question in 11:18a.[47] The catchword βασιλεία ["reign"] (vv. 17-18, 20) might be an indication in favor of this view, so that the reign of Satan and the reign of God are contrasted. But the use of "by the finger of God" is too obviously a counterpart to "by Beelzebul," and the more proximate point of reference for v. 20 is v. 19 rather than v. 15. Hence, v. 19 did not come into existence just at the time that 11:20 was attached to 11:17-18, and certainly not in the redaction of Q.[48]

Is 11:20 then a "commentary saying" that expounds on the distinctiveness of Jesus vis-à-vis Jewish exorcists (v. 19)?[49] The saying, however, does not contest the fact that they exorcise demons with the finger of God. Although the conditional sentence uses v. 19a as its pattern, its connection with the preceding verse is not especially strong. Rather, the urgent questions of v. 19 *and* v. 18 (connected by a catchword!) require a decisive answer that characterizes Jesus' activity in a positive way. One cannot avoid the conclusion that it was appended by the redaction that created the composition in Q 11:14-19.

(c) The metaphor of the binding of the strong man (11:21-22) describes a battle. For this reason it triggers the statement in v. 23 that implicitly is a summons to espouse the cause of Jesus. On the one hand, the verse is still determined by the controversy of 11:15-20 and unmasks those who slander Jesus as his adversaries. On the other, it uses the metaphor of gathering in addressing the envoys who, along with Jesus, are proclaiming the reign of God (cf. Q 11:20b with 10:9). [407] Does it thereby betray a certain appropriation of the conflict with Jewish opponents by early Christian missionaries? They were indeed indicted with the accusation leveled against Jesus when they engaged in exorcisms.

(d) Q 11:24-26 portrays a bitter experience with exorcisms and appears to be only superficially connected with the preceding debate. The prosaic saying represents a warning—directed to early Christian exorcists?—that the vacuum left by the unclean spirit must be filled with something posi-

46. This conclusion is inferred from the fact that 11:19 does not, like the metaphor [in 11:17-18], use Satan but instead speaks of Beelzebul, as does 11:15b. See also Schweizer 1973:184. Laufen's criticism of this position (1980:435 n. 76) does not distinguish sufficiently between tradition-historical and redaction-critical issues.

47. See Zeller 1977a, esp. 263. The discussion of this verse is muddied by the interest in recovering an authentic saying of Jesus.

48. Against Lührmann 1969:33; Laufen 1980:148; Merklein 1981:158–59. I cannot share their assumption that v. 20 is an independent saying. The adversative conditional sentence indicates all too clearly an alternative position.

49. Thus Wanke 1980:219. But does the verse in this form fulfill the requirements for an independent existence?

tive.[50] It intensifies the summons of Q 11:23: there is no neutral position when it comes to Jesus.

It has become more certain that the sayings cluster concerning the Beelzebul controversy, which was at first applied to the opponents, received a new ecclesial *Sitz im Leben*.[51] This new setting does not contradict the fact that with the pericope concerning the request of a sign (Q 11:29-32) the polemic against the unbelievers of this generation is taken up again. In Q 11:33-35, of course, it can likewise have a paraenetic conclusion.

INFERENCES ABOUT THE *SITZ IM LEBEN*

Although I have made only test probes in larger complexes, I can now venture a few tentative hypotheses concerning the redactional strata that have been highlighted and their respective *Sitze im Leben*.

1. The kernel of many of the sayings groups was composed and transmitted by wandering and wonder-working *missionaries*. This conclusion is certain with Q 10:3-16 but probable also with Q 12:22-31. For they could relate the sapiential admonition, "do not be anxious," to their problem of maintaining themselves and feel spurred on in their missionary activity as the seeking of the kingdom of God. The composition in Q 12:2-9 probably also had to do with the threat to life that these envoys in particular had to expect. Q 10:13-15 and 11:23 might indicate that they also transmitted material that polemicized against Israel. They could use it, so to speak, as ammunition where they ran into rejection, as Jesus did. The way that this circle of tradents handed on the sayings of Jesus, and perhaps were the first to write them down (in Aramaic), recalls the activity of prophetic schools (see Zeller 1977b:197–98).

2. This explanation should not now fall into the mistake of suspecting that the ethos of these poor, vagrant, and persecuted envoys of Jesus **[408]** is behind all the Q-material.[52] When the issue of possessions is raised, it is of course obvious that the collected sayings of Jesus are also intended to address well-to-do Christians. They are the only ones who are directly in danger of wanting to serve mammon (Q 16:13).[53] The saying in Q 12:33-34, which was probably placed after Q 12:22-31, encourages almsgiving by means of figurative speech and would be intended in the first place for those who were somewhat well-off.[54]

In addition, the subject of the first speech of Jesus in Q concerning con-

---

50. See the detailed discussion in Laufen 1980:140–42. My view is taken also by Hoffmann (1972:299) and Schenk (1981:69–70).

51. Fuchs (1979:106, 202) also remarks on the turn to the reader.

52. Thus Schottroff and Stegemann 1986:38–66, inspired by Hoffmann. But see Schottroff's qualifications (ibid., 39). [Schottroff is responsible for this portion of the book—ED.]

53. See also the temptation story, and on this story, my essay (Zeller 1980, esp. 71).

54. See Zeller 1977b:79–80 and my article on θησαυρός (Zeller 1991, esp. 150). Schottroff and Stegemann (1986:52–53) take a different view.

tact with people who are in part ill disposed should not be restricted to the situation of the envoys of Jesus.[55] There is indeed no reason to associate the larger collected units in the programmatic speech with the commissioning speech under the rubric of discipleship.[56] For to do this one would have to ignore the Baptist complex, whose position is scarcely the result of Lukan redaction.

Thus one may assume that the tradition of the itinerant preachers found a new *Sitz im Leben* in the *communities* that were founded by them.[57] In this setting, it was used partly for paraenetic purposes. The epilogue to the commissioning speech (10:21-22) shows how the community anchored its self-understanding as those who have received revelation through the design of God and the mediation of the Son.

3. The material that was formed in the midst of the conflict with the disciples of the Baptist (Q 3:7-9, 16-17; 7:18-23, 28) and the speeches directed against this unbelieving generation and its representatives (Q 11:14-23, 29-32; 11:39-52) appear in their present context to have been stripped of the immediate controversy. Christian catechumens could apply the summons to repentance in Q 3:7-9 to themselves; and even in the woes against the Pharisees and scribes, Q 11:42c offers a practical suggestion for the Christian audience.

The judgment of Israel continues to loom, but one gets the impression from many of the obviously later pericopae that the community had already written off its unbelieving contemporaries. On the one hand, it assured itself of its own patronage by the Son of Man; on the other hand, the faith that was wanting in the Jewish people legitimized openness to the Gentiles (see Q 7:1-10; 13:28-29; 22:28-30). **[409]**

4. Now we come to the question of the final redaction of the entire sayings source Q. Although it unquestionably took place, it is also risky to assign to it any of the particular redactional processes that have been discussed. One can see the effects of the final redaction best where relatively large interventions occur.[58] Often, the additional (and necessary!) tradition-historical and history-of-religions consideration settles the matter by indicating redaction in a Greek-speaking Jewish Christian environment.[59] One can say that the final redactor was hardly a creative prophet. The final literary assembling of material that is in part quite heterogeneous is best credited to early Christian teachers (see Zeller 1977b:198; Polag 1977:30).

5. Distinctions of the sort attempted above are not very popular at the present. What is preferred is the sensational and practical. But perhaps

---

55. Against Schottroff and Stegemann 1986:60–63, who on p. 61 misconstrue Q 11:9-13.
56. Against Lührmann 1969:58 and more recently Kuhn 1980:113–15.
57. See Zeller 1977b:192, with reference to the sapiential admonitions, and ibid., 198 for suggestions concerning the tradents in the community. Polag (1977:28–29) disagrees in part.
58. See above "Redactional Stages," §§2a, 3a, 3b, 4; "Test Cases," §§1b, 1e, 2a, 2e, 3d.
59. See Polag 1977:145–70, with reservations on particular details.

these distinctions have the useful function of affording an insight into the changing fates of the Q-material. From the radical, itinerant life-style of its first tradents, it succeeded in a sedentary community that directed its daily affairs by this material. The polemic against Israel now fulfilled another function: through it the Jewish Christian community discovered its own identity. In contrast to the majority of Israel, it subjected itself to the word of the Lord. Exegesis would do well to pay attention to the various redactional phases and the practical background that pertained to each.

8

Matthew 7:7-11 par. Luke 11:9-13

Evidence of Design and Argument in the Collection of Jesus' Sayings

RONALD A. PIPER

The predeliction of form criticism for the study of individual pericopae has frequently been at the cost of the study of collection of Jesus' sayings. Even the recognition of small and early collections of sayings has seldom been matched by much progress in explaining *how* these collections came into being and *what functions* they originally served. Such explanations have been still less forthcoming for collections which are predominantly composed of maxims and gnomic sayings,[1] for the well-defined, self-contained nature of such sayings can all too easily lead to the assumption that their collection is simply a loose conjunction of "variations on a theme." Catchword connections or topical associations may explain how some of these sayings have been brought together into larger units, but these considerations may obscure other, more important, motives of compilation. The search for such motives is as important for these collections as for others with more obvious theological interests.

The logia about asking and receiving in Q 11:9-13 are an important instance of a compact collection of gnomic sayings which is far from haphazard in its structure. On the contrary, it will be argued that it presents a carefully designed argument, the structure of which is not unique to this collection alone. Within the scope of this paper detailed attention can only be given to Q 11:9-13, but the wider implications of the argumentative design will be briefly noted in conclusion [see Piper 1989].

From Ronald A. Piper, "Matthew 7,7-11 par. Lk 11,9-13: Evidence of Design and Argument in the Collection of Jesus' Sayings," pp. 411–18 in Joël Delobel, ed., *Logia: Les Paroles de Jésus—The Sayings of Jesus: Mémorial Joseph Coppens*, BETL 59 (Leuven: Uitgeverij Peeters and Leuven Univ. Press, 1982). Piper usually refers to Q-texts by their Matthaean location. All have been converted into "Q" (i.e., Lukan) versification.

1. For recent studies of gnomic wisdom in the Synoptic tradition, cf. esp. Zeller 1977b; Küchler 1979:55–92; Carlston 1980.

Rudolf Bultmann rightly observed that one can no longer trace with confidence the stages by which the individual sayings in Q 11:9-13 were elaborated and joined together, although there is little doubt that some elaboration and uniting of material did occur (1968:87). The close parallelism between the threefold exhortations and promises in Q 11:9 ("Ask, and it will be given you; seek, and you will find; knock, and it will be opened to you") and the threefold proverbial statements in Q 11:10 ("For everyone who asks receives, and he who seeks finds, [412] and to him who knocks it will be opened") suggests that one unit has been modeled on the other, although it is not possible to decide with certainty which preceded.[2] It is also possible that the sayings on "seeking" and "knocking" are elaborations of the sayings on "asking," for it is clear that in the present context the theme of asking-receiving is dominant. It is this theme alone which holds Q 11:9-10 and 11:11-12 together. The original independence of the two units is confirmed by the self-contained nature of each and the presence of formal and thematic differences between the two.[3] Whereas the opening admonitions and maxims encourage hearers to "ask," "seek," and "knock" and emphasize the accompanying promises of receiving and finding, the rhetorical questions which follow in Q 11:11-12 show concern for the harmfulness or usefulness of what is received. The latter sayings also lack any reference to the images of "seeking" and "knocking," and introduce the new imagery of a father-son relationship. Finally, the concluding saying in Q 11:13 ("If you then, who are evil, know how to give good gifts to your children, how much more . . .") must either have been already united in the tradition with 11:11-12 or added at the time of the final compilation. It is doubtful that it could have existed as an independent unit since it required something to precede the a fortiori comparison.

Common to these varied sayings, however, is the high suitability of each for persuasive argument and popular appeal through the use of wisdom admonition, maxim, rhetorical question, and a fortiori comparison. Despite the imperative opening, all these sayings are suited to convince, not simply to demand or announce (cf. Zeller 1977b:128–30). This becomes evident not only as one looks at the individual forms, but even more so as one examines the development of the argument in the context of the collection.

1. The first stage of the argument comprises admonitions and promises in Q 11:9 which are almost embarrassing in the scope of what is [413]

---

2. Minear (1972:115) argues that Q 11:10 is "an innocuous and unnecessary restatement" in proverbial form of Q 11:9. This evaluation is rightly challenged by Zeller (1977b:128–29), although Zeller still considers Q 11:10 to have been modeled on 11:9.

3. Bultmann 1968:86; Minear 1972:117; also apparently Ott 1965:99–112 and Jeremias 1972:144–45. In contrast, Schulz 1972:163; Marshall 1978:465–66; and Zeller 1977b:128. Zeller's observation that "it is [Matt] v. 11 that first exposes the theological passive of v. 7" and that a catchword connection on αἰτεῖν ["ask"] and διδόναι ["give"] exists between the two units are hardly unambiguous arguments for original unity. Parallels to Q 11:9-10 alone are preserved in *Gos. Thom.* 2, 92, 94.

encouraged and promised.[4] There is no limitation of what is to be asked for or sought, and the threefold illustration accentuates the breadth of the admonition. It is also not immediately clear that petitionary prayer is how "asking" is to be interpreted. While the verbs δοθήσεται ["will be given"] and ἀνοιγήσεται ["will be opened"] are capable of being considered divine passives (Jeremias 1971:11), and while ζητεῖτε ["seek"] and κρούετε ["knock"] can be used figuratively of prayer (McNeile 1915:91–92; Marshall 1978:466–67), no such specific interpretation is at first demanded.[5] One must not lose the generality of these sayings by reading them too quickly in terms of what follows. Initially the appeal is wide and general.

2. The second unit consists of three maxims (Q 11:10) which run parallel to one another and to the opening admonition. The sole function of these maxims is to provide *additional* support for the preceding promises of receiving, finding, and opening, and significantly, the promises are now expressed in the form of general rules about human experience. Everyone (πᾶς) who asks receives.[6] That gnomic apperception, rather than religious insight or prophetic announcement, is the ostensible basis of appeal in this verse is demonstrated by the strikingly unqualified πᾶς, the predominance of habitual present rather than future tenses (λαμβάνει, εὑρίσκει ["receive," "find"]), and the continuing absence of clear references to divine agency. Indeed the change from δοθήσεται (v. 9) to λαμβάνει (v. 10) diminishes any suggestion of the theological significance of the passive.

The optimism of these maxims is of course striking. The promise of receiving, which is the main point of contention, may draw support, however, from its conjunction with the more familiar promise of "finding" for the one who seeks,[7] or the less contentious promise of the [414] "opening" to the one who knocks. In any case, maxims are never comprehensive generalizations about the world; they always express insights true to an aspect of experience rather than to human experience as a whole.[8]

3. The third stage of the collection, the rhetorical questions found in Q

4. Contrast the qualifications added in John 15:7; 1 John 3:22; 5:14-15, and Hermas, *Mand.* 9.4; *Sim.* 6.3.6b. Cf. also Minear 1972:114–15, 126–30.

5. "Seeking" can be with reference to God (Deut 4:29; Isa 55:6; Jer 29:13; cf. Greeven 1964: 892–93), to wisdom (Prov 8:17b), to the Law (Sir 32:15), or to entry into the kingdom (Matt 6:33). Similarly, "knocking" may serve as an image not only for prayer (*b. Meg.* 12b) but also for study of the Law (*Pesikta* 176a) and possibly for entry to the kingdom (Jeremias 1965:178). It is only in the light of the development of the argument, esp. in Q 11:13, that application to prayer is made clear.

6. Whether or not this was originally "beggar's wisdom" (cf. Jeremias 1972:159), it has been formulated as a general rule of experience. As argued below, one must not overstate the theological significance of the passive at this point (contra Zeller 1977b:129).

7. Cf. n. 5 above and Zeller 1977b:128–29. One may also conjecture that the well-attested application of "seeking" to wisdom (Prov 2:4-5; 8:17b; 14:6; Qoh 7:25; Sir 4:12; 24:34; 51:13; Wis 8:2, 17) further commended this saying to the interest of those clearly skilled in the use of practical wisdom. There is nothing to suggest, however, that this would have been more than a secondary interest.

8. Von Rad 1972:71, 87, 113, 311; Collins 1980:5–6.

11:11-12, marks a new departure in the argument, as indicated earlier. The preceding images of asking, seeking, and knocking are now confined simply to asking. The context for the asking also comes into clearer focus as it is now expressed within a father-son relationship. The note of assurance struck in the preceding verses is continued, since rhetorical questions permit no doubt as to their answer; but the assurance has now become that of not receiving something detrimental or useless. What is received will meet one's needs, here expressed in terms of requests for food. These new features provide the link between Q 11:9-10 and the final argument in Q 11:13, while maintaining the appeal to experiential evidence.

The actual details of the rhetorical questions are of course confused by the difference between Matthew and Luke at this point.[9] Luke may well be responsible for the substitution of πατέρα ["father"] for ἄνθρωπος ["person"] (cf. Luke 11:11) so as to improve the connection with the concluding sayings, but it serves only to make explicit what is already implicit in the common reference to υἱός ["son"] (Schulz 1972:162). The other differences are not critical to the structure of the argument.[10] The double rhetorical questions effectively indicate that a multiplicity of illustrations from daily life could have been drawn upon for support.

4. The final saying (Q 11:13) provides the interpretative key to all that has preceded, switching for an appeal to experience to an appeal to reason. The preceding example of a father's response to his son's request is made the basis for an a fortiori application to the heavenly Father. This is the first direct evidence in the compilation to God and therefore also the first clear reference to "asking" in terms of petitionary prayer. What has previously been phrased in the most general terms is at last made specific (Minear 1972:117). Assent to the general argument is carefully won before the specific application is made.

A major difficulty of interpretation, though, is the question of what is to be sought and received of God. First is the problem of the difference [415] between Matthew's ἀγαθά ["good things"] and Luke's πνεῦμα ἅγιον ["Holy Spirit"]. W. Ott has persuasively argued that Luke's version is the more likely to be secondary because the ambiguous reference to ἀγαθά and its openness to abuse would be incompatible with Luke's general outlook toward material possessions (Ott 1965:107–8; also Schulz 1972:162). H.-Th. Wrege, in contrast, has argued that the giving of the Spirit to the disciples prior to Easter would have been an unlikely Lukan introduction (Wrege 1968:108; also Marshall 1978:470). Luke, however, may be pointing forward in this passage to a post-Easter period by the use of the future tense δώσει. Just as the preceding Lord's prayer in Luke 11:1-4 is a prayer

---

9. Cf. Schulz 1972:161–62; Ott 1965:102–12.
10. All three questions have in common a request for an item of food. For a possible progression in imagery, however, see Ott 1965:109–11.

for the church, so also may the Holy Spirit here be a promise for the church.

One is still left with the problem of the meaning of ἀγαθά, however, if one accepts its originality. How far does ἀγαθά include material benefits? Certainly the rhetorical questions in Q 11:11-12 were expressed in terms of material benefits alone, albeit primarily directed to the meeting of physical needs, such as for food. The a fortiori comparison in Q 11:13 does not appear to apply to what is to be sought, but rather simply to the caring father-son relationship. In the absence of any other interpretative clues for ἀγαθά one seems compelled to allow at least for the meeting of physical needs in this promise.[11] Indeed if one has here only a vague promise of "spiritual blessing," it would hardly have required the extensive and persuasive argument which has been presented. The impression is that the persuasion is employed to counter doubts about very real problems of need facing followers. Just as human fathers, who are evil, know how to meet the physical needs of their sons, how much more will the heavenly Father be able to meet these requirements. That segments of the early church, especially in Palestine, actually had cause to doubt this benevolence is clearly indicated in Acts and the letters of Paul (cf. Acts 11:17-30; Rom 15:26; Gal 2:10).[12] The style of argument is therefore suggestive of its purpose and possibly of a *Sitz im Leben*.

This pattern of persuasion, however, is shared by other collections of gnomic sayings, particularly in the Q-tradition. These include the collections built around the admonitions to love one's enemies **[416]** (Q 6:27-29), not to be anxious about physical needs (Q 12:22-31), not to judge one's brother (Q 6:37-38, 41-42), and not to fear hostile opposition (Q 12:4-7), as well as the collection of maxims on the good and bad tree, applied to speech (Q 6:43-45).[13] Characteristic of these collections too is the pattern of progressing from general to specific application, the location of the interpretative key at the concluding stage of the argument, the use of (usually multiple) rhetorical questions at the center of the collection (cf. also Schulz 1972:163 n. 193), the change of imagery as the argument progresses, and the dominance of the appeal to experience and reason. In terms of the four stages of argument observed in Q 11:9-13, the other collections can be outlined as follows:

1. General opening sayings: Q 6:27, 35b;[14] 12:22; 6:37; 12:4; 6:43.
2. Sayings producing arguments directly in support of the initial instruction: Q 6:35c; 12:23; 6:37; 12:5; 6:44a.

---

11. So also Minear 1972:118; McNeile 1915:92; Ott 1965:108; Schweizer 1975:174.

12. Cf. Hengel 1974b:34; Theissen 1978:57; Jeremias 1969:121–23.

13. One may also include here Mark 8:34-38. This collection alone is found in the triple tradition, although the suggestion that it may derive from an earlier sayings tradition which also had contact with Q has been argued by Best (1976; 1981:30–31).

14. Piper argues that Matthew best represents Q's ordering of the sayings in Q 6:27-36, i.e., 6:27 (Matt 5:44); 6:35bc (Matt 5:45); 6:32-33 (Matt 5:46-47); 6:36 (Matt 5:48).—ED.

3. Rhetorical questions/new illustrations: Q 6:32-33; 12:24-28; 6:41-42a; 12:6-7a; 6:44b.
4. Final argument and application: Q 6:36; 12:29-31; 6:42b; 12:7b; 6:45.

The theme of each of these collections can be related to difficult practical problems confronting early Christians in which persuasion would have been of critical importance. The convergence of composition style, type of problem addressed, and source to which the collections are assigned provides a strong indication that these collections are to be attributed to a unique source of compilation within the Synoptic tradition.[15] They are not haphazard collections; they display a design and argument unique in the Synoptic tradition. [417]

These correspondences, however, also provide evidence for a tradition in early Christianity which was concerned to present Jesus' teaching from the perspective of practical wisdom. This observation is not a new one. J. M. Robinson (1971b; above, pp. 51–58) and R. A. Edwards[16] have been among those who have argued persuasively that Q has been influenced by such a perspective, as demonstrated by the quantity of logia of gnomic description which are assigned to Q and by the nature of the Q-collection as a whole. The present analysis provides a more limited and specific demonstration of how gnomic wisdom has proved attractive as a powerful, persuasive form of argument in the hands of those skilled in its use. This skill has been shown by several applications of a similar style of argument, yet with the emphasis remaining on the outlook of practical rather than speculative wisdom. Little support in this study of Q 11:9-13 can be found for the contention of S. Schulz that despite the artistry of the collection, it is best classified as "prophetic demand." Such a view runs contrary to the tone of the entire presentation.[17]

The absence of a prophetic or polemical tone in the present compilation, though, need not suggest that the tradition from which it derived had no

15. A correspondence in structure between some of these collections has also been briefly noted by Zeller (1977b:142). Zeller's concentration on wisdom admonitions, however, causes him to fail to include Q 6:43-45. Details of Zeller's analysis are also open to question, such as the apparent assignment of Q 11:13 to "the centerpiece" of the construction. Fundamentally, however, Zeller seems to understand these regularities in structure simply as the way in which *various* traditions *grew*: "These units grew in various sectors of tradition—only the sequence of Q 11:9, 11-13 shows itself to be relatively stable—through elaboration and amalgamation with larger compositions, which also display certain regularities." This fails to recognize the strong features of design and argument in these sayings collections and the predominance of such collections in Q alone, which suggests intentional and unique composition.
16. Edwards 1976:58–80. Also cf. Beardslee 1967; 1970:30–41.
17. Schulz 1972:163–64. Schulz particularly finds evidence of prophetic authority in two formulas, λέγω ὑμῖν ["I tell you"] and τίς ἐξ ὑμῶν ["which one of you"]. Curiously, Schulz recognizes the secondary nature of κἀγὼ ὑμῖν λέγω ["and I tell you"] in Luke, but still believes that such a formula *would* have introduced this unit of sayings. The formula τίς ἐξ ὑμῶν may (so Greeven) originate in prophetic tradition, but in the Synoptic tradition frequently introduces parabolic argument rather than prophetic accusation; cf. Matt 6:27; Luke 11:5; 14:28; 17:7. In Q 11:11 the force of the formula can hardly be an accusation (see also n. 19 below).

place at all for these other aspects of Jesus' teaching.[18] The nature of the argument is dependent as much on the nature of the problem addressed as on the wisdom orientation of the compiler(s). Both have their part to play. In Q 11:9-13, as in the collection of sayings in Q 12:22-31, the problem appears to be one of a response to a situation of physical need. Because such a situation could easily give rise to factious divisions among followers (cf. Acts 6:1ff.),[19] the preference shown for an encouraging, universally phrased presentation of instruction to either polemic or religious platitude is readily understandable. Similar sensitivities may underlie the instruction about judgmental attitudes toward one's brother in Q 6:36-37 and [418] about reactions in the face of hostile opposition in Q 12:4-7. The structure of these compilations therefore is testimony of early attempts by those learned in wisdom to apply Jesus' teaching to some of the most sensitive problems of the early Christian communities.

18. With respect to the combination of such traditions in Q, cf. Edwards 1976:*passim*.

19. Jeremias (1972:144–45) argued that Matt 7:9-11 was originally addressed to opponents. The connection with Matt 7:7-8, however, makes such an address unlikely for the collection as a whole, and the father-son relationship expressed in vv. 9-11 is also particularly appropriate for "insiders," despite the general reference to ὑμεῖς πονηροί.

9

The Formation of Q and
Antique Instructional Genres

———————————— JOHN S. KLOPPENBORG

[443] Prior to the influential essay of James M. Robinson, "ΛΟΓΟΙ ΣΟΦΩΝ: Zur Gattung der Spruchquelle Q," which appeared in the Bultmann *Festschrift* (1964; ET 1971b),[1] the question of the literary genre and hermeneutic of Q had received little more than passing reference. The basic contours of Robinson's proposals are well-known: Q is to be located upon a trajectory of sapiential sayings genres whose origins are found in biblical collections such as Proverbs 30, 31, and 22:17—24:22—all of which bear the term *logoi* in their respective incipits[2]—and ultimately in Near Eastern collections such as Amenemope and Ahikar. The genre found more recent expression in Christian ("Q"), rabbinic (*m. 'Abot*), and gnostic (*Gospel of Thomas*) circles, but in each case it was supplanted by other genres: the Gospel form in Christianity, halakic debate and haggadah in early rabbinism, and the post-resurrection dialogue in Gnosticism.

Robinson accounted for the ultimate displacement of the genre *logoi sophōn* from Christian usage by arguing that the tendency immanent in the genre was gnosticizing. The presence of wisdom sayings in the Jesus tradition opened the possibility of framing those sayings as *logoi sophōn*. This placed the sayings tradition on a theological and generic trajectory which tended to associate the speaker of the wise sayings with the heavenly Sophia—a development already seen in Q 7:35; 10:21-22; 11:49-51.[3]

From John S. Kloppenborg, "The Formation of Q and Antique Instructional Genres," *JBL* 105 (1986) 443–62.

1. All references will be to the English version.
2. Prov 30:1: *dibrê 'āgûr*, 31:1: *dibrê lĕmû'ēl*, 22:17: λόγοις σοφῶν παράβαλλε σὸν οὖς ..., *BHK* restores the incipit as *dibrê ḥăkāmîm*.
3. This paper will use the convention adopted by the SBL Q consultation for citing Q-texts. Q-texts are cited by their *Lukan* location, e.g., Q 7:35 = Matt 11:19 // Luke 7:35.

When this in turn was coordinated with "the trajectory from the hypostatized Sophia to the gnostic redeemer" (1971b:113; above, p. 58), the sayings of Jesus could easily become the "hidden sayings" of Gnosticism. The ease with which this genre could [**444**] undergo gnosticizing distortions explained, in Robinson's view, the fact that "orthodox" circles came to prefer other, less dangerous genres.[4]

The term *logoi sophōn* has been accepted by many as a suitable generic designation for Q, the *Gospel of Thomas,* and other similar literature.[5] But the importance of Robinson's contribution goes far beyond the coining of a term. In the first place, he recognized clearly that the transition from oral to written stages of tradition was enabled by the mediation of literary genres. Moreover, he addressed the important questions of why Jesus' sayings came to be transmitted in such a genre and what theological influence the genre itself exerted upon the interpretation of those sayings. Finally, the introduction of the idea of a *Gattungsgeschichte*, which is fundamental to his approach, represents a methodological advance since it takes into account diachronic change within the field of genres and allows the interpreter to situate a document not on a static grid of generic characteristics but in terms of the inner dynamisms and tendencies expressed within the entire range of documents of a certain class.

Despite the impressive acceptance of Robinson's basic proposal regarding the sapiential nature of Q, detractors are not wanting. There has been considerable reluctance to grant that the immanent tendency of the genre is gnosticizing. It is repeatedly pointed out, for example, that of all of the examples cited, only the *Gospel of Thomas* reveals any explicit gnosticizing tendency.[6] And there have been attempts to distinguish Q from the *Gospel of Thomas* on generic as well as hermeneutical grounds. M. Devisch, rather unconvincingly, sought to drive a wedge between Q and the *Gospel of Thomas* by characterizing the former as a "composition théologique" and the latter as "un simple recueil" (Devisch 1972:85). [**445**] More recently, B. Dehandschutter disputed the propriety of grouping Q with the *Gospel of Thomas* on more cogent grounds. First, it cannot, in his view, be demonstrated that "the first traditions of the *logia* belong exclusively to a

---

This should not, however, be taken to imply that the Lukan wording is necessarily that of Q or that the Lukan location of the text is in all cases to be preferred.

4. Elsewhere Robinson speaks of the gnosticizing proclivity of the genre itself: Robinson 1965:135; 1971a:43.

5. See, e.g., Carlston 1978; 1982:111–12 (where he places Q in a "tradition [not *Gattung*] of 'wise men's sayings.'" Also Polag 1977:21 n. 58; Küchler 1979:562–63; Lührmann 1969:89–92 [pp. 62–65 in this volume]; Schenke 1978:360–61; Vielhauer 1975:316; S. Davies 1983:13–17.

6. Lührmann 1969:91 [p. 64 in this volume]; Schenke 1978:361; Küchler 1979:562–63. It is, of course, a matter of debate whether and to what extent the *Gospel of Thomas* can be called "gnostic." See most recently, S. Davies 1983:18–35.

sapiential stream."[7] Moreover, dialogical elements and indications of the context of the sayings (i.e., conversation with the disciples) play a greater role in the *Gospel of Thomas* than in Q and unlike Q, the *Gospel of Thomas*'s teachings are represented as secret sayings transmitted by Jesus to the disciples (Dehandschutter 1982:512–13). Frans Neirynck dismisses Robinson's thesis by asserting that the *Gospel of Thomas* is dependent upon the canonical Gospels, and that "its literary genre is most probably of a later origin." Q he declares to be a primitive Christian genre sui generis (Neirynck 1976).

In considering the relationship of Q to the *Gospel of Thomas,* the question of their *genetic* relations must be distinguished carefully from their *generic* relations. Even if the *Gospel of Thomas* depends literarily upon the Synoptics—and that conclusion is far from certain[8]—it is certainly not dependent upon them for its genre. The *Gospel of Thomas* does not need to be related to Q source-critically in order to share generic features. And it remains to be seen whether the idea of "secret sayings" in need of special interpretation falls outside the idiom of sapiential genres. It would seem, on the contrary, that this represents one possible expression of the characteristic notion that wise sayings require skilled interpretation (e.g., Sir 39:1-3). One suspects that the attempts to rescue Q from the company of the *Gospel of Thomas* may rest more upon theological and apologetic motives than sound literary comparisons.

The association of Q with sapiential genres has been questioned from another quarter. While conceding several points of similarity, Howard C. Kee holds that the radical eschatological comportment of Q distinguishes it from the pragmatic or Law-oriented wisdom characteristic of Sirach and other Jewish wisdom collections (1977:80–81). To this observation it could be added that the recipients of wisdom in Q are defined in more exclusive terms (Q 10:21-22, 23-24) than is the case in much of the sapiential corpus. These are surely important differences, but do they impinge on the problem of genre? There are dozens of examples of sapiential genres which do not share a purely pragmatic outlook or one founded on the equation of wisdom and the Law. Moreover, recent work on Egyptian and biblical wisdom collections [446] has convincingly challenged the naive view that their counsels are those of pure pragmatism or unprincipled opportunism. Egyptian wisdom, on the contrary, has a profound theological orientation and basis in the idea of Ma'at, the divine ground of all cosmic and human order.[9] Proverbs and Sirach reflect very similar views. For both Egyptian and biblical wisdom, human behavior should be grounded in divinely established order. Although Q is obviously distinctive in its eschatology, the

---

7. Dehandschutter 1982, quote from 510 [trans. by editor]. Recently Quispel (1981) has argued that the formative element in the *Gospel of Thomas* is a collection of Hermetic sayings.
8. See Wilson 1982:297.
9. See, e.g., Fox 1980.

kingdom as a manifestation of a new, divinely instituted order may be seen as functioning analogously to Ma'at and Wisdom as the basis for the (re-) ordering of human affairs.

It is also true that Q defines "wisdom" in exclusive, sectarian terms. Yet the presence of a wisdom psalm at Qumran (11QPs[a] 154) shows that other sapiential genres were amenable to sectarian usage. In the case of wisdom genres, at least, it seems unwise to tie the definition of genre too closely either to a particular set of motifs or to a particular social setting.

Another consideration should be given yet greater weight. Robinson's thesis that Proverbs, *m. 'Abot*, Q, and the *Gospel of Thomas* are comparable in form and belong on the same line of generic development is predicated on the fact that all of these collections are comprised of wisdom sayings and that they are represented as the pronouncements of various sages. It must be recognized that almost all of the examples which Robinson adduces are, from a form-critical and history-of-traditions standpoint, much more homogeneous than Q. Q in fact is a composite of not only wisdom sayings, but chriae, prophetic and apocalyptic words, and the temptation story. Is such variety compatible with a sapiential genre? The answer to this question is, I think, a qualified yes. However, it is necessary to answer Dehandschutter's question, namely, whether the most primitive traditions in Q belong to the sapiential current.[10] One must establish more clearly the range of forms which sapiential genres permitted and describe the inner dynamisms of those genres. In this regard Robinson's focus on primarily Jewish sapiential collections tended to obscure the international context of wisdom collections and to constrict unnecessarily the context in which to view Q.

The problem posed by form-critical diversity within Q was faced squarely by Helmut Koester in a series of articles.[11] Invoking a methodological principle that the so-called apocryphal gospels are not merely to be [**447**] dismissed out of hand as late corruptions of earlier works but may, on the contrary, reveal the *primary* tendencies of those genres, Koester argued that, as a collection of wisdom sayings, legal pronouncements, prophetic sayings, and parables, the *Gospel of Thomas* is a better representative than is Q of the genre *logoi sophōn*, or "wisdom gospel," as he prefers to call it. Central to the hermeneutic of the genre is

> the authority of the word of wisdom as such, which rests in the assumption that the teacher is present in the word which he has spoken. If there is any "Easter experience" to provide a Christology congenial to this concept of the *logoi*, it is here the belief in "Jesus, the Living One" (incipit of the *Gospel of Thomas*). (1971a:138–39)

10. Contrast the view of Schulz (1972:55–175), who characterized the earliest layer of Q as prophetic in nature.

11. Koester 1971a, esp. 135–36; 1971b, esp. 166–87 (above, pp. 35–50); 1971c; 1980; 1982:147–55.

Or again:

> Faith is understood as belief in Jesus' words, a belief which makes what Jesus proclaimed present and real for the believer. The catalyst which has caused the crystallization of these sayings into a "gospel" is the view that the kingdom is uniquely present in Jesus' eschatological preaching and that eternal wisdom about man's true self is disclosed in his words. (1971b:186; above, p. 50)

In contrast, the addition of apocalyptic Son of Man sayings to Q effectively attenuated the radicalized soteriology proper to its genre and moved Q in a more "orthodox" direction. Hence, the domestication of the tradition of the sayings of Jesus began not with absorption of Q into the Markan narrative framework but much earlier, within the redaction history of Q itself:

> If the genre of the wisdom book was the catalyst for the composition of sayings of Jesus into a "gospel" and if the christological concept of Jesus as the teacher of wisdom and as the presence of heavenly Wisdom dominated its creation, the apocalyptic orientation of the *Synoptic Sayings Source* with its christology of the coming Son of Man is due to a secondary redaction of an older wisdom book. (1980:113)

Some of the suggestions of Koester have been developed along rather different lines by two recent authors. In what is perhaps the most systematic attempt to defend the thesis that oracles of Christian prophets made their way into the Synoptic tradition as sayings of Jesus, M. Eugene Boring has argued that a substantial number of Q-sayings (twenty-two by his count) are the products of Christian prophets and almost as many (twenty) have been reformulated or re-presented by such prophets.[12] But Q not only [448] contained oracles; it should be understood as *the address of the Risen Lord to his community*. It is an oracle collection. Boring does not deny that there are some historicizing forms in Q: he acknowledges the presence of some chriae, which he regards as historicizing in form. But the dominant *Tendenz* of Q is contemporizing:

> While the dissolution of the word of the historical Jesus into the word of the heavenly Jesus had not yet occurred in Q, the center of gravity had shifted, so that Q was moving in the direction of a collection of "sayings of the living Jesus" such as the Gospel of Thomas. (1982:182)

Werner Kelber makes a similar point (1983). From Robinson he adopted

---

12. Boring 1982:137–79, 180. The following are designated by Boring as oracular: Q 6:22-23; 10:3, 4, 5-12, 13-15, 16, 21-22; 11:29b-30, 39-52; 12:8-9, 10, 11-12; 13:34-35; 16:17; 22:28-30. Prophetic reformulations include: Q 6:20b-21; 10:2, 16(?), 23-24; 11:14-23, 29a, 31-32; 12:2-3, 4-7, 22-34, 51-56, 57-59; 13:23-30; 17:22-37. This accounts for 53 percent of Q or 49 percent of the actual word count (p. 198).

the view that Q functioned in the *Sitz* of the oral transmission of Jesus' sayings. In fact, "Q represents an oral genre."[13] The hermeneutical situation envisaged for Q is its "oral performance" within the community, a performance which makes present the exalted Lord. Hence, it is not the historical figure of the past who authorizes the preachers to continue the proclamation of the kingdom (Q 10:9) but the Risen Lord who speaks through their words.

Both Boring and Kelber try to distinguish between the "historicizing" and "contemporizing" tendencies within the Q-material. Numerically and hermeneutically the contemporizing forms, typified by the λέγω ὑμῖν ["I tell you"] mode of address, take precedence over the historicizing or καὶ εἶπεν αὐτοῖς ["and he said to them"] form.[14] Boring rejects the appropriateness of Robinson's term *logoi sophōn* on the grounds that Q is neither timeless gnomic wisdom nor words of some historic authority. Instead it is the prophetic address of the exalted Jesus. Q is closer to Jeremiah in genre than it is to Proverbs (1982:180–81). More sympathetic to Robinson's term, Kelber argues that "Jesus' identity as prophetic speaker of words of wisdom could easily modulate into that of a gnostic redeemer, bringer of secret sayings" (1983:200). With Koester he affirms the gnosticizing proclivity of the genre. Even before the explicitly gnosticizing transformation of the sayings, Q's "oral ontology" was regarded suspiciously by the wider church. Several factors point in this direction: "the canonical rejection of the sayings genre *in its own right*, Paul's defensive attitude in 1 Corinthians, the paucity of sayings in Mark, Matthew's and Luke's absorption of the oral genre into gospel textuality, and its privileged status in gnosticism" (199, emphasis original).

One comment is in order here. The "oral" nature of Q is asserted rather than proved. **[449]** Both Kelber and Boring presumably accept the *opinio communis* that Q was a document. Its "oral" nature of the genre resides, apparently, in the fact that it was intended for "oral performance." But what then is the precise relationship of the document to the oral performance? Was it a memory aid? Or a casual transcription of what had been performed orally? It is apparently the latter which Kelber has in mind.[15] But this brings us back to all of the problems raised by the idea of *Kleinliteratur* as surrogate oral literature, a concept which has been roundly criticized by, among others, Kelber himself.[16] Nor is this model capable of explaining the careful *literary* stylization which is present in Q. Moreover, the analogy

---

13. Kelber 1983:201. Robinson 1971b:102–3: "With the final discontinuation of the oral transmission of Jesus' sayings, the *Sitz im Leben* of the gattung [*logoi sophōn*] was gone; hence orthodoxy contented itself with the canonical gospels."

14. Kelber 1983:202; Boring 1982:181.

15. Kelber 1979:22: "Oral traditions can fixate into texts, while texts in turn may stimulate oral impulses. A case of the former would be the possible transfer of the sayings source Q into literary form."

16. See Güttgemanns 1979:95–257; Kelber 1979; Shuler 1982:6–15.

of the *Gospel of Thomas* sabotages the hypothesis that the genre as such presupposed oral performance. As the incipit of the *Gospel of Thomas* clearly
shows, its hermeneutic is explicitly *scribal*: interpretation and appropriation
of the "truth" of the sayings is accomplished not by oral performance but
by penetration of the opacity of the written word:

> These are the secret sayings which the living Jesus spoke and which Didymos
> Judas Thomas *wrote down*. And he said, "Whoever finds the interpretation of
> these sayings will not experience death." (Lambdin 1977:118; emphasis
> added)

Progress can be made, I believe, if we return to the basic insight of
Robinson regarding the sapiential nature of Q, keeping in mind the fact
that redactional interventions may have effected important transformations
of the generic direction and hermeneutic of Q.[17] The first step in the un-
ravelling of the literary and hermeneutical puzzle that is Q is to determine
the nature of the literary stratum that was formative for Q *as a document*.
Then we will be in a position to establish the relationship of this stratum to
antique literary genres.

THE FORMATIVE COMPONENT IN Q

The starting point for tracing the *Gattungsgeschichte* of Q must be the determination of its formative components. This task necessarily entails redaction or composition history. Obviously, such a major analysis cannot [450]
be conducted in the space available here. I will, however, sketch a thesis
that may point to a possible solution.[18]

Dieter Lührmann long ago demonstrated that opposition to "this generation" was a prominent redactional theme in several extended portions of Q
(1969). This judgment has received confirmation and additional support
from the outstanding study of Arland Jacobson, who has documented the
use of the Deuteronomistic view of history as an organizational motif in
one major stratum of Q-materials (1978, 1982b; above, pp. 98–115).

It is clear that at least four clusters of Q-texts have been composed with
this polemic against "this generation" in view: (1) Q 3:7-9, 16-17; (2) Q
7:1-10, 18-23, 24-28, (16:16?),[19] 31-35; (3) Q 11:14-15, 17-26, 16, 29-32,
33-36, 39-52; and (4) Q 17:23-37. These clusters display a remarkable uniformity in "projected audience," constituent forms, and dominant motifs.
The actual audience of all of these clusters is, of course, the Q-community
itself. However, in each case, the projected or ostensible audience are those

---

17. See further my comments in Kloppenborg 1984.
18. I have treated the question of the formative component of Q in much greater detail
elsewhere (Kloppenborg 1987).
19. There is dispute whether Q 16:16 should be located in its present Lukan context (thus
J. Weiss 1892:192; J. Schmid 1930:284–85) or in its Matthaean context (thus Lührmann
1969:27-28; Jacobson 1978:62–83; Fitzmyer 1981:662).

who refuse the call to repentance, invoking national privilege (Q 3:8), the "children" who perversely reject the summons of John and Jesus (Q 7:31-35), the opponents who fail to comprehend the signs of the presence of the kingdom (Q 11:19-20, 30, 31-32), the vaticides and opponents of the kingdom (Q 11:49-51; 16:16), and those who act oblivious to the impending destruction which will attend the parousia (17:23-37).

The forms most typical of these clusters are the prophetic judgment saying and the apocalyptic word. Q 3:7-9, 16-17; 11:19b, 31-32, 47-51 (a woe oracle in almost classical form!), and 17:34-35 are all examples. All of Q's "prophetic correlatives"[20] occur here: 11:30; 17:24, 26-27, 28-30. There are, in addition, several sayings which, although not of prophetic origin, are turned to prophetic use in Q-redaction and made to serve Q's announcement of judgment: 11:20, 23, 24-26, 33, 34-36, and 17:34b. It goes without saying [451] that these clusters of Q-sayings display a variety of prophetic and Deuteronomistic motifs (Jacobson 1982b:383–88; above, pp. 109–14). It is additionally important that in both 7:1-10 and 11:31-32 the Deuteronomistic view of history is transformed by means of the notion that positive Gentile response to preaching is an *Unheilszeichen* for Israel.[21]

Although prophetic forms and motifs dominate these portions of Q, it is noteworthy that the Q-sayings are frequently framed as *chriae*, and, more specifically, as circumstantial or responsorial chriae: Q 3:7-9; 7:1-10, 18-23, 24-26; 11:14-15, 17-18a; and 11:16, 29. There is, in other words, a hierarchy of forms to be observed: prophetic and apocalyptic sayings may form the content of Jesus' words, but these sayings are not represented as the contemporizing, oracular utterances of the exalted Lord. They are, on the contrary, framed as sayings of Jesus on a particular occasion. This is in no way to mitigate the powerful effect that these words had as they were employed in the community. Q 10:16 evidences the conviction of a functional unity between the exalted Lord and those who repeat his words. But the sayings are, nonetheless, framed as chriae, not as oracles.

The fundamental coherence which exists among the four above-mentioned clusters of Q-sayings allows us to conclude that they derive from the same compositional layer of Q.[22] But do these belong to the for-

20. This term, coined by Daryl Schmidt (1977), is preferable to R. A. Edwards's "eschatological correlative" (1969), since it situates the Q-form in a broader context of prophetic speech. In addition to Schmidt's list of Septuagintal correlatives, 1Q27 1:6 and 4QpsDanA[a] [= 4Q246] 2:1-2 should be noted as examples.

21. It is disputed whether the tradents of the Q-materials were engaged in a mission to the Gentiles. Schulz (1972:243–44) and Jacobson (1978:69) contend that Q 7:1-10 does not constitute evidence of a Gentile mission. However, Q contains several other texts which repeat the theme that (actual or predicted) Gentile faith signals condemnation for Israel: 10:13-15; 11:31-32; 13:28-29. This constellation of texts makes more plausible the suggestion that the Q-group at least *knew* of the positive results of a Gentile mission (thus P. Meyer 1970). And in view of the apparently disappointing results of Q's mission to Israel, the possibility of a Q Gentile mission must be taken seriously.

22. For further discussion of redaction-critical methodology appropriate to the study of Q, see Jacobson 1978:10; Kloppenborg 1984:54–57; and Zeller 1982, esp. 396–99 [pp. 117–20 in

mative stage in Q's literary history? Are the opposition to "this generation" and the Deuteronomistic preaching of repentance the motifs that account for the crystallization of the Q-materials into a written form? In order to answer these questions, it is necessary to look at several other "clusters" of Q-sayings.

Significant blocks of Q-sayings are either untouched or only minimally influenced by the motifs of the Deuteronomistic view of God's relation to Israel, the announcement of judgment, and the condemnatory ramifications of Gentile faith. These include Jesus' inaugural sermon (Q 6:20-49); a collection of discipleship and mission sayings (9:57-60 [61-62?]; 10:2-16, 21-24); and instructions on prayer (11:2-4, 9-13), anxiety in the face of persecution (12:2-12), and concern over daily necessities (12:22b-31, 33-34). [452] No less than the redactional stratum described above, these clusters of sayings also display a coherence in forms, projected audience, and motifs. These "speeches" are not formulated with outsiders in view, but are community-directed, serving as programmatic statements of self-definition and fundamental comportment toward the world (6:20b-49; 11:2-4, 9-13; 12:22b-31, 33-34) as well as more specific instructions regarding discipleship and mission (9:57-62; 10:2-16; 12:2-12).

Before pursuing the description of this redactional stratum, it is worthwhile to raise the question of the relationship between those blocks of sayings crystallized around the theme of the preaching of repentance and the announcement of judgment, and the community-directed sayings. Instructive in this respect are sayings such as Q 6:23c; 10:(12), 13-15; and 12:8-9, 10, all of which occur in the middle of blocks of community-directed speeches. It is widely held that 6:23c is a secondary addition to the "persecution beatitude" (Q 6:22-23b).[23] Moreover, Jacobson rightly points out that 6:23c evinces the Deuteronomistic notion of the persecution of the prophets,[24] a motif which characterizes Q 3:7-9, 16-17; 7:1-35; 11:14-52; and 17:23-37. Q 6:23c can in no way be considered as the formative or compositional motif for all of 6:20b-49; it is clearly a gloss inserted into a pre-existing speech.

The same appears to be the case with Q 10:13-15. In these verses, the addressees shift abruptly from those engaged in mission (9:57-62; 10:2-11) to those who have rejected the preaching of the kingdom. The connection of the woes (10:13-15) with the mission speech is obviously due to the mention of the possibility of rejection in 10:10-11. Lührmann is probably correct that 10:12 is a piece of Q-redaction formed on the analogy of 10:14 and used to effect the transition.[25] Moreover, the addition of vv. 12, 13-15

---

this volume].

23. Steck 1967:258–59; Schulz 1972:456 n. 404; Jacobson 1978:53.

24. Jacobson 1978:53–54; 1982b:384–85 (above, pp. 110–11); also Steck 1967:257–60.

25. Lührmann 1969:62; similarly, Hoffmann 1972:288; Laufen 1980:274–75, 286. For a contrasting view, see Bultmann 1968:112.

appears to have broken an original catchword connection between 10:10 and 10:16.[26] The intrusive nature of the woes and the artificial nature of the transition from 10:2-11 to 10:13-15 are such as to suggest that the woes are an insertion [453] into originally community-directed instructions.[27] Three features suggest that Q 10:13-15 should be connected with the redactional stratum that emphasized the coming judgment. First, like many of the sayings deriving from that stratum, Q 10:13-15 is a prophetic form; second, tradition-historically it belongs to the orbit of the Deuteronomistic preaching of repentance; and third, like 7:1-10 and especially 11:31-32, these woes contrast Jewish response unfavorably with (hypothetical) Gentile response and award to Gentiles a higher status in the judgment. Predicted Gentile faith becomes an *Unheilszeichen* for Israel.

A third community-directed speech has undergone similar expansion. Q 12:2-12 is directed at a community whose missionaries are subject to persecution and death threats. The core of sayings about which this "speech" is constructed is the essentially sapiential admonition in 12:4-7.[28] This has been augmented in two ways: by the addition of a wisdom saying (12:2) and an admonition to preach openly,[29] and by the addition of a "Sentence of Holy Law" (12:8-9) and a threat issued to those who speak against the Spirit (12:10). Q 12:2 serves an important function. As a wisdom saying disclosing the "natural" or inevitable course of events (i.e., revelation of what is hidden), it interprets the mission presupposed in 12:4-7 and commanded in 12:3 // Matt 10:27. This is not a human undertaking, subject to ordinary failures, but is itself an expression of the ineluctable (and divinely motivated) apocalyptic manifestation of what is hidden, namely, the kingdom. It is for this reason that the Q-missionaries have no need of fear or anxiety. Hence the wisdom sentence Q 12:2 assumes a programmatic function with respect to the imperatives that follow.

---

26. Both Matt 10:14 // Luke 10:10 and Matt 10:40 use δέχομαι, whereas Matt 10:14 and Luke 10:16 use ἀκούω. Long ago T. W. Manson (1949:77) remarked that 10:16 followed "more effectively" after 10:12 than it did after 10:13-15. On this basis he concluded that the original order of Q was 10:12, 16, 13-15; but the more likely solution is that interpolation has interrupted an original connection.

27. Jacobson (1982a) takes a different view: 10:3-16 forms the core of a composition that conceived of mission in terms of a call to repentance, with 10:2 and 10:7b (both expressions of later missionary praxis) as additions. He admits that 10:(12), 13-15 is not original to the mission sayings but argues that its addition was antecedent to the additions of 10:2 and 10:7b.

28. Q 12:4-7 is itself the product of the combination of several smaller units. On this see Zeller 1977b:95-96.

29. Here I take the Matthaean formulation of the verse to represent Q better than Luke 12:3. As J. Schmid (1930:272) points out, Luke 12:4 begins a new theme (for Luke), while 12:2-3 conclude the previous section on the hypocrisy of the Pharisees and scribes. Luke 12:3 represents as still future what Matt 10:27 and Luke 12:4-7 require in the present, namely, the disclosure of "what was spoken in the dark." Luke can alter the sense of 12:3 because for him it refers to hypocrisy rather than preaching, as it does for both Matthew and Q. See further, Laufen 1980:162-63; Wanke 1980:222; P. Meyer 1967:39-40; Strecker 1966:190. Favoring Lukan wording: Hoffmann 1972:156; Lührmann 1969:50; Manson 1949:106; Schulz 1972:462.

With Q 12:8-9 and 12:10 the case is rather different. As Lührmann [454] (1969:52) notes, 12:8-9 has to do with *confession* rather than with *preaching*. Moreover, the focus is strongly christological, whereas in 12:2-7 the subject is the disclosure of the kingdom. Formally, 12:8-9 belongs to the realm of prophetic speech,[30] and materially it moves beyond the essentially sapiential rhetoric of 12:2-7. Along with 12:10, Q 12:8-9 is directed not at the preachers of the kingdom, but at those who reject that preaching: both are apocalyptic threats. But in 12:11-12 another abrupt shift in addressee and tone occurs. Of course, 12:11-12 describes the forensic scene that the two preceding sayings presuppose. But formally and materially, Q 12:11-12 coheres better with 12:4-7 and with the following "speech" (12:22-31, 33-34) than it does with the prophetic sayings in 12:8-9, 10. Q 12:2-7, 11-12 forms a coherent speech, unified by its mode of address (second-person plural imperative), tone (hortatory and comforting), setting (anticipation of persecution), and function (encouragement to fearless preaching). As was the case with Q 10:13-15, Q 12:8-9, 10 appear to be secondary insertions into a pre-existing speech—and indeed, insertions that bear the theological stamp of the other major stratum of Q-redaction.

The thrust of my argument should by now be clear. Analysis of the Q-materials reveals two major types of sayings: on one hand, prophetic sayings (often framed as chriae) which announce the impending judgment of this generation and which evince the Deuteronomistic understanding of history; and, on the other, community-directed exhortations concerning self-definition and general comportment toward the world, discipleship and mission, and the prospect of persecution and death. There is no reason to suppose that the latter crystallized only under the influence of the motifs characteristic of the polemical stratum of Q. On the other hand, each of these community-directed speeches bears the marks of secondary interpolation (Q 6:23c; 10:12, 13-15; 12:8-9, 10). The most natural inference to be drawn from these facts is that these interpolations along with the other materials that cohere with them (3:7-9, 16-17; 7:1-10, 18-35; 11:14-52; 17:23-37) derive from a secondary expansion of an original collection of community-directed speeches.

Among the community-directed speeches I include not only 6:20b-49, 9:57-62 + 10:2-11, 16, and 12:2-7, 11-12 but also 11:2-4, 9-13[31] and 12:22b-31, 33-34, which bear the same features as the "speeches" outlined above. The latter has also undergone expansion through the addition of apocalyptic warnings (12:39-40, 42-46, 49, 51-53, 54-56, 58-59). In this case the secondary materials were not inserted into the middle of the speech but were [455] appended to it by the use of the catchwords κλέπτης ["thief"] and διορύσσω ["dig"] (Q 12:33, 39). It is worthwhile noting that

---

30. See Käsemann 1969c:77; Boring 1982:165–66.

31. On this, see the excellent article of Piper (1982 [chap. 8 in this volume]), who has demonstrated the sapiential nature of this cluster of sayings.

the expansion of the other speeches was accomplished in precisely the same way: the interpolated materials were connected either by catchword or by thematic association. This may be illustrated by the accompanying table.

Interpolation	Mode of Association	Connected with
1. Q 6:20b-49		
6:23c	thematic: persecution	6:22-23b
2. Q 9:57-62; 10:2-16,		
21-24		
10:12, 13-15	thematic: rejection	10:10-11, 16
10:21-24	thematic: acceptance/ rejection:	10:16
10:21-24	catchword: ἀκούω ["hear"]	10:16
10:21-24	catchword: πάτερ ["father"]	11:2-4
10:21-24	thematic: prayer/ thanksgiving	11:2-4
3. Q 12:2-12		
12:8-9,10	thematic: forensic scene	12:4-7, 11-12
12:10	catchword: ἅγιον πνεῦμα ["Holy Spirit"]	12:11-12
4. Q 12:22b-31, 33-34		
12:39-40	catchwords: κλέπτης, διορύσσω	12:33-34

Thematic and catchword connections may also provide partial explanations for the insertion of the larger judgment speeches between the wisdom speeches.[32] The connection between the inaugural sermon and the following judgment speech (beginning with 7:1-10) may be due to the catchwords κύριε ["sir," "Lord"] (6:46; 7:6) and λόγος ["word"] (6:47, 49; 7:7).[33] Similarly, the Beelzebul Accusation/Request for a Sign complex may have been attached to the preceding speech (11:2-4, 9-13) because of the catchword *kingdom* present in both the instruction on prayer and in the Beelzebul accusation (11:2, 17, 18, 20). [**456**]

---

32. The connection between 12:2-12 and 12:22b-34 (both "wisdom speeches") is clearly both catchword (μὴ μεριμνᾶτε, vv. 11, 22, 26, 29) and thematic (words of comfort to a community which assumes a vulnerable and defenseless posture).

33. Lührmann (1969:58) argues that the connection of 7:1-10 with the inaugural sermon is not accidental since the narrative serves as a paradigm of the relation between hearing and action which is required in 6:46-49; similarly, Jacobson 1978:70. But 7:1-10 goes considerably beyond the didactic thrust of the sermon. Like Q-texts such as 11:14-23 and 11:29-32, it focuses on the recognition of Jesus' ἐξουσία by *outsiders*, not members of the community (as is the case in 6:46-49).

THE FORMATIVE COMPONENT OF Q AS "INSTRUCTION"

Compositional analysis suggests that the formative component of Q consisted of several "speeches": Q 6:20b-49 (without 6:23c); 9:57-62; 10:2-11, 16; 11:2-4, 9-13; 12:2-7, 11-12; and 12:22b-31, 33-34. The didactic nature and community orientation of these have already been noted. From a form-critical standpoint, these speeches are also distinctive. A large number of the constituent sayings should be classified as sapiential admonitions[34] taking the form of second-person plural (or, less commonly, singular)[35] imperatives with or without a motive clause. Some are introduced by λέγω ὑμῖν, also a sapiential locution.[36] The attached motive clauses include a wide variety of sapiential forms: rhetorical questions appealing to ordinary human reason (Q 6:32-35; 11:11-13; 12:6-7, 23, 25), apodoses that express the symmetry between act and consequence (6:37-38; 11:4, 9), and appeals to the observation of nature (6:35c; 12:6-7, 24, 26-28, 25, 30, 33). In addition to sapiential admonitions, this stratum of Q contains other wisdom forms: beatitudes (6:20b-21, 22-23b),[37] proverbs and wisdom sayings (6:39, 40, 43, 44, 45c; 10:7b; 11:10; 12:2, 34), sayings introduced by τίς ἐξ ὑμῶν ["who among you"][38] (11:11-13; 12:25), and parables (6:47-49). [**457**]

It must be emphasized that these "speeches" are not simply an agglomeration of unrelated admonitions and wisdom sayings. On the contrary, the sayings are thematically organized, and the speeches display enough com-

---

34. See Zeller 1977b:*passim*.

35. Plural: Q 6:27-28, 31, 35ab, 36, 37-38; 11:9-10; 12:3-4, 6-7, 22b-23, 24, 25, 26-28, 29-31, 33-34; 13:24. Singular: Q 6:29, 30, 41-42.

36. Q 6:27; 11:9 (diff. Matt); 12:4 (diff. Matt), 5 (diff. Matt), 22. While some consider λέγω ὑμῖν to be the earmark of prophetic speech, a fundamental distinction should be observed between those instances in which the formula introduces information that necessarily presupposes special insight into divine workings or the future (e.g., Q 11:51c; 13:35; 17:34 [omit Matt]) and those cases in which it introduces an imperative (and motive clause). The latter usage appears in Prov 24:23: ταῦτα δὲ λέγω ὑμῖν τοῖς σοφοῖς, in paraenetic sections of 1 Enoch 91.3; 94.1, 3, 10, and frequently in *Testaments of the Twelve Patriarchs* with a following imperative: *T. Reu.* 4.5 (mss); 6.5 (mss); *T. Levi* 16.4 (mss); *T. Naph.* 4.1 (mss); *T. Gad* 5.2; *T. Benj.* 9.1 (mss); *T. Jud.* 14.1 (mss). Several related formulae are attested: διδάσκω ὑμῖν + imperative: *T. Reu.* 3.9; διὰ τοῦτο ἐντέλλομαι ὑμᾶς + infinitive/ἵνα: *T. Reu.* 6.8; *T. Sim.* 7.3; *T. Levi* 13.1; *T. Jud.* 13.1; 17.1; *T. Benj.* 12.1; (παρ)αγγέλλω ὑμῖν + imperative/infinitive: *T. Jud.* 21.1 (mss); *T. Zeb.* 5.1; παραινῶ ὑμῖν + imperative: *T. Gad* 6.1; παρακαλῶ ὑμᾶς + imperative: *T. Reu.* 4.5 (mss); ὀρκῶ ὑμᾶς τὸν θεόν + infinitive: *T. Reu.* 6.9; ἐπιμαρτύρομαι ὑμῖν + infinitive: *T. Reu.* 1.6. See further Zeller 1977b:155–57.

37. The Q-beatitudes, of course, differ from typical sapiential beatitudes such as Prov 3:13; Ps 1:1, which are semantically equivalent to admonitions; but equally, Q 6:20b-23 differ from most apocalyptic beatitudes, which function as conditions of salvation or exhortations to faithfulness, wisdom, and the like (2 Enoch 42:7-14; 44:4; *Pss. Sol.* 4:26; 1 Enoch 82:4; etc.) Betz (1978; ET 1985:17–36, esp. 33) terms them "anti-beatitudes" since they stand in contrast to the conventional wisdom that the affluent and secure are blessed.

38. Although Greeven (1952) and Jeremias (1972:103) adduce the presence of the formulae in prophetic literature (Isa 42:34; 50:10; Hag 2:3), there it introduces a *real question*. Berger (1973:31–33) points out that in the Synoptic materials the formula expects an answer "no one" and is thus semantically equivalent to a statement introduced by οὐδείς ["no one"]. Locutions of this sort can be found in sapiential literature (Prov 18:14; Sir 10:29; 12:13-14; *T. Job* 37:6) and in Hellenistic popular philosophy (Epictetus, *Diss.* 1.22.1; 1.27.19; 2.17.8).

mon structural elements to invite the conclusion that they were redacted together. Three of the speeches begin with a programmatic pronouncement in the form of a wisdom saying or a declaratory sentence: 6:20b-23b (three beatitudes); 9:57-58 (a Son of Man saying framed as a chria), and 12:2 (a wisdom saying). In each instance, the saying sets the tone for the following speech. Q 6:20b-22b announces the transvaluation of norms which the kingdom brings and which the following speech attempts to inculcate; Q 9:57-58 describes the mode of existence of the Son of Man as homologous with the behavior that the following speech enjoins on his followers and envoys;[39] and 12:2 grounds the admonitions to fearless preaching (Q 12:4-7, 11-12) aphoristically by asserting that the manifestation of the kingdom is a matter of the inevitable eschatological disclosure of what is hidden. Q 11:2-4, 9-13 is in some respects comparable. It begins the instructions on prayer with a paradigm of prayer. Since Q 11:2b-4 is *Jesus'* prayer, the filial attitude of utter confidence expressed therein functions programmatically with respect to the rest of the instruction and buttresses the exhortations of 11:9-13.

Not only are there structural similarities in the introductions of the Q-speeches; two of the instructions conclude in a similar fashion. The inaugural sermon closes with a symmetrically constructed parable describing the benefits of adherence to the teacher's words and the dangers in their neglect (6:47-49), and 12:33-34 offers a similar symmetrical admonition relating to the body of the preceding instruction on concern over the necessities of day-to-day living.

If such was the formative component of Q, what may be said about the *literary patterns* which governed the composition of this formative stratum? And what may be said of the literary, theological, and hermeneutical tendencies of this stratum?

Although Q contains many wisdom sayings such as proverbs, it is in no way comparable to proverb collections like Prov 10:1—22:16. Nor does the sapiential form of dispute or dialogue (such as "The Dispute of a Man with [458] His Ba," "The Eloquent Peasant," or Job) offer close analogies. Q is neither an anthology of proverbs, nor is it concerned with the "reflective" side of wisdom—the place of humankind within the universe, the meaning of piety or suffering, etc.

The major form of prescriptive wisdom in both Egypt and the Near East is the *instruction*. This form is very widely attested in Egyptian wisdom literature,[40] and well represented in other Near Eastern literature. As William

---

39. See Theissen 1978:26–27. The programmatic nature of 9:57-58 has been recognized by Schürmann (1975:132; p. 83 in this volume).

40. For a description of the form see Brunner 1970; H. Schmid 1966:8–84. A catalog and synopsis of the variety of instructions is conveniently supplied by Kitchen 1979. Instructions not treated by Kitchen: "The Counsels of Piety of Sansnos" (published in Bernand 1969:165); "Shube-awilum" (published in Nougayrol and Laroche 1968 and Smith 1975).

McKane has properly stressed (McKane 1970:3; similarly Lang 1972:31–36), the fundamental form-critical unit of the instruction is the imperative or admonition. Where wisdom sentences or proverbs occur, their function is ancillary. The admonitions may be monostichic (as is common in Demotic collections)[41] or binary, and they may or may not have a motive clause attached. Although some instructions display little in the way of internal coherence, organization of admonitions into clusters by thematic association, catchword, or formal analogy is observed in such diverse collections as Amenemope, Ptahhotep, the Instructions of Aniy, the Counsels of Piety of Sansnos, Ankhsheshonq, Papyrus Insinger, the Babylonian Counsels of Wisdom, and portions of Aramaic Ahikar, Proverbs 1–9, and Sirach.[42]

Besides the basic compositional unit, the imperative, there are two other fairly constant features of the instruction. First, the overwhelming majority of collections for which incipits survive are ascribed to named sages, usually of some prominence. Anonymous instructions are rare. Second, the authorial fiction is usually governed by the metaphor of parental instruction. Ascription of the sayings to a sage of some reputation [459] appears to serve a legitimating function: although imperatives are buttressed by motive clauses, it would be wrong to assume that the acceptability of their counsels depended solely upon the persuasiveness of their rhetoric. Association of the admonitions with an experienced practitioner of wisdom was the rule, not the exception. The introductions of these instructions are often replete with laudatory descriptions of the sage or novelistic prologues stressing his wisdom, endurance, and self-control.

The other constant—the metaphor of parental instruction—is particularly appropriate to the generally conservative and traditional posture of most Near Eastern instructions. Commenting on the use of this metaphor in biblical wisdom genres, J. G. Williams notes:

> The point where the individual meets the tradition is in relationship with the "father," a figure which includes the parent but which is also a metaphor of several kinds of guides. The individual internalizes the voice of the fathers and obeys it by guarding himself against disorder (folly). (Williams 1981:42)

Egyptian instructions are governed by one fundamental hermeneutical principle: instruction establishes and preserves Maʻat (order) both historically and at every level of society. In biblical wisdom order in human affairs is to be achieved by pursuit of the primordial order created by God. In both cases the metaphor of parental instruction aptly comprehended the "hori-

---

41. On this see Lichtheim 1979, 1983. Lichtheim suggests that the preponderance of monostichoi in Demotic collections may be due to the influence of Menander's *monostichoi* and has documented the influence of Greek gnomologia and Near Eastern wisdom collections (esp. Ahikar) on Demotic instructions.

42. For bibliographical details, see n. 40.

zontal" aspect of order—the continuity of historical transmission—and at the same time its "vertical" dimension, namely, that order must permeate every level of society (and ultimately of the cosmos).

More variable are other aspects of the instruction form. We have already noted that imperatives may be buttressed with motive clauses. In addition, clusters of admonitions may be prefaced by programmatic statements (as in Merikare and Sirach (2:1, 5)[43] or conditionals (Ptahhotep), and the imperatives are sometimes strengthened by rhetorical questions or concluding maxims or both.

Several instructions contain prologues, providing details regarding the supposed occasion for the instruction (Khety, Ptahhotep, Shuruppak, Shube-awilum), or even biographical data about the sage. Of particular interest are the exordiums of Ankhsheshonq and Aramaic Ahikar for which the motif of the ordeal or testing of the sage is basic to the narrative introduction. Both relate tales of the unjust imprisonment of the sage, his endurance of this misfortune, and the instruction of his son (or adoptive son) while in prison. The function of such biographical exordiums should [460] be seen in the context of the basic requirement of the genre for legitimation. These ordeal or testing stories demonstrate in the sage the presence of some of the basic sapiential virtues: self-control, equanimous acceptance of trying circumstances, and patient endurance of suffering. Such prologues treat in narrative form what Sirach puts aphoristically:

My son, if you come forward to serve the Lord,
prepare yourself for temptation. . . .
For gold is tested in fire
and acceptable men in the furnace of humilitation. (Sir 2:1, 5)

Another common strategy of legitimation consists in associating the sage with the source of wisdom itself. Egyptian instructions, regardless of whether they are framed as instructions to kings, crown princes, the highest levels of officialdom, or to a more general audience (as is the case with Ankhsheshonq), are regularly ascribed to sages close to the throne (and sometimes to the pharaoh himself). This is intelligible once it is recognized, first, that teaching is never considered to be the *creation* of the sage but only something which he transmits and which his experience confirms (Brunner 1970:118), and, second, that for Egyptian theology the king is the very source of Ma'at. Association of the teaching with the king serves the theological role of grounding it in divinely established order. A similar strategy of legitimation is observed in Shube-awilum, whose exordium states that the sage's wisdom was given him by Enlilbanda himself (I 1-6),

---

43. W. Roth (1980:60–61) has demonstrated that the first half of Sirach consists of four units (1:1—4:10; 4:11—6:17; 6:18—14:19; 14:20—23:27), each beginning with a programmatic statement concerning Sophia and her pursuit (1:1—2:18; 4:11-19; 6:18-37; 14:20—15:10).

and in the prologues of Proverbs 1–9 and Sirach, which effectively identify the voice of the sages with the voice of Sophia.

It should be clear that there is much in common between the Near Eastern instruction and the earliest stratum of Q. The preponderance of imperatives and the use of programmatic statements, rhetorical questions, and aphoristic conclusions suggest that this stratum of Q was framed as an instruction. Since the incipit of Q, where one normally expects indications of the position and status of the putative teacher, is not extant, we must rely upon internal features to determine various hermeneutical aspects of the collection. Q 6:40 and 6:46 present the speaker as a teacher or master. In Q 9:57-58 the radical life-style of the speaker is held out as a model for imitation, and the same is implied by Q 14:26, 14:27, and 17:33.[44] Although the metaphor of Jesus as a teacher or master is central in Q, there are indications of his association with God or Sophia. Q 10:3, 16 present Jesus as the one who initiates the eschatological harvest and the one whose message, as it is presented by his envoys, is equivalent to the voice of God. Steck has rightly [461] noted that 10:16 effectively places Jesus in the position of God or Sophia, as the sender of the eschatological envoys to Israel (Steck 1967:286 n. 9).

The hermeneutic which this stratum of Q presupposes is similar to that of the instruction. In contrast to critics who caricatured the sapiential admonition as advisory and debatable rather than categorical,[45] McKane rightly notes that the instruction "demands unreserved acceptance and is not offered for critical consideration" (1970:51). On the other hand, sapiential admonitions do not have the force of "law"; the student's task is not simply to memorize and repeat the admonitions but to perceive and assimilate the basic ethos that informs individual imperatives. In Egyptian idiom, the goal of instruction is to "speak Ma'at, do Ma'at." C. Kayatz has rightly underscored the centrality of an idea akin to Ma'at operative in Proverbs 1–9 (1966:76–134). The intention of the genre is to inculcate a perception of divinely ordained order and to promote action in accord with that order. Submission to the authority of the teacher is the beginning of the initiation into that order.

In the case of Q, the "order" into which the student is initiated is not an eternally present order, but a new eschatological existence. In accordance with the apocalyptic idiom of Q, this order is described as a reversal and radical transformation of old values and principles. Nonetheless, the hermeneutic of Q is comparable to that of the instruction genre. Submission to the instructions of the teacher/Sophia leads to assimilation of the ethos of the kingdom. As Q 6:35 puts it: ἀγαπᾶτε τοὺς ἐχθροὺς ὑμῶν . . . ,

---

44. I take these three sayings as belonging together in Q (and hence as one of the few instances in which Luke has dislocated a Q-saying) and as part of the sapiential, community-directed stratum.

45. For example, Zimmerli 1976:180. For a summary of the criticisms of this view, see Crenshaw 1971.

καὶ ἔσεσθε υἱοὶ ὑψίστου, ὅτι αὐτὸς χρηστός ἐστιν ἐπὶ τοὺς ἀχαρίστους καὶ πονηρούς ["Love your enemies . . . , and you will be children of the Most High, for he is gracious to the ungrateful and the evil"].

Not only is the association of Jesus with Sophia intelligible, given the internal dynamics of the genre, but later developments within Q may also be seen as the result of the tendencies immanent in the genre. In the major expansion of the instructional speeches described above, several sayings were introduced that imply a functional unity between Jesus and Sophia: Q 7:35 represents Jesus and John as Sophia's children; 11:49-51a places an oracle of Sophia on Jesus' lips, and the same appears to be the case in 13:34-35; and, most dramatically, 10:22 draws upon the mythologoumena of Sophia and employs them in the description of the relation of the "Son" to the "Father" (see Kloppenborg 1978). [462] Hence, Q's second (polemical) stage represents an expression of the generic potentialities at work already in the first stratum.

The use of "ordeal" or "testing" stories as prefaces for instructions makes intelligible another development in Q. The temptation account (Q 4:1-13), long considered anomalous in Q, may be regarded as functioning in the same way as the narrative prologues of Ankhsheshonq and Ahikar: to demonstrate the reliability, self-control, and endurance of the sage in trying circumstances and hence to provide further legitimation for his sayings.[46]

There are two notable departures from the typical form of the instruction. Q does not represent itself as parental instruction (as far as can be determined), and its teaching is far from conservative or traditional. These two features are obviously related. The metaphor of parental instruction would be quite inapposite for instructions that enjoin the severing of family ties, abandonment of home and hearth, and the rejection of behavioral modes normally sanctioned by society.

These two features are not, however, sufficient to disqualify the formative components of Q as an instruction. It would be more appropriate to regard the first stages of Q as an application of the instruction genre to the special circumstances of a sectarian community with a strong orientation toward the dawning kingdom. The hermeneutic characteristic of the Near Eastern instruction was easily adaptable to this theological datum, and the morphology of the genre was quite appropriate to the community's needs. The potential of the genre to associate the speaker with the divine voice responded well to the legitimating needs of a community which espoused a radically countercultural life-style, and which experienced widespread rejection of its preaching. To adapt Koester's dictum: "If there is any 'Easter experience' to provide a Christology congenial to this genre, it is the reorienting of believers to a new mode of eschatological existence by means of the instruction of Sophia through her agent Jesus."

---

46. Space does not permit a thorough analysis of the redactional stratum to which Q 4:1-13 belongs, and its function within Q as a whole. Along with Jacobson (1978:36–46, 93) I regard it as the latest addition to Q.

10

The Shape of the
Q-Source

MIGAKU SATO

THE WRITTEN NATURE OF Q

The presupposition of the following study is the essential correctness of the two-document hypothesis. The majority of scholars have rightly assumed that the Q-source was written. The three main arguments for this can be summarized briefly.

1. The high degree of *verbatim agreement* of the texts that Matthew and Luke have in common. Let us take for the moment the textual basis that Robert Morgenthaler assumes: Approximately 49 percent of Markan material in Matthew is taken over verbatim from Mark; about 50 percent of the ostensible Q-text of Matthew agrees verbatim with that of Luke. Similarly, Luke has reproduced verbatim about 40 percent of the material taken from Mark, while approximately 51 percent of the ostensible Q-material in Luke agrees with that of Matthew (1971:163, 165, 258–61). This is a striking result insofar as the proportion of verbal agreement both in Matthew's and Luke's Q-material is higher than that in their respective reproductions of Mark. The assumption of a written source is, therefore, plausible.

2. The *doublets* of Mark in Matthew/Luke, and *parallel traditions* between Mark and Matthew/Luke: Synoptic comparison elsewhere illustrates the tendency—especially in Luke—to avoid doublets (Schürmann 1968b:272–78, 279–89; Morgenthaler 1971:128–60). For this reason it is all the more probable that doublets and parallel traditions are due to the existence of two sources—Mark and Q—that were already written.

3. Agreements in the *order* of Q-pericopae in Matthew and Luke.

Excerpted and translated from Migaku Sato, "Die Gestalt der Q-Quelle," pp. 16–47, 62–65 of *Q und Prophetie: Studien zur Gattungs- und Traditionsgeschichte der Quelle Q*, WUNT 2/29 (Tübingen: Mohr [Siebeck], 1988).

Vincent Taylor has demonstrated that Matthew preserved within his five discourses the sequence of Q-pericopae as they occur in Luke (V. Taylor 1953, 1959). [17] One might also compare the revealing table of W. G. Kümmel (1975:65–66) and the even more extensive tables of Morgenthaler (252–54). Morgenthaler has illustrated how the agreement between Matthew's and Luke's order becomes stronger in the longer pericopae (254). This common sequence represents the most important indication of the written character of Q.

4. In addition, there have been attempts to confirm the existence of a written, Aramaic Q-source by means of a list of visual mistakes in the Greek translation. For example, Philipp Vielhauer, following Julius Wellhausen, mentions that δότε ἐλημοσύνην ("give alms") in Luke 11:41 incorrectly read the original Aramaic word דכו ("cleanse"—which Matt 23:26 correctly renders with καθάρισον) as זכו ("give alms").[1] This attempt, however, is not very effective; convincing "mistakes" are found too seldom and sporadically. They may have been caused accidentally or by parallel Aramaic traditions that circulated orally. Such evidence by itself does not suffice to demonstrate the existence of a document *composed in Aramaic*.

THE EXTENT OF Q

The table on pp. 158–61 represents the extent of Q presupposed in this study. The sequence of pericopae in Q is to be derived in the main from Luke; as is well-known, because of his tendency to treat Markan and non-Markan materials in "blocks," Luke must have preserved Q better than Matthew (who treats his source materials with greater freedom) and in particular has arranged them into five large discourses of Jesus (chaps. 5–7; 10; 13; 18; 23–25).[2]

THE PROCESS OF THE FORMATION OF Q

1. Recent Hypotheses Concerning the "Redaction" of Q

[28] With the application of form and redaction criticism to Gospel research, there have been several attempts to describe more precisely the origins of Q. Here I review the most important of these.

1. Following Bultmann, Dieter Lührmann distinguished between "collection" and "redaction" (Lührmann 1969:15–16, 19; Bultmann 1968:322–28). To the earlier "collections" he ascribes individual units (e.g., Q 6:20-49; 11:33-36; 12:22-34). The complete Q-document was brought into existence only by a subsequent "redaction" characterized primarily by the

---

1. Vielhauer 1975:312–13; see also Wellhausen 1905:36 and further examples in Black 1967:191–92, 194; Bussby 1954.
2. See Kümmel 1975:68–69. Possible departures of the Q-order from Luke's current order are marked with an askerisk (*) in the table.

OVERVIEW OF Q

Matthew		Luke	Clusters	Redaction	Q^Lk	Q^Mt
(3:1-6?)	The Baptist's Appearance	(3:2-4?)				
3:7-12	John's Preaching	3:7-9, 16-17			3:10-14	
(3:13,16-17)	Jesus' Baptism	(3:21-22)				
4:1-11	The Temptation of Jesus	4:1-13				
(4:13?)	Return to Nazareth	(4:16?)			(4:16-30)	
(5:1-2?)	Intro. to the Sermon	(6:20a?)				
5:3-4,6	Blessed Are the Poor	6:20b-21				5:5.7-9
5:11-12	Blessed Are the Persecuted	6:22-23		A	6:24-26	
5:44-48	Love of Enemies	6:27-28,32-36				
5:39-42	No Retaliation	6:29-30				
7:12	Golden Rule	6:31				
7:1-2	Judge Not	6:37-38			6:37b-38b	
15:14	Blind Guides	6:39*				(7:2a)
10:24-25	Disciples and Master	6:40*				7:6
7:3-5	Mote in the Eye	6:41-42				
7:16-20/12:33	Tree and Fruit	6:43-44		C		
12:34-35	Treasures of the Heart	6:45				
7:21	Lord, Lord	6:46				
7:24-27	Two Builders	6:47-49				
8:5-10,13	Centurion from Capernaum	7:1-2, 6b-10			7:3-6a	
11:2-6	The Baptist's Question	7:18-23				
11:7-11	Opinion of John	7:24-28				

((21:32?))	Tax Collectors Believe	((7:29-30?))	7:29-30	
11:16-17	Children in the Market	7:31-32		
11:18-19	Baptist and Son of Man	7:33-35		
8:19-22	Candidates for Discipleship	9:57-60	9:61-62	
9:37-38; 10:(5b-6? 23?), 10:7-16	Mission Instructions	10:2-12 (+ Matt 10:5b-6? 23?)		(10:5b-6) (10:23)
11:21-23	Against the Galilean Cities	10:13-15		
10:40	Everyone Who Hears You	10:16	10:18-19	
11:25-26	Jesus' Thanksgiving	10:21		
11:27	Sayings about Revelation	10:22		11:28-30
13:16-17	Blessed Are the Witnesses	10:23-24		
(22:35-40?)	Greatest Commandment	(10:25-28?)		
6:9-13	Lord's Prayer	11:2-4	11:5-8	
7:7-11	Seek, Pray	11:9-13		
(9:32-34)	Beelzebul Controversy	11:14-23		
12:22-30	Return of the Demon	11:24-26		
12:43-45	Sign of Jonah	11:29-30		
12:38-40	Queen of the South, Jonah	11:31-32		
12:41-42	Light on the Lampstand	11:33	11:36	
5:15	Eye and Light	11:34-35		
6:22-23	Woes against Jewish Leaders	11:39b-44, 46-48,52		(23:15- 19,24)
23:4,6-7, 13,23-33	Sophia Saying	11:49-51		
23:34-36	Hidden-Revealed	12:2-3		
10:26-27				

B

Matthew		Luke	Clusters	Redaction	Q^{Lk}	Q^{Mt}
10:28-31	Fear Not	12:4-7				
10:32	Confession and Denial	12:8-9				
12:32	Blasphemy of the Spirit	12:10				
10:19-20	Confession by the Spirit	12:11-12				
6:25-33	Do Not Be Anxious	12:22-31			12:16-21	6:34
6:19-21	Gathering Treasure	12:33-34			12:32	
24:43-44	Housebreaker	12:39-40			12:35-38	
24:45-51	Faithful and Evil Servants	12:42b-46		?	12:47-48	
	Fire and Baptism	(12:49-50)				
10:34-36	Divisions	12:51-53				
((16:2-3?))	Appearance of the Sky	12:54-56			(12:54-56)	
5:27-28	Swift Agreement	12:57-59				
13:31-32	Parable of the Mustard	13:18-19			(13:1-5)	
13:33	Parable of the Leaven	13:20-21			(13:6-9)	
7:13-14	Narrow Gate	13:23-24				
7:22-23	Turned Away from the Door	13:25-27		C		25:1-12
8:11-12	Expelled from the Kingdom	13:28-29				
((20:16?))	Last, First	((13:30?))				
23:37-39	Jerusalem, Jerusalem	13:34-35				
((12:11-12))	Cow in a Pit	((14:5?))				
((23:12?))	Exaltation, Humiliation	((14:11/18:14?))				
(22:1-14?)	Great Supper	(14:16-24?)			(14:16-24)	(22:1-14)
(10:37?)	Hate for Jesus' Sake	(14:26?)			(14:26)	(10:37)
(10:38?)	Bearing the Cross	(14:27?)			(14:27)	(10:38)
(5:13?)	Salt Saying	(14:34-35?)			(14:34-35)	(5:13)

(18:12-14?)	(15:4-7?)	Lost Sheep	(15:4-7)	(18:12-14)
(6:24)	(16:13)*	Serving Two Masters		
(11:12-13?)	(16:16?)	Plundering the Kingdom	(16:16)	(11:12-13)
(5:18?)	(16:17?)	Validity of the Law	(16:17)	(5:18)
(5:32?)	(16:18?)	Divorce Prohibition	(16:18)	(5:32)
(18:7?)	(17:1?)	Necessary Scandals	(17:1)	(18:7)
(18:15,21-22?)	(17:3-4?)	Unlimited Forgiveness	(17:3-4)	(18:15,21-22)
(17:20?)	(17:6?)	Faith like Mustard Seed	(17:6)	(17:20)
(24:26-28, 37-41)	17:23-24,26-27, 30,34-35,37	Eschatological Speech	17:28-29	
(10:39?)	(17:33?)*	Losing, Gaining	(18:2-8)	
(25:14-30?)	(19:12-27?)	Talents/Minas	(19:12-27)	(25:14-30)
((21:15-16?))	((19:39-40?))	People Crying Out		
((23:11?))	((22:26?))	Life Servants		
(19:28?)	(22:28-30?)	Judging the Twelve Tribes		

Sigla

(. . .) Probably in Q

(. . .?) Possibly in Q

((. . .)) Probably not in Q

* Position in Q is unclear

⌐ Smaller clusters of sayings

⌐ Redactional groupings

In the QMt and QLk columns, texts in parentheses cannot be assigned to QMt and QLk with certainty.

"opposition between Jesus and this generation" and "the announcement of judgment against Israel" (or against all who reject the message of Jesus) (1969:84 [p. 59 in this volume]).

One might ask, however, whether such a simple partition of Q's composition history into "collection" and "redaction" can adequately account for the complexity of Q. Lührmann himself postulates that Q is the end result of "a long process of tradition" (1969:84; above, p. 59). How was the process completed? From the compositional history of Q, one should also investigate the community that, according to Lührmann, was responsible for Q. Hence Lührmann's initial exploration requires further discussion. [29]

2. In contrast, Siegfried Schulz rightly assumes that there was historical development in Q. He distinguishes two strata: the older, Palestinian, prophetic, and enthusiastic stage,[3] which is deeply influenced by end expectation and by post-Easter enthusiasm about the Spirit; and a more recent, Syrian, and Hellenistic Jewish stage (containing the remainder of Q), characterized in particular by a cessation of prophetic enthusiasm, awareness of the delay of the parousia, polemic against Israel, reflection on the earthly Jesus, and so forth.[4]

In spite of the exhaustive detail of Schulz's work, one must ask whether this schematic division is appropriate. Recent research has seen the traditional distinction between the "Palestinian Jewish Christian" and the "Hellenistic Jewish Christian" realms—both in a geographical and in a traditional-historical sense—as extremely problematic. Furthermore, Schulz assumes that Luke's order of Q is the more original (1972:27) but fails to infer from this order any conclusions about tradition history or compositional history. Neither is it clear how the "final Q-redaction" (1972:481; also 24, 482) relates to the second stratum. Should it be placed after the second stratum—a "Gentile Christian final redaction" (1972:484)? Finally, Schulz does not inquire at all into the Q-prophets' relation to Jesus. Only in a later essay does he mention (in passing) that the oldest Q-material is "broadly identical with the message of the historical Jesus" (1973:57). But what does "broadly identical" mean?

3. By contrast, Heinz Schürmann (1975:140-47; see above, pp. 89–97 for a revised version of what follows) postulates more stages for Q. On the basis of observations of the use of the Son of Man title, he posits four stages:

(a) "Isolated sayings," by which he distinguishes "the oldest stratum" from the "secondary stratum," at which stage Son of Man sayings

---

3. Q 6:20b-21, 27-28, 32-36, 29-30, 31, 37-38, 41-42; 11:2-4, 9-13, 39, 42-44, 46-48, 52; 12:4-7, 8-9, 22-31, 33-34.

4. On the older material, see Schulz 1972:57–164; on the more recent stage, see esp. pp. 47-53, 481-89.

were added as "commentary sayings."[5] [**30**] This process occurred in a Palestinian locale (1975:130–40, 146 and n. 119).

(*b*) "Clusters of sayings," where sayings that use the Son of Man title appear in a concluding section "as if by themselves," without any particular emphasis, or that occasionally are "deliberately placed at the end of a sayings cluster" (1975:142 and nn. 102–4).

(*c*) "Discourses," where "the title appears 'on its own' in concluding formulations, and as such, obviously has no particular redactional stress" (e.g., Q 7:[18-30], 31-35) (1975:143 and n. 106).

(*d*) The "final redaction," in which the Son of Man title no longer has any decisive christological significance but is "merely transmitted"; this stage occurs on "Hellenistic soil."[6] Later Schürmann seems to have combined the first two stages as the "early stage" and the last two as the "late stage" (Schürmann 1982:132 and n. 65).

This developmental schema from "isolated sayings" to the "final redaction" seems at first glance to be quite plausible as a model for the growth of a document such as Q—but only as a model. How does Schürmann know that the document underwent a *final* redaction? In my view, only from his model. Moreover, he has not yet applied the schema concretely to all of the material in Q; he has tested it only on the kingdom sayings (Schürmann 1982).[7] Furthermore, the function of the Son of Man sayings in the later period should perhaps be interpreted differently, as we shall soon see. In any case, Schürmann's observation that the Son of Man sayings appear mainly at the beginning or at the end of a complex deserves special attention.

4. Athanasius Polag also posits several stages of development in Q. He assumes three main strata: the "primary tradition," the "principal collection," and a "late redaction."[8] In a thorough review, Polag subdivides the entire process into five stages: [**31**] (*a*) The "primary tradition," which circulated in Aramaic, originated broadly speaking in the pre-Easter circle of disciples. This material "reveals a conceptual field that is completely 'open' in respect to Christology" (1977:198; cf. also 34–35, 194–95). (*b*) The "secondary stage of tradition" is oriented toward both the "preservation,

5. For example, Q 6:22-23 (added to 6:20b-21); 7:33-34 (added to 7:31-32); 9:57-58 (added to 9:59-60); 11:30 (added to 11:29); 12:8-9 (added to 12:[1], 2-7); 12:10 (added to 12:[1], 2-9); Q//Matt 10:23 (added to 12:11-12); Q 12:40 (added to 12:[35-]39); 17:24 (added to 17:23); 17:26-27, 28-30 (added to 17:24).

6. Schürmann 1975:144–47 and n. 112. Zeller (1982:399–402; above, pp. 120–23 and n. 103) recently proposed a very similar schema: "Appending of 'Commentary Sayings' "; "Formation of Thematic Sayings Complexes"; "Juxtaposition of Macro-Texts"; "Arrangement of the Macro-Texts." The final redactor belongs "in a Greek-speaking Jewish Christian environment" (409).

7. In the meantime, Schürmann has worked out his model on the Q-woes (1986).—ED.

8. Polag 1977, esp. 198–99 (summary). His licentiate thesis (1966) marks the actual beginning of the redaction-critical investigation of Q, but this work need not be summarized in order to present Polag's current position.

explanation, and expansion of the material as dominical sayings" and the "formation of smaller clusters of sayings." Polag probably has in mind the clusters in Q 6:20-21, 27-36; 6:37-38 (31); 10:4-11, 16; 11:9-13; 11:14-23; 12:4-7; 12:22-31 (1977:23, 129 and n. 377). This stage is not discussed further.

Of special importance is (c) the first redactional stage, the "principal collection," which arranged the corpus of Q in Greek. It reveals the compositional motifs of "comfort and encouragement," "warning"—there are already indications of the delay of the parousia—and "polemic" with a few redactional formulations (e.g., 17:30; 11:30; 1977:130–31, 133; cf. 10–15). This stage is "not characterized first of all by christological reflection but instead refers to the church's faithfulness to its confession" (1977:144).

The "later interpolations" (d) into the main collection form a further stage that displays an interest in the situation of the community, polemic against false teachers and false prophets, and the situation of the disciples in reference to community leaders. From this stage comes Q 6:43-45 (?); 9:57-62; 10:2; 11:1b-13; 12:1b; 14:16-24, 26-35; 16:17; and 17:1-2. The texts that address Jesus as "Lord" (mostly only in Luke) also come from this stage: Q 11:1b, 45; 12:41; 13:23; 14:15; 17:5; 17:37 (1977:13–15, 131).

Finally, there is (e) a "late redaction," which represents a scribal, amplified edition: Q 3:7-9, 16-17, 21-22; 4:1-13; 7:1-10, 27, 28; 10:21-22, 23-24; 12:10; 12:47-48, 49-53 (Q/Matt 5:19); 19:12-27, as well as various framing elements (1977:15–17, 23, 30, 145). "The basic components of these pericopae reflect early tradition, but there is a greater degree of reworking than in the rest of the Q-material" (1977:167). This stage "contains clear indications of christological reflection that is concerned with Jesus' relation to God" (cf. the titles "Son of God" and "the Son," etc.) (15–17). With this stage, Q achieved the form that Matthew and Luke used. [32]

The position taken by Polag seems to me to be especially appropriate insofar as it assumes a successive development of Q. It is certainly correct for a document with smaller units of sayings that gives no indication of a single author with a personal style (as is the case with the Gospels) but that must have had a decade-long history. Polag is also right, in my view, to take Q's order (following Luke) more seriously. So it is all the more regrettable to me that he does not make more use of this order. As far as is possible, one should ask about the sense that is intended by this order. For it is from the style and manner in which the material has been arranged that one can derive concrete conclusions regarding the formation of Q. But instead of using such features, Polag has been guided generally by his own conception of the development of the Q-community and Q-Christology.

As far as Christology is concerned, this may have been an important redactional principle from an early stage onward—as we will soon see. It does not explain why in the "primary tradition" Jesus can remain "completely open" from a christological perspective even though he occupies a "key position in the kingdom event" (1977:198). For the post-Easter tradents of the "primary tradition," the question of what Jesus claimed— "Christology of the demand" (1977:127)—is scarcely separable from the other question of who Jesus was. Related to this point is the significance of the Son of Man title, which according to Polag had "not been worth emphasizing" even for the main Q-collection, in spite of the apocalypticizing of the title that first occurred at this point (1977:135, see also 134).

Another question arises: whether one can fit the redaction of Q into these *two* large stages ("primary tradition" and "main collection") without difficulty. How does one know that there was only a single main collection? Even in the "later redaction" it is difficult to see why a saying such as Q 10:23-24, which evinces a realized eschatology, would be placed in the same redactional stage as Q 19:12-27 (the parable of the entrusted money), with its express allusion to the problem of the delay of the parousia and interim ethics. One cannot get along simply by using the rubric of "expansion." Here Polag owes us further explanation.

Finally, his definition of the extent of Q should be mentioned. It seems to me that he is far too optimistic in ascribing many uncertain texts to Q. This caution applies in particular to the sayings that occur in only one Gospel. For it is impossible to find any plausible grounds for Matthew to have omitted texts such as Luke 9:61-62; 11:5-8, 37-39a; 12:32, 35-38, 47-48; 14:28-32; 15:8-10; 17:7-10 (see 1977:2–5). Related to this problem is the fact [33] that Polag nowhere in his work discusses the possibility that Luke and Matthew each have a different recension of Q.

I have assembled many views. I now attempt to sketch my own view of the development of Q.

2. The Model of Q's Development

1. Terminology

(*a*) I refer to the smallest units of sayings material as *independent sayings* that existed separately and were first transmitted orally. This material, however, also includes longer units that can be called short *discourses*.

(*b*) A *sayings cluster* arises from connecting two or even four or five independent sayings on the basis of formal features (catchwords, similar or related form) or because of a topical relationship. This connection often occurs with the intention of indirect "commentary" on a saying through association with another saying[9] or to allow the sayings to comment on each other. The sayings cluster can be formed either at the oral stage or at a written stage. Up to this stage, origins in the pre-Easter period are possible.

---

9. On the notion of "commentary sayings," see Schürmann 1975 (above, pp. 74–97) and esp. Wanke 1980. In my view the relationship between the saying that is the point of reference (*Bezugswort*) and the commentary saying (*Kommentarwort*) is not always one-sided; is it not the case that the sayings in the combinations Q 11:33, 34-35 or 12:8-9, 10 comment on each other?

(c) A *sayings collection* is a more complex written compilation of sayings. This collection can occur by means of the same principles mentioned in (b), occasionally with a clear logical progression.[10]

(d) *Redaction* has to do with an independent, written corpus, edited from a consciously chosen perspective, which is furnished with other materials besides sayings.

It should be underlined explicitly that this is a heuristic schema. The boundary between sayings clusters and sayings collections is fluid; the same is the case between sayings collections and redaction.

2. Analytical Survey of Q

1. The Baptist Complex, Q 3:2—7:35. Q begins with sayings of John (Q 3:[2-4?], 7-9, 16-17), followed probably by the narrative of Jesus' baptism (Q 3:21-22) and certainly by the temptation story (4:1-13). This story flows into [34] the "programmatic discourse" (Q 6:20-49). Then follows the apophthegm about the centurion from Capernaum (7:1-10). An incidental theme in this story of Jesus' miracle working creates a bridge to the next section about the inquiry of the Baptist (Q 7:18-23: miracles of Jesus in v. 22).[11] At this point emerges the topic of the Baptist, which is continued in Q 7:24-27, to which is attached the sayings cluster of Q 7:31-35. With this cluster the theme of the Baptist comes to an end. The appearance of the Son of Man title in 7:34 probably signals the conclusion of a complex. In the next Q-passage (9:57-60) something completely new begins (discipleship and mission).

This first complex in Q did not come into being all at once. In the first place, the connection of 7:31-35 with the preceding corpus (ending in 7:28) appears to be very loose: it is achieved only through the word *John* in 7:33, which is not itself a theme of the parable in 7:31-32.[12] Moreover, the audience changes: up to 7:28 it is a willing public that is addressed, but in 7:31-35 the unbelieving masses appear. Correspondingly, the concern of 7:31-35 is rather new: the complaint against "this generation." Hence the connection is a secondary one. If the concluding verse (7:35)—the "children of wisdom"[13]—designates in particular the people of the Q-circle who have accepted the message of John and Jesus, there is also a bridge to the next complex on the "disciples" (9:57—10:24). The connection of 7:31-34 with 7:35 in this position is probably the result of an overarching redaction.

10. On the notion of "collection," see Bultmann 1968:322.

11. Matthew has rearranged the corresponding Q-pericope (Matt 11:2-19) so that Matt 11:5-6 is anticipated better by Matt 8-9 (and 10).

12. This means that the connection of 7:33-34 with 7:31-32 occurred early and only after that did the connection of 7:31-35 happen. On this matter, see Schürmann 1975:131-32 (above, pp. 81-82); Wanke 1980:216.

13. Matthew's version, "the works of wisdom" (11:19b), is, as most assume, due to Matthaean redaction.

What is the situation with the main corpus ending at 7:28? Q 7:28 ("[Amen] I say to you … the smallest in the kingdom of God is greater than he") explictly and solemnly concludes the foregoing train of thought. Moreover, it is interesting that one can detect a multifaceted framework that compasses the whole complex. This framework can be seen first of all in the general framing that occurs through the theme of the Baptist in Q 3:[2-6], 7-9, 16-17; and 7:18-28. The Baptist's question in 7:19 ("are you the one who is to come?") obviously picks up on his earlier saying in Q 3:16 ("the one who is to come"). If, in addition, Luke 3:3 ("the whole region of the Jordan," "in the wilderness" [?]) [35] already belonged to Q as an indication of the setting, Jesus' explicit reference to the place of baptism in 7:24 ("what did you go out to the wilderness to see?") would also belong to the framing of Q. Moreover, one should note that in both the initial and closing saying of this complex (6:20b; 7:28) the "kingdom of God" is expressly mentioned—which is an additional kind of framing by means of an extremely important catchword. Furthermore, Q 7:22b ("the poor have the good news brought to them") should certainly be connected in its current context with Jesus' saying in 6:20b ("Blessed are the poor, for yours is the kingdom of God"), especially since the word πτωχοί occurs in Q only in these two places. There are additional references: the sayings of Jesus in Q 6:20b-49, especially in 6:27-49 (warnings), could be read as further specifications of the demands of the Baptist "to bring forth the fruit worthy of repentance" (Q 3:8). At the same time the pericope about the centurion from Capernaum (7:1-10) appears to be connected with Q 7:18-23; the healing miracle (7:10) prepares for the answer to the Baptist's question (Q 7:22). This pericope, which makes a non-Israelite conspicuous (cf. 3:8b) by his complete trust in Jesus' word and status, can at the same time provide a convenient illustration of the warning to recognize Jesus (7:23, 28). Finally, one should take note of the strong apophthegmatizing of the entire complex. It is therefore probable that the finished complex represents a consciously composed literary unity, which has in view the relationship of Jesus to the Baptist in particular. I call this complex *Redaction "A."*

But this corpus is not unitary. Immediately before Q 7:28 stands the unique verse Q 7:27, a citation that fuses Mal 3:1a (or 3:22-23 = ET 4:4-5) and Exod 23:30 with an introductory formula, γέγραπται. This formula is found elsewhere in Q only in the temptation story (Q 4:4, 8, 10, 12). Both presuppose scribal activity. Moreover, Q 7:27 interrupts the thematic association between 7:26 and 7:28. Besides, Q 7:27 is the only place in Q where John is implicitly associated with the figure of Elijah as the precursor of the Messiah: one should note the reminiscence of Mal 3:22-23 (ET 4:4-5) and the use of the word κατασκευάσει, which also appears in the Elijah-John connection in Luke 1:17. Elsewhere in Q, all Elijah motifs refer to Jesus himself.[14] In all probability, Q 7:27 is a later interpolation.

---

14. See Sato 1988:404-5.

At the same time, there are indications that the temptation story (4:1-13) also originated later. This pericope has no obvious [36] connection with the theme of the Baptist. Reference has been just made to the citation formulae that are unique in Q. In addition, the Septuagint is explicitly used only here.[15] What we encounter here is probably scribalism used in the service of paraenesis. Moreover, Q 4:1-13 is also very difficult to classify from a formal point of view, but in any event, in Q it is a foreign construction. The christological title "Son of God" (4:3, 9) is unique in Q. This pericope perhaps originated after Redaction "A"; someone probably later elaborated the originally shorter narrative of the testing of Jesus (like the one found in Mark 1:12-13 // Luke 4:1-2a), which had been obtained through an interrelation with Mark 1:(2-6), 7-15.

In the body of Redaction "A" there is yet another older *sayings collection*, Q 6:20b-49 (the "programmatic discourse"), which was itself formed from several sayings clusters: Q 6:20-23, with the established form of beatitudes, was originally independent of the subsequent sayings clusters and sayings in 6:27-49. Q 6:27 signals the real beginning with "I tell you"; from the point of view of content, the conclusion (6:47-49, "whoever hears my words and *does* them . . .") has the hortatory or monitory sayings of Q 6:27-46 in view. The affixing of the beatitudes (6:20b-23) to the admonitions in 6:27-49 is motivated both by the topical association of mistreatment or persecution at the hands of enemies (cf. μισέω in Luke 6:22 // 6:27 or διώκω in Matt 5:11 // 5:44) and by the fact that beatitudes are frequently found at the beginning of a work or complex.[16] Besides, the position of the kingdom saying in Q 6:20b and the Son of Man saying in 6:22-23 cannot have been irrelevant at the beginning of a sayings collection.[17] In the section Q 6:27-49, Q 6:37 marks a turning point in the tone: from this point on, warnings to believers are more strongly emphasized. Does this observation perhaps suggest that the individual sayings and sayings clusters in Q 6:27-49 were, from a tradition-historical standpoint, successively arranged after the original admonitions on the subject of love of enemies (6:27-36)? Finally, the question remains whether 6:39, 40 were originally in the position Luke has them. Considering Matthew's order in Matt 7:1-5, one has the impression that Q 6:39-40 may be a secondary interpolation between Q 6:38 and 6:41.

The Baptist sayings in Q 3:7-9, 16-17 are a noteworthy *sayings cluster* in Redaction "A."

[37] Thus one can already see in the first complex of Q how the protracted process of formation is illustrated.

---

15. The clearest indication that Q uses the LXX rather than the MT is the second-person singular in Q 4:12 (contrast the second-person plural in the MT of Deut 6:16).

16. Cf. Ps 1:1; Prov 8:32; Job 5:17; Isa 56:1-2; Rev 1:3, etc.

17. In this sayings cluster (Q 6:20b-21 + 22-23) two key concepts are juxtaposed: "kingdom" and "Son of Man"—an index of the fact that the early tradition saw a close connection between the two.

2. The Mission Complex, Q 9:57—10:24. The next complex begins with the apophthegm Q 9:57-60, in which preparedness for discipleship is tested. This apophthegm forms an introduction to the mission speech (Q 10:2-16 + Matt 10:5b-6?, 23?). Then comes another apophthegmatized introduction in 10:21a, "At this time, Jesus said. . . ." One might ask what "at this time" means. This puzzling temporal reference would have meaning if one sees the first apophethegm in Q 9:57-60 and the apophthegmatized 10:21 as related within a framework: Jesus twice tests the preparedness of the disciples for a radical mission (9:57-60), then sends them out with his instructions (10:2-16), and following this thanks his heavenly Father for his disciples (10:21). The occurrence of ταῦτα in 10:21b, which is remarkable in itself, should be taken to signify the eschatological, but now available, salvation—the peace mentioned in Q 10:5-6 and the "kingdom" in Q 10:9. Finally, Jesus pronounces the disciples blessed because of the eschaton that has just broken in (Q 10:23-24).[18] Concluding a unit with beatitudes is not uncommon.[19] Another indication of a conclusion in 10:23-24 is the solemn formula "I tell you" (as above in Q 7:28). Finally, the saying about the homeless "Son of Man" (Q 9:58) at the beginning of the unit anticipates the free-as-a-bird itinerant mission of the disciples in 10:3-16. What is said about salvation in 10:21-24 corresponds—as a complement—to the arduous nature of discipleship in 9:57-60. With this saying, the section seems to have come to a close. Since the connection with Q 3:2—7:28 was probably created secondarily through Q 7:(31-34), 35, I hold Q 9:57—10:24 to be an independent redaction (*Redaction "B"*), whose main focus is the commissioning of the disciples. If this is so, it means that redaction "B" deliberately placed the apophthegm containing the Son of Man saying at the beginning of the whole unit. Accordingly, it is probable that the Son of Man saying was most important at the level of redaction in the introductory and concluding sections and in no way got into the redactional framework "on its own" as a leftover of earlier stages (against Schürmann 1975:142–47; see above, pp. 91–97). [38]

Two units in this complex may have been interpolated at a later date: Q 10:22 and 10:(12), 13-15. Q 10:22 is unique with the christological title "Son" (used absolutely), which is nowhere else clearly attested in Q. One might note the similarlity to the "Son of God" in the temptation story (Q 4:3, 9). The narrative of the baptism of Jesus with the heavenly voice ("You are my son," Q 3:22), which was incorporated earlier, may be presupposed by both Q 10:22 and Q 4:1-13. Q 10:22 may therefore have been inserted later. In the context, the pericope expresses the three-stage revelation (God–Jesus–disciples) seen in Q 10:16, stresses the exclusive nature of the revela-

---

18. In Matthew the corresponding verses (Matt 13:16-17) are placed in the context of the parables discourse.

19. For example, Isa 32:20; Sir 50:28; *T. Naph.* 10.9 (Hebrew); Rev 1:3; *Sib. Or.* 4.192; cf. also above, on Q 7:23.

tion of Q 10:21, and furnishes—in an anticipatory way—the christological justification for the blessing of the disciples in Q 10:23-24. Q 10:22 therefore is probably a secondary construction that arises from the context.

The other pericope is the saying in Q 10:13-15, which is foreign to the context. The impenitent Galilean cities appear quite unexpectedly as addressees. This woe oracle is connected to Q 10:10-11 by means of topical considerations (on the judgment of a certain city).[20] The intervening verse (10:12) is a construction that is foreign as far as form is concerned: formally it seems to be a pronouncement of doom, but no one is actually addressed. The verse was probably formulated on the pattern of Q 10:14 (ἀνεκτότερον ἔσται ἤ) and at the same time interpolated into the text along with Q 10:13-15, as an illustration of Q 10:10-11. The reference to notorious Sodomites, long ago destroyed, is an intensification when compared with the mention of the (merely) gentile cities of Tyre and Sidon (v. 14).[21]

But the remaining part of this section is also not unitary in origin. Within it can be seen a tightly bound complex—the mission discourse that ends with the authorizing saying in 10:16: Q 10:2-11, 16 (+ Matt 10:5b-6? 23?).[22] In any event, Q 10:16 was surely an independent saying at one point, as the parallels with Mark 9:37; John 12:44-45; 5:23b; 13:20 indicate. Q 10:2 also appears to have been an originally isolated saying that was secondarily introduced at this point, no doubt at the time of Redaction "B." The verse envisages a larger audience than merely the commissioned disciples (from 10:3 on); the use of ὑπάγετε in 10:3 probably signals the beginning of the original mission complex. Hence Q 10:3-11 can be designated as an early *sayings collection* on the topic of mission.

3. The Great Commandment (Luke 10:25-28).

[39] If it is true that the following pericope (Luke 10:25-28) in fact belonged to Q, its position would be quite uncertain. Is it perhaps to be connected with the following Q-units concerning prayer (Q 11:2-4, 9-13)? In this case, two important themes of discipleship would be treated here: law and prayer.[23] But the word (ἐκ)πειράζων ["testing"] in Luke 10:25 does not fit well with this analysis. Because of this uncertainty, Luke 10:25-28 will be left out of further consideration.

4. Prayer and Petition (Q 11:2-4, 9-13).

Here, by contrast, it is probable that Q 11:2-4 and 11:9-13 formed a special *sayings cluster* on the topic

---

20. For considerations of content, Matthew has removed the saying from the context of the commissioning of the disciples and inserted it at Matt 11:21-24.

21. On the secondary character of Q 10:12, see esp. Lührmann 1969:62 and n. 1.

22. If Matt 10:5b-6, 23 belonged to Q, one might tentatively place 10:5b-6 between Q 10:7 and 10:8, and Matt 10:23 before Luke 10:17.

23. On the connection of law (esp. the Shema—cf. Luke 10:27) and prayer (or praise), see *m. Ber.* 1:4; 2:2; 3:4; *m. Meg.* 4:3, 5.

of "prayer or petition." The catchword *father* in 11:2, 11, 13 constitutes the leitmotif and framework. Moreover, one should compare the request for bread in Q 11:3 with that in 11:12 (//Matt 7:9).[24] That this sayings cluster in fact stood at this position in Q is made probable by the agreement in order between Luke 11:2-4, 9-13, 14-23 and Matt 6:9-13; 7:7-11; 12:22-30.[25] This position is completely unmotivated, however, and the pericope cannot be connected meaningfully either with what precedes it or with what follows it. The compositional or redactional hand responsible for the introduction of this sayings cluster remains obscure.

5. The Miracle Chain (Q 11:14-32). The chain of materials that follow (Q 11:14-23, 24-26, 29-32) comes under the general rubric of "miracle." It has a sharper christological focus: the forensic authority of Jesus, which has been mounting, culminates in the sayings that pronounce doom on "this generation" (Q 11:29-30, 31-32). In addition, the motif of Sophia appears here—just as in Q 7:31-32, 33-35—along with the term *Son of Man* (11:30). Here it can be seen how important the Son of Man title is in the concluding portion of a redactional complex (contrast Schürmann 1975; above, pp. 74-97). In this combination one can surely discern the hand of the same redactor who joined Q 3:2—7:28 (Redaction "A") and Q 9:57—10:24 (Redaction "B"). That this hand did not earlier insert a *pronouncement* of doom in 7:33-35 is explicable from the perspective of a compositional plan that entailed intensification. I provisionally designate this stage of composition—which stresses the bitter indictment or pronouncement of judgment on the whole of Israel ("this generation"), connected with the Sophia motif—as *Redaction "C"*[40].

6. The Sayings on Light (Q 11:33-35). The location of the next *sayings cluster* (Q 11:33-35) is not completely clear, but precisely because the couplet of sayings seems so mysterious in the Lukan sequence, it probably also stood here in Q. Indeed, it would be conceivable that Q 11:33-35 belonged with 12:2-3, (4-7); one might consider the possible catchword connection εἰς κρύπτην (Q 11:33)–κρυπτόν (Q 12:2); φῶς + σκότος (Q 11:35)–φῶς + σκοτία (Q 12:3); perhaps also σῶμα (Q 11:34//12:4, 6) (Zeller 1984:72-73). But then it would not be entirely intelligible why the sayings cluster would have stood here. It is neither a direct continuation of Q 11:29-32 nor an introduction to the woes that follow (11:39-52).[26]

24. On the original nature of "bread/stone" in Matt 7:9, see the arguments of Schulz 1972:162 and n. 185.

25. On grounds of content, it is understandable why Matthew separated the important instructions to disciples in 6:9-13 and 7:7-11 from the "Beelzebul controversy" and incorporated them into his "Sermon on the Mount," which is a programmatic instruction of Christians.

26. Even if Q 16:13 originally stood after 11:35 (see Sato 1988:24), the mystery of the position of 11:33-35 would not be solved.

7. The Woes (Q 11:39-52).   Q 11:39-52 is a long string of seven woes, with the key word *kingdom* at the end (Q 11:52).[27] The sevenfold woes correspond to the same number in the series of woes in Isa 5:8-23; 10:1-3.[28] Especially from the third woe on, there is an intensification of sinful responsibility:

v. 43   being ambitious
v. 44   making the people unclean
v. 46   burdening the people
vv. 47-48   responsibility for the murder of the prophets
v. 52   locking up the kingdom

Thus the existence of an earlier *sayings collection* with these seven woes is very probable.

Q 11:49-51 is a foreign intrusion. This saying of doom was first interpolated between the seventh woe (11:47-48) and the last woe because of a catchword or topical association (murder of the prophets). Again one notes a striking convergence in motifs: first, a Sophia motif (11:49a), then the indictment, or rather the pronouncement of doom and the damning of "this generation" (11:50-51). It is probable therefore that Redaction "C" is responsible for this interpolation. At the same time, one ought to make the same hand responsible for the ordering of Q 11:14-32 and 11:39-52. These verses would constitute a larger block of [41] polemical and judgment sayings (notwithstanding 11:33-35). From the point of view of content it is also appropriate that the pronouncements of judgment in 11:29-32 and—even more vehemently—11:49-51 (along with the woes) come only after the polemic in Q 11:14-23.

8. Sayings of Consolation and Warning (Q 12:2-34).   The next series picks up the theme of "persecution" from the preceding verses (11:47-48, 49-51). For itself, however, the series in Q 12:2-34 has another focus: consolation and warning for the disciples. The Q-order is not completely certain, although Luke's sequence seems to reproduce it: Luke 12:2-9 is attested also by Matthew's sequence (Matt 10:26-33), and Luke 12:22-34 corresponds closely to Matt 6:19-21 + 6:25-33. An obviously early set of catchword associations is telling: "the Son of Man" (Luke 12:8-9 // 12:10), "the Holy Spirit" (Luke 12:10 // 12:12), "do not be anxious" (Luke 12:11 // 12:22). Q 12:33-34 seems to have been placed here as a commentary on the content of 12:22-31 (freedom from possessions/possessions in heaven). But whoever is responsible for this arrangement cannot be ascertained.

It has often been rightly asked whether there is not an even earlier *say-*

---

27. The phrase ἡ κλείς τῆς γνώσεως (thus Luke) is secondary, since one cannot "enter" γνῶσις as one can the "kingdom" (thus Matt 23:13).

28. For similar woes that were gathered together at an early date one can also refer to Amos 5:(7), 16, 18; 6:1 (13); and Hab 2:6b-19.

ings cluster within this series of sayings. This idea seems plausible, at least in the case of Q 12:4-12, where acute danger from persecution is envisaged. Formally, the two prohibitions ("fear not" in 12:4 and "do not be anxious" in 12:11) provide a framework. In addition, the fact that the Son of Man sayings (12:8-9, 10) are not used either as introductions or as conclusions (contrast Schürmann 1975:135–37; above, pp. 84–87) point to a nonredactional, early connection of the sayings. Both Q 12:2-3 and Q 12:22-31 may have been added subsequently, where the point of view is that of the difficulties faced by impoverished, itinerant preachers.

9. Eschatological Parables (Q 12:39-46).   The two following eschatological parables (Q 12:39-40, 42-46) may have formed an early cluster, based on their common theme. The "Son of Man" emerges again at the beginning (12:40). This cluster is connected with the preceding saying by means of catchword association: κλέπτης and διορύσσω (Q 12:33// 12:39).[29]

10. Isolated Sayings (Q 12:49—13:21).   From Q 12:49 to Q 13:21 the sayings show no clear connection, presuming that the order of Luke reproduces that of Q. The threatening tone, [42] which was previously seen in 12:39-40, 42-46, is found again only in Q 12:58-59. As ἦλθον sayings, Q 12:49-50 and 12:51-53 form a special sayings cluster; but it is incomprehensible why they are placed here. The position of the pair of parables in Q 13:18-19, 20-21 is all the more puzzling.

11. Threatening Sayings (Q 13:23-35).   A series of sayings appears in Luke 13:23-24, 25-27, 28-29 that clearly corresponds to the order of Q.[30] These sayings are also coherent thematically: they represent a threat made pointedly in Q 13:28-29 in a pronouncement of doom (against the Israelites). This series probably comes to its climax in the lament spoken against Jerusalem—and, *pars pro toto*, against all Israel—in Q 13:34-35. To be sure, the position of Q 13:34-35 is not certain, but in view of the similarity in form the sequence of Q 13:28-29 (pronouncement of doom)—13:34-35 (saying of doom) can be assumed. In any case, Q 13:34-35 cannot be located after Q 11:49-51,[31] for the reiterated, concluding woe against the Pharisees in Q 11:52 would be too isolated after two long doom sayings (Q 11:49-51 + 13:34-35), and especially after the address to Jerusalem (Q 13:34).[32]

29. The latter word is found only the Matthew's version (6:19), but it is probably original there.
30. Note the agreements in order between Luke and Matthew from Luke 12:57-59 on: Luke 12:57-59 // Matt 5:25-26; Luke 13:23-24 // Matt 7:13-14; Luke 13:25-27 // Matt 7:22-23; Luke 13:28-29 // Matt 8:11-12; Luke 13:34-35 // Matt 23:37-39.
31. Thus Lührmann 1969:48 and many others.
32. Polag (1977:5; 1979:25, 66) places Q 13:34-35 after 12:57-59. This placement, which

It is possible that Q 13:23-24, 25-27, 28-29, 34-35 (in this order) constituted a *sayings cluster* (or *sayings collection*). The motif of "entrance" connects Q 13:23-24 and 13:25-27;[33] the catchword ἔξω (Q 13:25 [only in Luke]//Q 13:28) joins 13:25-27 and 13:28-29 together. In addition, there is an escalation in the harshness of the judgment, ending in Q 13:34-35. Finally, "the one who comes in the name of the Lord" (Q 13:35) in Q certainly refers to Jesus as the judge of the world, so that we have a concluding verse equivalent to the Son of Man endings. Luke and Matthew, however, diverge sharply in Q 13:23-24 and 13:25-27 with respect to wording; this divergence should warn us about drawing any further conclusions. [43]

It is an important question whether Redaction "C" is responsible for the placement of 13:23-35, or even for its very composition. The common theme of indictment or announcement of judgment against Israel is clearly recognizable as the overarching theme, especially in Q 13:28-29, 34-35. The expression "this generation," of course, does not appear, but it can be inferred from the content. In addition, Q 13:34-35 has the characteristics of a discourse of the personified Wisdom. In this case, however, there is a difficulty: assuming that Redaction "C" inserted the large sayings collection in Q 12:2-34 en bloc after Q 11:52 because it was available as an established unit of paraenesis for disciples, one must ask why the material in Q 12:39 onward, in particular from 12:49 to 13:21, is arranged in so mysterious a manner from the point of view of content. These sayings contain no indictment of Israel. Two responses are possible. Either Redaction "C" arranged these individual materials casually and without a plan of composition; or the obscure organization derives not directly from Redaction "C" but from various, unsystematic interpolations and additions from a later—or earlier?[34] —period. The second alternative seems better to me. This explanation is quite possible in view of the continuing influence of oral tradition, which can be committed to writing as the circumstance requires.

12. Uncertain Sayings (Luke 14:16—17:6).

12. Uncertain Sayings (Luke 14:16—17:6). I have already expressed the view that it is not certain that the verses occurring after Luke 13:35 (14:16-24, 26, 27, 34-35; 15:4-7; 16:16, 17, 18; 17:1, 3-4, 6) belong to Q (Sato 1988:23–24). The sequence of the sayings in Luke and that in Matthew diverge considerably. Even if Luke's order of the sayings reproduces that of Q, there would exist no clear line of thought. Only three verses, Luke 16:16, 17, 18, seem to form a distinct cluster on the subject of

---

is not supported by either Matthew or Luke, appears quite arbitrary.

33. The catchword connection with θύρα in Luke 13:24 and 13:25 unfortunately depends on a secondary alteration in Luke 13:24; Matt 7:13-14 (with πύλη) is more original.

34. Were the sayings in Q 12:39-40, 42-46, 49-53; 13:18-21 added successively after the sayings collection in Q 12:2-34?

the "Law."[35] The significance of this association, however, is still quite obscure. One cannot speak of a comprehensive redaction.

13. The Eschatological Discourse (Q 17:23-37). Only in Q 17:23-37 does one again encounter a distinct Q-complex, one that probably concluded the source. These sayings (Q 17:23-24, 26-27, 30, [33?], 34-35, 37) contain direct statements on the topic of [44] the end of the world with the typical motif of "suddenness." The obscure metaphor in Q 17:37 about the unavoidable nature of the judgment rounds off the entire composition. The saying about the Son of Man (Q 17:23-24) stands at the beginning. Thus, these sayings formed a *sayings collection* quite early. The present position at the end of the entire source might indicate just how central the expectation of Jesus as the Son of Man coming to judge was for Q as a whole.

One should ask who was responsible for the position of the sayings collection in Q 17:23-37. Redaction "C"? On the one hand, the usual motifs of the "C" stage of redaction (judgment against Israel; Sophia imagery) are obviously missing. On the other hand, the perspective of a universal judgment does not fit at all badly with the principal preoccupations of Redaction "C." The absence of the usual motifs is explained by the fact that Q 17:23-27 was an early sayings collection that was already fixed when Redaction "C" incorporated it en bloc. Redaction "C" perhaps placed the collection Q 17:23-37 here as a conclusion to the corpus.

If other material were present in Q between Q 13:23-35 and 17:23-37, its presence there would indicate that the concluding nature of 17:23-37 was clearly recognized, and that verses were added not after it but always before it. The image of the coming of the Son of Man in the concluding section may have functioned additionally as a compositional principle.

14. Disputed Sayings (Q 19:12-27; 22:28-30). These verses, even if they belonged to Q, cannot be ascribed to a definite redactional stratum; therefore they can be left out of consideration.

15. Results. One can make the following observations as a result of this survey of the Q-source:

(a) There are three recognizable redactional blocks: "A," "B," and—less clearly—"C." These do not, however, account for all the Q-material.

(b) To a large degree, Redaction "A" shaped the first complex (Q 3:2—7:28) and did so with a interest in the significance and place of Jesus especially in relation to the Baptist.

(c) Redaction "B" is restricted to the formulation of the second large corpus in Q, namely the commissioning complex (Q 9:57—10:24). It is

---

35. Polag (1977:13) includes Q 16:13 using the same catchword, though with some hesitations (1977:5). But it is not clear how this verse relates to the "Law."

quite possible that Redactions "A" and "B" derived from the activities of the same redactor (or from the same circle). The techniques of framing and of creating apophthegms can be found in both. Moreover, the emphasis on the present as the time of salvation (Q 7:18-23; 10:21, 23-24) [45] is shared by both. But in other respects, the two complexes are independent of each other. Since they surely had different *Sitze im Leben*, one may with justification assume two different redactions.

(d) By contrast, Redaction "C" not easily comprehended as a stratum. It did not produce a fixed redactional block like Redaction "A" or "B." Rather, it has brought together the two existing large blocks, by revising a sayings cluster (Q 7:31-35) and interpolating it between them. Characteristic of Redaction "C" are the polemical indictment or announcement of judgment against the entire people of Israel and an emphasis on the motif of divine Wisdom. In addition, one can regard the sequences in Q 11:14-32, 39-52 and probably also those in Q 13:23-35 as arranged by this redaction. These sayings, along with Q 7:31-35, produce in this sequence a certain intensification. It is also possible that Redaction "C" positioned the large collection on discipleship paraenesis (Q 12:2-34) between Q 11:52 and 13:23. One may also surmise that the interpolation of Q 10:13-15 along with 10:12, with a similar theme, derives from this stratum, although there can be no certainty. The same redaction possibly placed the pre-existing sayings collection Q 17:23-37 at the end of the Q. Only in this way can Redaction "C" be considered a "complete redaction."[36] What else was added by this hand is obscure.

(e) Following (or even before) Redaction "C" there were probably additional unsystematic accretions and additional strings (thus, e.g., the isolated sayings found between Q 12:39 and 13:21). One cannot completely exclude the possibility that the sayings collection in Q 17:23-37 came to be at the end of Q in this way. This growth of material occurs mainly in the latter parts of Q (i.e., after Q 10:24), obviously because the first two complexes in their finished forms would permit only minor encroachments. Among these few additions are the pericopae Q 4:(1-2a), 2b-13 and Q 7:27. Q 10:22 also probably originated from later christological reflection. Occasionally, there are units in the programmatic discourse that are more recent than Redaction "A" (e.g., Q 6:43-45 or 6:39, 40).

(f) Christological interest plays an important role in the composition of Q. This is not only the case in Redaction "A," which was already characterized by Christology in its content, but also true of the other redactions and revisions. The importance of Christology can be [46]

---

36. In this respect my thesis of a Redaction "C" is a modified version of the insight of Lührmann (above p. 162).

inferred from the position of the Son of Man (and similar) sayings: one should note Q 3:16 at the beginning of Redaction "A," Q 6:22 at the beginning of the programmatic discourse (Q 6:20-49), Q 7:34 at the end of the John complex (due to Redaction "C"), Q 9:57-58 at the beginning of Redaction "B," Q 13:35 at the end of the series in Q 13:23-35 (probably due to Redaction "C"), and Q 17:24, 26, 30 at the beginning of the sayings collection in Q 17:23-37, or at the end of Q as a whole. The common interest in Christology means that one can assume a relatively strong degree of continuity among those persons responsible for transmitting Q.

(g) From all of this one can conclude the following. The document Q was not fixed redactionally all at once but came into being through a long process of collection, addition, redaction, and editing. Q is characterized by *successive reformulation*. We have been able to detect a few steps in this process; a more detailed description of Q's process of growth is hardly possible.

3. Geographical and Temporal Location

Nothing in Q indicates an extra-Palestinian provenance. Even such sayings as Q 7:1-10; 13:28-29, which are favorable to the Gentiles, do not presuppose an actual mission to the Gentiles outside Palestine. The observation that according to rabbinic texts (*m. Kil.* 3:2; also *t. Kil.* 2.8) the planting of mustard in gardens (Q 13:19, in Luke's version) points to "non-Palestinian horticulture"[37] is hardly decisive: that the Mishnah expressly *forbids* the planting of mustard in seedbed indicates, on the contrary, that this practice was common in Palestine. Even if it were not, the text may always have been altered in the pre-Lukan tradition (or even by Luke himself).

As the use of the Septuagint in Q 4:4, 8, 10-11, 12 indicates, Q was composed in Greek. But composition in Greek does not necessitate an origin outside Palestine; Greek was in use at that time in Palestine, especially in the cities and in the area of Galilee.[38] When the translation of sayings or clusters of sayings into Greek was made cannot be ascertained; possibly it happened quite early and, of course, over a period of time and in an unsystematic way. Hence Q probably came into existence in Palestine (or in areas nearby). The Galilean city names (Q [4:16]; 7:1; 10:13-15) might suggest a center in the north. [47]

As far as date is concerned, the form available to us comes from before 70 C.E., since the destruction of Jerusalem is nowhere clearly reflected, and the temple and the temple system are still presupposed (Q 4:9; 11:42). Q

37. Schulz 1972:299; Jeremias 1972:27 and n. 11.
38. On the dissemination of the Greek language in Palestine, see Sevenster 1968, e.g., 186; Hengel 1974a:58–65, 103–6; Mussies 1974–76.

13:34-35 does not supply any indication that the saying originated as an *ex eventu* prophecy.

Q AS A NOTEBOOK?

[62] How is it possible to imagine paleographically such a continuously developing document? With each respective large insertion, did the entire scroll have to be recopied? How would the document Q have looked?

1. The Writing Medium

I have suggested that the Q-sayings—viewed heuristically—had been combined slowly, from the stage of "individual sayings" to that of "sayings collections." The form of a scroll is scarcely suitable for writing down smaller independent sayings and sayings clusters. Notebooks are the most probable medium. For this purpose, papyrus pages might have served well, especially since they are also mentioned in the Mishnah (*m. Kel.* 24:7) as a writing medium. Parchment pages, however, would have been even more suitable. Perhaps such pages formed the basis for Q.[39]

2. Q as a "Looseleaf Book"?

[64] It is not difficult to understand: A (parchment) fascicle that is amenable from the beginning to expansion in its extent fits very well with the external form of Q, which was never composed as a finished book. One might ask whether, if Q existed as a loose fascicle, it would have had from the beginning the form of a *codex*. This possibility cannot be rejected from the outset, for one redaction—be it "A," "B," or "C"—could have newly transcribed the existing material into a notebook during the process of revision. The two recensions further attest to the fact that there was at least one exemplar to be copied; the copying could have resulted at the same time in a codex fascicle. Moreover, additional pages can also be inserted into a codex without great difficulty.[40] But since the growth of Q cannot be reduced to a couple of redactional insertions, the following possibility presents itself. A redactor may have carefully laid the pages of existing notebooks on top of each other, and like wax tablets, bound them together with a cord or a ring. The notebook pages from parchment (second cen-

---

39. Sato (1988:62–64) includes a detailed excursus on the literary and archaeological evidence of the use of notebooks in antiquity. He quotes Lieberman: "rabbinic sayings and decisions were written down in epistles, in private rolls and, above all, on πίνακες, codices (or single tablets which could subsequently be bound in a codex). Most of the Rabbis who are reported to have put down the *Halakhot* of their masters on codices flourished in the first half of the third century. But the practice itself is undoubtedly much older. The employment of the note-book was the most suitable way of indicating that they were writing the Oral Law for private, or unofficial use, and not for publication" (1962:204–5).—ED.

40. See examples of this procedure in E. Turner 1977:64.

tury) that were mentioned above[41] but also schoolbooks made of papyrus (fourth century) [65] serve as examples of such a procedure. Q then would have been a kind of "looseleaf book." It is also possible, however, that what was assembled were partly individual pages and partly (newly written) sheets folded in the middle.

In any case, a working hypothesis is possible: Q came into existence from notebooks, possibly parchment, which were successively collected into a loosely bound fascicle that was always amenable to further additions.[42]

SUMMARY

Q developed over a period of decades (in Palestine prior to 70 C.E.); some three phases of important redaction can be recovered. In time, development proceeded in at least two directions: Q-Matthew and Q-Luke, so that the evangelists Matthew and Luke received Q, each in a different form. Q-Luke developed to a much greater degree than Q-Matthew. The external form of Q—as a well as that of Q-Matthew and Q-Luke—was probably a kind of loosely connected fascicle, which had facilitated the growth of its contents.

41. In excursus 1 in Sato 1988:62–64.—ED.

42. Two suggestions may be noted: Lieberman (1962:205) says: "Now the Jewish disciples of Jesus, in accordance with the general rabbinic practice, wrote the sayings which their master pronounced *not* in the form of a book to be published, but as notes in their *pinaces*, codices, in their note-books (or in private small rolls). . . . In line with the foregoing we would naturally expect the *logia* of Jesus to be originally copied in codices" (emphasis original). Moreover, Roberts and Skeat (1983:59) remark: "It is possible . . . that papyrus tablets were used to record the Oral Law as pronounced by Jesus, and that these tablets might have developed into a primitive form of codex."

Abbreviations

AB	Anchor Bible
AJBI	*Annual of the Japanese Biblical Institute*
ALBO	Analecta lovaniensia biblica et orientalia
AnOr	Analecta orientalia
ATANT	Abhandlungen zur Theologie des Alten und Neuen Testaments
ATD	Das Alte Testament Deutsch
BBB	Bonner biblische Beiträge
BETL	Bibliotheca ephemeridum theologicarum lovaniensium
BGBE	Beiträge zur Geschichte der biblischen Exegese
BHK	*Biblia hebraica*, ed. R. Kittel
Bib	*Biblica*
BibLeb	*Bibel und Leben*
BibS(F)	Biblische Studien (Freiburg)
BJRL	*Bulletin of the John Rylands University Library of Manchester*
BR	*Biblical Research*
BTB	*Biblical Theology Bulletin*
BZ	*Biblische Zeitschrift*
BZAW	Beihefte zur *Zeitschrift für die alttestamentliche Wissenschaft*
BZNW	Beihefte zur *Zeitschrift für die neutestamentliche Wissenschaft*
CBQ	*Catholic Biblical Quarterly*
CG	Coptic Gnostic
CRAIBL	*Comptes rendus de l'Académie des inscriptions et belles-lettres*
CRINT	Compendia rerum iudaicarum ad novum testamentum
EDNT	*Exegetical Dictionary of the New Testament*, ed. H. Balz and G. Schneider
ET	English translation

ETL	*Ephemerides theologicae lovanienses*
ETS	Erfurter theologische Studien
EvQ	*Evangelical Quarterly*
EvT	*Evangelische Theologie*
ExpTim	*Expository Times*
FB	Forschung zur Bibel
FRLANT	Forschungen zur Religion und Literatur des Alten und Neuen Testaments
HibJ	*Hibbert Journal*
HTKNT	Herders theologischer Kommentar zum Neuen Testament
HTR	*Harvard Theological Review*
HUCA	*Hebrew Union College Annual*
IDBSup	*Interpreter's Dictionary of the Bible,* Supplementary volume
Int	*Interpretation*
IRT	Issues in Religion and Theology
JAAR	*Journal of the American Academy of Religion*
JBL	*Journal of Biblical Literature*
JES	*Journal of Ecumenical Studies*
JSNTSup	*Journal for the Study of the New Testament*—Supplement Series
JTS	*Journal of Theological Studies*
LCL	Loeb Classical Library
LTK	*Lexicon für Theologie und Kirche*
LTP	*Laval théologique et philosophique*
LXX	Septuagint
Mus	*Le Muséon*
NHC	Nag Hammadi Codices
NIGTC	New International Greek Testament Commentary
NovT	*Novum Testamentum*
NTAbh	Neutestamentliche Abhandlungen
NTD	Das Neue Testament Deutsch
NTOA	Novum Testamentum et Orbis Antiquus
NTS	*New Testament Studies*
OBO	Orbis biblicus et orientalis
OTL	Old Testament Library
PTMS	Pittsburgh Theological Monograph Series
PWSup	Pauly-Wissowa, *Real-Encyclopädie der classischen Altertumswissenschaft,* Supplement
RB	*Revue biblique*
RGG	*Religion in Geschichte und Gegenwart*
RSV	Revised Standard Version
SANT	Studien zum Alten und Neuen Testament
SBLASP	Society of Biblical Literature Abstracts and Seminar Papers
SBLMS	SBL Monograph Series
SBLTT	SBL Texts and Translations

SBS	Stuttgarter Bibelstudien
SBT	Studies in Biblical Theology
SE	*Studia Evangelica*
SJLA	Studies in Judaism in Late Antiquity
SNT	Studien zum Neuen Testament
SNTSMS	Society for New Testament Studies Monograph Series
SUNT	Studien zur Umwelt des Neuen Testaments
TBü	Theologische Bücherei
TDNT	*Theological Dictionary of the New Testament*, ed. G. Kittel and G. Friedrich
TLZ	*Theologische Literaturzeitung*
TP	*Theologie und Philosophie*
TRev	*Theologische Revue*
TRu	*Theologische Rundschau*
TS	*Theological Studies*
TTZ	*Trierer theologische Zeitschrift*
TU	Texte und Untersuchungen
USQR	*Union Seminary Quarterly Review*
VC	*Vigiliae christianae*
WD	*Wort und Dienst*
WMANT	Wissenschaftliche Monographien zum Alten und Neuen Testament
WUNT	Wissenschaftliche Untersuchungen zum Neuen Testament
ZAW	*Zeitschrift für die alttestamentliche Wissenschaft*
ZNW	*Zeitschrift für die neutestamentliche Wissenschaft*
ZTK	*Zeitschrift für Theologie und Kirche*

Bibliography

(In the case of translated works, the date of the original appears in brackets following the entry.)

ALAND, Kurt, ed.
1985   *Synopsis Quattuor Evangeliorum: Locis parallelis evangeliorum apocryphorum et patrum adhibit.* 13th ed., revised. Stuttgart: Deutsche Bibelgesellschaft.

AUNE, David E.
1987   *The New Testament in Its Literary Environment.* Library of Early Christianity 8. Philadelphia: Westminster.

BACON, B. W.
1923–24   "The Nature and Design of Q, the Second Synoptic Source." *HibJ* 22:674–88.
1930   *Studies in Matthew.* New York: Holt.

BAILLET, Maurice
1961   "Un Recueil liturgique de Qumrân, grotte 4: 'Les paroles des luminaires.'" *RB* 68:195–250.

BAMMEL, Ernst
1964   "Erwägungen zur Eschatologie Jesu." *SE* 3 (TU 88):3–32.
1970   "Das Ende von Q." Pp. 39–50 in *Verborum Veritas: Festschrift für Gustav Stählin zum 70. Geburtstag,* ed. O. Böcher and K. Haacker. Wuppertal: Rolf Brockhaus.

BARNS, J.
1950   "A New Gnomologium: With Some Remarks on Gnomic Anthologies (I)." *Classical Quarterly* 44:126–37.
1951   "A New Gnomologium: With Some Remarks on Gnomic Anthologies (II)." *Classical Quarterly* n.s., 1:1–19.

BARTH, Hermann, and Odil Hannes Steck
1978   *Exegese des Alten Testaments: Leitfaden der Methodik.* 8th ed. Neukirchen-Vluyn: Neukirchener Verlag.

BARTSCH, Hans Werner
1959–60   "Das Thomas-Evangelium und die synoptischen Evangelien." *NTS* 6:249–61.

BAUMGARTNER, W.
1914   "Die literarischen Gattungen in der Weisheit des Jesus Sirach." *ZAW* 34:161–98.

BEARDSLEE, William A.
1967   "Wisdom Tradition and the Synoptic Gospels." *JAAR* 35:231–40.
1970   *Literary Criticism of the New Testament.* Guides to Biblical Scholarship. Philadelphia: Fortress.

BERGER, Klaus
1973   "Materialien zu Form und Überlieferungsgeschichte neutestamentlicher Gleichnisse." *NovT* 15:1–37.
1976   *Die Auferstehung des Propheten und die Erhöhung des Menschensohnes: Traditionsgeschichtliche Untersuchung zur Deutung des Geschickes Jesu in frühchristlichen Texten.* SUNT 13. Göttingen: Vandenhoeck & Ruprecht.
1977   *Exegese des Neuen Testaments: Neue Wege vom Text zur Auslegung.* Uni-Taschenbücher 658: Theologie. Heidelberg: Quelle & Meyer.

BERNAND, Etienne
1969   *Inscriptions métriques de l'Egypte gréco-romaine: Recherches sur la poésie épigrammatique des Grecs en Egypte.* Besançon Université, Annales littéraires 98. Paris: Belles Lettres.

BEST, Ernest
1976   "An Early Sayings Collection." *NovT* 18:1–16.
1981   *Following Jesus: Discipleship in the Gospel of Mark.* JSNTSup 4. Sheffield: JSOT.

BETZ, Hans Dieter
1978   "Die Makarismen der Bergpredigt (Matthäus 5,3–12)." *ZTK* 75: 3–19.
1979   *Galatians: A Commentary on Paul's Letter to the Churches in Galatia.* Hermeneia. Philadelphia: Fortress.
1985   *Essays on the Sermon on the Mount.* Philadelphia: Fortress.

BITZER, Lloyd F.
1968   "The Rhetorical Situation." *Philosophy and Rhetoric* 1:1–14.

BLACK, Matthew
1967   *An Aramaic Approach to the Gospels and Acts.* 3d ed. Oxford: Clarendon.

BLANK, Josef
1969   "Zur Christologie ausgewählter Wunderberichte." Pp. 112–17 in *Schriftauslegung in Theorie und Praxis*, ed. Josef Blank. Biblische Handbibliothek 5. Munich: Kösel.

BÖHLIG, Alexander, and Pahor C. Labib, ed. and trans.
1963   *Koptisch-gnostische Apokalypsen aus Codex V von Nag Hammadi im Koptischen Museum zu Alt-Kairo.* Halle and Wittenberg: Wissenschaftliche Zeitschrift der Martin-Luther-Universität.

BORING, M. Eugene
1982   *Sayings of the Risen Jesus: Christian Prophecy in the Synoptic Tradition.* SNTSMS 46. Cambridge: Cambridge Univ. Press.

1991   *The Continuing Voice of Jesus: Christian Prophecy and the Gospel Tradition.* Louisville: Westminster/John Knox.

BORNKAMM, Günther

1958   "Evangelien, synoptisch. 2a. Spruchquelle." *RGG*³ 2:758–60.

1960   *Jesus of Nazareth,* trans. Irene McLuskey, Fraser McLuskey, and James M. Robinson. Preface by James M. Robinson. New York: Harper & Row [1956].

1961   *Die Vorgeschichte des sogenannten zweiten Korintherbriefes.* Sitzungsberichte der Heidelberger Akademie der Wissenschaften, Philosophisch-historische Klasse 2. Heidelberg: Winter.

1963   "End-Expectation and Church in Matthew." Pp. 15–51 in Günther Bornkamm, Heinz Joachim Held, and Gerhard Barth, *Tradition and Interpretation in Matthew,* trans. P. Scott. Philadelphia: Westminster; London: SCM [1960].

1968   "Die Verzögerung des Parusie." Pp. 46–55 in *Geschichte und Glaube.* Part 1. Gesammelte Aufsätze 3. Munich: Kaiser.

1971a   "The Risen Lord and the Earthly Jesus: Matthew 28.16–20." Pp. 203–29 in *The Future of Our Religious Past: Essays in Honor of Rudolf Bultmann,* ed. James M. Robinson. Trans. C. E. Carlston and R. P. Scharlemann. London: SCM [1964].

1971b   "Die Vorgeschichte des sogenannten zweiten Korintherbriefes." Pp. 162–94 in *Geschichte und Glaube.* Part 2. Gesammelte Aufsätze 4. Munich: Kaiser.

BORNKAMM, Günther, Heinz Joachim Held, and Gerhard Barth

1963   *Tradition and Interpretation in Matthew,* trans. P. Scott. Philadelphia: Westminster; London: SCM [1960].

BRETSCHER, Paul G.

1967   "Whose Sandals? (Matt 3:11)." *JBL* 86:81–87.

BRUEGGEMANN, Walter

1968   "The Kerygma of the Deuteronomic Historian." *Int* 22:387–402.

BRUNNER, Helmut

1970   "Die Lehren." Pp. 113–39 in *Handbuch der Orientalistik.* Part 1, Vol. 1 *Ägyptologie.* Section 2. *Literatur.* 2d ed., ed. Hermann Kees. Leiden and Köln: Brill.

BULTMANN, Rudolf K.

1913   "Was lässt die Spruchquelle über die Urgemeinde erkennen?" *Oldenburgisches Kirchenblatt* 19:35–37, 41–44.

1923   "Der religionsgeschichtliche Hintergrund des Prologs zum Johannesevangelium." Pp. 3–26 in ΕΥΧΑΡΙΣΤΗΡΙΟΝ: Festschrift Hermann Gunkel, ed. Hans Schmidt. FRLANT 36. Göttingen: Vandenhoeck & Ruprecht.

1931   *Die Geschichte der synoptischen Tradition.* FRLANT 29. 2d ed. Göttingen: Vandenhoeck & Ruprecht.

1951–55   *Theology of the New Testament,* trans. K. Grobel. 2 vols. New York: Charles Scribner's Sons [1948–1953].

1962   "The Study of the Synoptic Gospels." Pp. 11–76 in *Form Criticism: Two Essays on New Testament Research,* ed. Rudolf K. Bultmann and Karl Kundsin. Trans. Frederick C. Grant. New York: Harper & Row.

1968   *The History of the Synoptic Tradition*, trans. John Marsh. Rev. ed. Oxford: Blackwell [1931].

1971a   *Die Geschichte der synoptischen Tradition: Ergänzungsheft*. 4th ed., ed. Gerd Theissen and Philipp Vielhauer. Göttingen: Vandenhoeck & Ruprecht.

1971b   *The Gospel of John: A Commentary*, trans. G. W. Beasley-Murray. Oxford: Blackwell [1941].

1986   "The History of Religions Background of the Prologue to the Gospel of John." Pp. 18–35 in *The Interpretation of John*, ed. John Ashton. Issues in Religion and Theology 9. Philadelphia: Fortress; London: SPCK [1923].

BUSSBY, F.
1954   "Is Q an Aramaic Document?" *ExpTim* 65:272–75.

BUSSMANN, Wilhelm
1929   *Synoptische Studien*. Vol. 2. *Zur Redenquelle*. Halle [Saale]: Buchhandlung des Waisenhauses.

BUTTS, James R.
1986   "The Chreia in the Synoptic Gospels." *BTB* 16:132–38.
1987   "The 'Progymnasmata' of Theon: A New Text with Translation and Commentary." Ph.D. diss., Claremont Graduate School.

CAMERON, Ron
1990   " 'What Have You Come Out to See?' Characterizations of John and Jesus in the Gospels." Pp. 35–69 in *The Apocryphal Jesus and Christian Origins*, ed. Ron Cameron. Semeia 49. Atlanta: Scholars Press.

CARLSTON, Charles E.
1978   "On Q and the Cross." Pp. 27–33 in *Scripture, Tradition and Interpretation: Essays Presented to Everett F. Harrison*, ed. W. W. Gasque and W. S. LaSor. Grand Rapids: Eerdmans.
1980   "Proverbs, Maxims, and the Historical Jesus." *JBL* 99:87–105.
1982   "Wisdom and Eschatology in Q." Pp. 101–19 in *Logia: Les Paroles de Jésus—The Sayings of Jesus: Mémorial Joseph Coppens*, ed. Joël Delobel. BETL 59. Leuven: Uitgeverij Peeters and Leuven Univ. Press.

CHARLES, Robert H., ed.
1912–13   *The Apocrypha and Pseudepigrapha of the Old Testament in English: With Introductions and Critical and Explanatory Notes*. Oxford: Clarendon.

CHRIST, Felix
1970   *Jesus Sophia: Die Sophia Christologie bei den Synoptikern*. ATANT 57. Zurich: Zwingli.

COLLINS, John J.
1980   "Proverbial Wisdom and the Yahwist Vision." Pp. 1–17 in *Gnomic Wisdom*, ed. John Dominic Crossan. Semeia 17. Chico, Calif.: Society of Biblical Literature.

COLPE, Carsten
1970   "Der Spruch von der Lästerung des Geistes." Pp. 63–79 in *Der Ruf Jesu und die Antwort der Gemeinde: Exegetische Untersuchungen für Joachim Jeremias zum 70. Geburtstag*, ed. Eduard Lohse, Christoph Burchard, and Berndt Schaller. Göttingen: Vandenhoeck & Ruprecht.

1972   "ὁ υἱὸς τοῦ ἀνθρώπου." *TDNT* 8:400–77.

1981   "Neue Untersuchungen zum Menschensohn-Problem." *TRev* 77: 353–72.

COLSON, F. H.

1921   "Quintilian I.9 and the 'Chria' in Ancient Education." *Classical Review* 35:150–54.

CONYBEARE, Frederick C., James R. Harris, and Agnes S. Lewis, eds.

1913   *The Story of Ahikar from the Aramaic, Syriac, Arabic, Armenian, Ethiopic, Old Turkish, Greek and Slavonic Versions.* 2d ed., enlarged and corrected. Cambridge: Cambridge Univ. Press.

CONZELMANN, Hans

1960   *The Theology of St. Luke*, trans. Geoffrey Buswell. New York: Harper & Row [1953].

1969   *An Outline of the Theology of the New Testament*, trans. John Bowden. London: SCM [1967].

COPPENS, Joseph

1961   *Le Fils de l'homme et les saints du Très-Haut en Daniel VII, dans les apocryphes et dans le Nouveau Testament.* ALBO 3/23. Leuven: Leuven Univ. Press.

1973   "De Mensenzoon-Logia in het Markus Evangelie." Pp. 3–55 in *Medelingen van de Koninklijke Academie voor Wetenschappen.* Klasse der Lettern 33/3. Brüssel: Koninklijke Academie voor Wetenschappen.

1976   "Le Fils de l'Homme dans l'évangile johannique." *ETR* 52: 28–81.

1979   *La relève apocalyptique du messianisme royal.* Vol. 1. *La Royauté—le règne—le royaume de Dieu: Cadre de la relève apocalyptique.* BETL 50. Leuven: Uitgeverij Peeters and Leuven Univ. Press.

1981a   *La relève apocalyptique du messianisme royal.* Vol. 3. *Le Fils de l'homme neotestamentaire*, ed. Frans Neirynck. BETL 55. Leuven: Uitgeverij Peeters and Leuven Univ. Press.

1981b   "Les logia du fils de l'homme dans l'évangile de Marc." Pp. 109–49 in *La relève apocalyptique du messianisme royal.* Vol. 3. *Le Fils de l'homme neotestamentaire*, ed. Frans Neirynck. BETL 55. Leuven: Uitgeverij Peeters and Leuven Univ. Press.

1983   *La relève apocalyptique du messianisme royal.* Vol. 2. *Le Fils d'homme vétéro—et intertestamentaire*, ed. J. Lust. BETL 61. Leuven: Uitgeverij Peeters and Leuven Univ. Press.

CRENSHAW, James L.

1971   "*'eṣā and dabar*: The Problem of Authority/Certitude in Wisdom and Prophetic Literature." Pp. 116–23 in *Prophetic Conflict: Its Effect upon Israelite Religion.* BZAW 124. Berlin: de Gruyter.

CROSSAN, John Dominic

1973   *In Parables: The Challenge of the Historical Jesus.* New York: Harper & Row.

1983   *In Fragments: The Aphorisms of Jesus.* San Francisco: Harper & Row.

CULLMANN, Oscar

1959   *The Christology of the New Testament*, trans. Shirley C. Guthrie and Charles A. M. Hall. Philadelphia: Westminster [1953].

1960   "Das Thomasevangelium und die Frage nach dem Alter der in ihm
              enhaltenen Tradition." *TLZ* 85:321–34.

1962   "The Gospel of Thomas and the Problem of the Age of the Tradi-
              tion Contained Therein: A Survey." *Int* 16:418–38 [1960].

DAVIES, Stevan L.

1983   *The Gospel of Thomas and Christian Wisdom.* New York: Seabury.

DAVIES, William D.

1966   *The Setting of the Sermon on the Mount.* Cambridge: Cambridge Univ.
              Press.

DEHANDSCHUTTER, B.

1982   "L'Évangile de Thomas comme collection de paroles de Jésus." Pp.
              507–15 in *Logia: Les Paroles de Jésus—The Sayings of Jesus: Mémorial
              Joseph Coppens,* ed. Joël Delobel. BETL 59. Leuven: Uitgeverij
              Peeters and Leuven Univ. Press.

DELLING, Gerhard

1970   "Geprägte Jesus-Tradition im Urchristentum." Pp. 100–75 in *Studien
              zum Neuen Testament und zum hellenistischen Judentum: Gesammelte
              Aufsätze 1950–1968.* Göttingen: Vandenhoeck & Ruprecht.

DELOBEL, Joël, ed.

1982   *Logia: Les Paroles de Jésus—The Sayings of Jesus: Mémorial Joseph
              Coppens.* BETL 59. Leuven: Uitgeverij Peeters and Leuven Univ.
              Press.

DENAUX, Adelbert

1982   "Der Spruch von den zwei Wegen im Rahmen des Epilogs der
              Bergpredigt (Mt 7,13–14 par. Lk 13,23–24)." Pp. 305–35 in *Logia:
              Les Paroles de Jésus—The Sayings of Jesus: Mémorial Joseph Coppens,* ed.
              Joël Delobel. BETL 59. Leuven: Uitgeverij Peeters and Leuven
              Univ. Press.

DEVISCH, Michel

1972   "Le document Q, source de Matthieu: Problématique actuelle." Pp.
              71–97 in *L'Évangile selon Matthieu: Rédaction et théologie,* ed. M.
              Didier. BETL 29. Gembloux: Duculot.

1974   "La relation entre l'évangile de Marc et le document Q." Pp. 59–91
              in *L'Évangile selon Marc: Tradition et rédaction,* ed. M. Sabbe. BETL
              34. Leuven: Leuven Univ. Press; Gembloux: Duculot.

DIBELIUS, Martin

1935   *From Tradition to Gospel,* trans. B. L. Woolf. New York: Charles
              Scribner's Sons [1933].

1953   *Botschaft und Geschichte.* Tübingen: Mohr (Siebeck).

1959   *Die Formgeschichte des Evangeliums.* 3d ed., with a postscript by
              Gerhard Iber. Tübingen: Mohr (Siebeck).

1976   *James: A Commentary on the Epistle of James.* Revised by Heinrich
              Greeven. Trans. Michael A. Williams. Hermeneia. Philadelphia:
              Fortress [1964].

DOUGLAS, Rees Conrad

1990   "Once Again, 'Love Your Enemies': Rhetorical and Social Scientific
              Considerations of a Familiar Passage." Paper presented at the 1990
              annual meeting of the Society of Biblical Literature, Q Session,
              New Orleans, November 18.

DRESSLER, Wolfgang
1972   *Einführung in die Textlinguistik*. Konzepte der Sprach- und Literatur-
wissenschaft 13. Tübingen: Niemeyer.

DUNGAN, David L.
1970   "Mark—The Abridgement of Matthew and Luke." Pp. 51–97 in
Jesus and Man's Hope: Pittsburgh Festival on the Gospels, vol. 1., ed.
David G. Buttrick. Perspective 11. Pittsburgh: Pittsburgh Theological Seminary.

EBERHARTER, A.
1911   *Der Kanon des Alten Testaments zur Zeit des Ben Sira*. Alttestament-
liche Abhandlungen 3/3. Münster: Aschendorff.

EDWARDS, Richard A.
1969   "The Eschatological Correlative as Gattung in the New Testament."
ZNW 60:9–20.
1971   *The Sign of Jonah in the Theology of the Evangelists and Q*. SBT 2/18.
London: SCM.
1976   *A Theology of Q*. Philadelphia: Fortress.

EISSFELDT, Otto
1965   *The Old Testament: An Introduction. Including the Apocrypha and
Pseudepigrapha*, trans. Peter R. Ackroyd. New York: Harper & Row
[1964].

FARMER, William R.
1975   "A Fresh Approach to Q." Pp. 39–50 in *Christianity, Judaism and
Other Greco-Roman Cults: Essays for Morton Smith at Sixty*, ed. Jacob
Neusner. SJLA 12/1. Leiden: Brill.
1976   *The Synoptic Problem: A Critical Analysis*. Dillsboro, N.C.: Western
North Carolina Press (1st ed., New York: Macmillan, 1964).

FARRER, Austin M.
1957   "On Dispensing with Q." Pp. 57–88 in *Studies in the Gospels in
Memory of R. H. Lightfoot*, ed. D. E. Nineham. Oxford: Blackwell.

FEUILLET, André
1955   "Jésus et la sagesse divine d'après les évangiles synoptiques." *RB*
62:161–96.

FITZMYER, Joseph A.
1959   "The Oxyrhynchus Logoi of Jesus and the Coptic Gospel According to Thomas." *TS* 20:505–60.
1981   *The Gospel According to Luke I–IX*. AB 28. Garden City, N.Y.:
Doubleday.

FOHRER, Georg, F. W. Hoffmann, F. Huber, L. Markert, and G. Wanke
1973   *Exegese des Alten Testaments*. Uni-Taschenbücher 267. Heidelberg:
Quelle & Meyer.

FOX, Michael V.
1980   "Two Decades of Research in Egyptian Wisdom Literature."
Zeitschrift für Ägyptische Sprache und Altertumskunde 107:120–35.

FRIDRICHSEN, Anton
1972   *The Problem of Miracle in Primitive Christianity*, trans. Roy A.
Harrisville and John S. Hanson. Minneapolis: Augsburg [1925].

FUCHS, Albert
1979   *Die Entwicklung der Beelzebulkontroverse bei den Synoptikern: Traditions-*

geschichtliche und redaktionsgeschichtliche Untersuchung von Mk 3,22–27 und Parallelen, verbunden mit der Rückfrage nach Jesus. Studien zum Neuen Testament und seiner Umwelt, B 5. Linz: Berger Verlag and Studien zum Neuen Testament und seiner Umwelt.

GARITTE, G.

1960a   "Les 'Logia' d'Oxyrhynque et l'apocryphe copte dit 'Évangile de Thomas.' " *Mus* 73:151–72.

1960b   "Les 'Logia' d'Oxyrhynque sont traduits du copte." *Mus* 73:335–49.

GÄRTNER, Bertil E.

1961   *The Theology of the Gospel According to Thomas*, trans. Eric J. Sharpe. New York: Harper and Brothers [1960].

GEIGER, Ruthild

1973   *Die lukanischen Endzeitreden, Lukas 17,20–37; 21,5–6: Studien zur Eschatologie des Lukas-Evangeliums*. Europäische Hochschulschriften 23, series Theologie 16. Bern and Frankfurt: Herbert Lang.

GEORGI, Dieter

1986   *The Opponents of Paul in Second Corinthians: A Study of Religious Propaganda in Late Antiquity*, trans. Dieter Georgi. Philadelphia: Fortress [1964].

GIBLIN, Charles H.

1968   "Theological Perspectives and Matthew 10,23b." *TS* 29:637–61.

GILBERT, George H.

1911–12   "The Jesus of 'Q'—The Oldest Source in the Gospels." *HibJ* 10:533–42.

GNILKA, Joachim

1970   *Jesus Christus nach frühen Zeugnissen des Glaubens*. Biblische Handbibliothek 8. Munich: Kösel.

GOPPELT, Leonard

1981–82   *Theology of the New Testament*, trans. John E. Alsup. 2 vols. Grand Rapids: Eerdmans [1975–1977].

GOULDER, M. D.

1989   *Luke: A New Paradigm*. JSNTSup 20. Sheffield: JSOT.

GRANT, Robert M., and David Noel Freedman

1960   *The Secret Sayings of Jesus*. Garden City, N.Y.: Doubleday.

GRÄSSER, Erich

1969–70   "Jesus in Nazareth (Mark VI. 1–6a): Notes on the Redaction and Theology of St. Mark." *NTS* 16:1–23.

1973   "Nachfolge und Anfechtung bei den Synoptikern." Pp. 44–57 in *Angefochtene Nachfolge: Beiträge zur theologischen Woche 1972*, ed. V. Alsen. Bethel 11. Bethel: Verlagshandlung der Anstalt; repr. as pp. 168–82 in *Der Alte Bund im Neuen: Exegetische Studien zur Israelfrage im Neuen Testament*. WUNT 35. Tübingen: Mohr (Siebeck), 1985.

GREEVEN, Heinrich

1952   " 'Wer unter euch . . . ?' " *WD* 3:86–101.

1964   "ζητέω." *TDNT* 2:892–96.

1982   " 'Wer unter euch . . . ?'" Pp. 238–55 in *Gleichnisse Jesu: Positionen der Auslegung von Adolf Jülicher bis zur Formgeschichte*, ed. Wolfgang Harnisch. Wege der Forschung 365. Darmstadt: Wissenschaftliche Buchgesellschaft.

GRIESBACH, Johann Jakob

1789–90   *Commentatio qua Marci Evangelium totum e Matthaei et Lucae commentariis decerptum esse monstratur.* 2 vols. Jena: Goepferdt.

GRUNDMANN, Walter

1977   "Weisheit im Horizont des Reiches Gottes: Eine Studie zur Verkündigung Jesu nach der Spruchüberlieferung Q." Pp. 175–99 in *Die Kirche des Anfangs. Für Heinz Schürmann*, ed. Rudolf Schnackenburg. Freiburg: Herder.

GUILLAUMONT, Antoine, ed. and trans.

1959   *The Gospel According to Thomas: Coptic Text.* Leiden: Brill; New York: Harper & Row.

1960   "Les Logia d'Oxyrhynchos sont-ils traduits du copte?" *Mus* 73: 325–33.

GÜTTGEMANNS, Erhardt

1979   *Candid Questions Concerning Gospel Form Criticism: A Methodological Sketch of the Fundamental Problematics of Form Criticism*, trans. William G. Doty. PTMS 26. Pittsburgh: Pickwick [1970].

HAENCHEN, Ernst

1961a   *Die Botschaft des Thomas-Evangeliums.* Theologische Bibliothek Töpelmann 6. Berlin: Töpelmann.

1961b   "Literatur zum Thomasevangelium." *TRu* 27:147–78, 306–38.

1966   *Der Weg Jesu: Eine Erklärung des Markus-Evangeliums und der kanonischen Parallelen.* Berlin: Töpelmann.

HAHN, Ferdinand

1965   *Mission in the New Testament*, trans. Frank Clarke. SBT 1/47. London: SCM [1963].

1969   *The Titles of Jesus in Christology: Their History in Early Christianity*, trans. Harold Knight and George Ogg. London: Lutterworth [1963].

1974   *Christologische Hoheitstitel: Ihre Geschichte im frühen Christentum.* FRLANT 83. 4th ed. Göttingen: Vandenhoeck & Ruprecht.

HARNACK, Adolf von

1907   *Sprüche und Reden Jesu: Die zweite Quelle des Matthäus und Lukas.* Beiträge zur Einleitung in das Neue Testament 2. Leipzig: Hinrichs.

1908   *The Sayings of Jesus: The Second Source of St. Matthew and St. Luke*, trans. John Richard Wilkinson. New Testament Studies 2. London: Williams & Norgate; New York: G. P. Putnam's Sons [1907].

HAUFE, Günther

1966   "Das Menschensohn-Problem." *EvT* 26:130–41.

HELD, Heinz Joachim

1963   "Matthew as an Interpreter of the Miracle Stories." Pp. 165–300 in Günther Bornkamm, Heinz Joachim Held, and Gerhard Barth, *Tradition and Interpretation in Matthew*, trans. P. Scott. Philadelphia: Westminster; London: SCM [1960].

HENGEL, Martin

1974a   *Judaism and Hellenism: Studies in Their Encounter in Palestine during the Early Hellenistic Period*, trans. John Bowden. London: SCM; Philadelphia: Fortress [1969].

1974b   *Property and Riches in the Early Church: Aspects of a Social History of Early Christianity*, trans. John Bowden. London: SCM [1973].

1981   *The Charismatic Leader and His Followers*, trans. J. C. G. Greig.
              Edinburgh: T. & T. Clark; New York: Crossroad [1968].

HENNECKE, Edgar
1963   *Gospels and Related Writings*. Vol. 1. *New Testament Apocrypha*, ed.
              Wilhelm Schneemelcher. Trans. R. McL. Wilson. Philadelphia:
              Westminster [1959].

HERFORD, R. Travers
1962   *Pirke Aboth: The Ethics of the Talmud: Sayings of the Fathers*. 4th ed.
              New York: Schocken.

HIGGINS, A. J. B.
1975   "Menschensohn oder Ich in Q: Lk 12,8–9/Mt 10,32–33." Pp.
              117–23 in *Jesus und der Menschensohn: Für Anton Vögtle*, ed. Rudolf
              Pesch and Rudolf Schnackenburg. Freiburg: Herder.

HILL, David
1973–74   "On the Evidence for the Creative Role of Christian Prophets."
              NTS 20:262–74.

HOCK, Ronald F., and Edward N. O'Neil
1986   *The Progymnasmata*. Vol. 1. *The Chreia in Ancient Rhetoric*. SBLTT
              27, Graeco-Roman Religion Series 9. Atlanta: Scholars Press.

HOFFMANN, Paul
1969   "Die Anfänge der Theologie in der Logienquelle." Pp. 134–52 in
              Gestalt und Anspruch des Neuen Testaments, ed. Josef Schreiner.
              Würzburg: Echter.
1970   "Jesusverkündigung in der Logienquelle." Pp. 50–70 in *Jesus in den
              Evangelien*, ed. Josef Blinzler and Wilhelm Pesch. SBS 45. Stuttgart:
              Katholisches Bibelwerk.
1972   *Studien zur Theologie der Logienquelle*. NTAbh n.s., 8. Münster:
              Aschendorff (2d ed., 1975; 3d ed., 1980).
1975   "Besprechung von S. Schulz, *Q: Spruchquelle der Evangelisten*." *BZ*
              n.s., 19:104–15.

HOFIUS, O.
1960   "Das koptische Thomasevanglium und die Oxyrhynchus-Papyri Nr.
              1, 654 und 655." *EvT* 20:21–42, 182–92.

HORNA, K., and K. von Fritz
1935   "Gnome." PWSupp 6:74–90.

HULTGREN, Arland J.
1979   *Jesus and His Adversaries: The Form and Function of the Conflict Stories
              in the Synoptic Gospels*. Minneapolis: Augsburg.

HUMPHREY, Hugh M.
1991   "Temptation and Authority: Sapiential Narratives in Q." *BTB*
              21:43–50.

HUMPHRIES, Michael
1988   "The Beelzebul Pericope in Q as an Elaborated Chreia." Paper pre-
              sented to the fall 1988 meeting of the Westar Institute.

HUNZINGER, Claus-Hunno
1960a   "Aussersynoptisches Traditionsgut im Thomas-Evangelium." *TLZ*
              85:843–46.
1960b   "Unbekannte Gleichnisse Jesu aus dem Thomas-Evangelium." Pp.

209-20 in *Judentum, Urchristentum, Kirche: Festschrift für Joachim Jeremias*, ed. Walther Eltester. BZNW 26. Berlin: Töpelmann.

INTERNATIONAL Q PROJECT

1990   "The International Q Project Work Session 17 November 1989." *JBL* 109:499–501.

1991   "The International Q Project Work Session 16 November 1990." *JBL* 110:494–98.

JACOBSON, Arland D.

1978   "Wisdom Christology in Q." Ph.D. diss., Claremont Graduate School.

1982a   "The Literary Unity of Q: Lc 10,2–16 and Parallels as a Test Case." Pp. 419–23 in *Logia: Les Paroles de Jésus—The Sayings of Jesus: Mémorial Joseph Coppens*, ed. Joël Delobel. BETL 59. Leuven: Uitgeverij Peeters and Leuven Univ. Press.

1982b   "The Literary Unity of Q." *JBL* 101:365–89.

1987   "The History of the Composition of the Synoptic Sayings Source." Pp. 285–94 in *Society of Biblical Literature 1987 Seminar Papers*, ed. David J. Lull. SBLASP 26. Atlanta: Scholars Press.

1992   *The First Gospel: An Introduction to Q.* Foundations and Facets: Reference series. Sonoma, Calif.: Polebridge.

JEREMIAS, Joachim

1965   "θύρα." *TDNT* 3:173–80.

1967   "Die älteste Schicht der Menschensohn-Logien." *ZNW* 58:159–72.

1969   *Jerusalem in the Time of Jesus: An Investigation into Economic and Social Conditions during the New Testament Period*, trans. F. H. Cave and C. H. Cave. London: SCM; Philadelphia: Fortress [1962].

1971   *New Testament Theology: The Proclamation of Jesus*, trans. John Bowden. London: SCM; New York: Charles Scribner's Son [1971].

1972   *The Parables of Jesus.* Rev. ed. Trans. S. H. Hooke. New York: Charles Scribner's Sons; London: SCM [1970].

JÜLICHER, Adolf

1900   *Einleitung in das Neue Testament.* 2d ed. Tübingen: Mohr (Siebeck).

1904   *An Introduction to the New Testament*, trans. J. P. Ward. London: Smith, Elder [1900].

KALLMEYER, Werner, W. Klein, Rudolf Meyer-Hermann, K. Netzer, and H. J. Siebert

1974   *Lektürekolleg zur Textlinguistik, Bd. 1: Einführung.* 3d ed. Frankfurt: Athenaeum-Fischer-Taschenbuch.

KÄSEMANN, Ernst

1964   "The Problem of the Historical Jesus." Pp. 15–47 in *Essays on New Testament Themes*, trans. W. J. Montague. SBT 41. London: SCM [1954].

1969a   "The Beginnings of Christian Theology." Pp. 82–107 in *New Testament Questions of Today*, trans. W. J. Montague. London: SCM [1960].

1969b   "On the Subject of Primitive Christian Apocalyptic." Pp. 108–37 in *New Testament Questions of Today*, trans. W. J. Montague. London: SCM [1962].

1969c   "Sentences of Holy Law in the New Testament." Pp. 66–81 in *New Testament Questions of Today*, trans. W. J. Montague. London: SCM [1955].

KATZ, Friedrich
1973   "Lk 9,52–11,36: Beobachtungen zur Logienquelle und ihrer hellenistisch-judenchristlichen Redaktion." Diss., University of Mainz.

KAYATZ, Christa
1966   *Studien zu Proverbien 1–9. Eine form- und motivgeschichtliche Untersuchung.* WMANT 22. Neukirchen-Vluyn: Neukirchener Verlag.

KEARNS, Rollin
1978   *Vorfragen zur Christologie. I: Morphologische und semasiologische Studie zur Vorgeschichte eines christologischen Hoheitstitel.* Tübingen: Mohr (Siebeck).
1980   *Vorfragen zur Christologie. II: Überlieferungsgeschichte und rezeptionsgeschichtliche Studie zur Vorgeschichte eines christologischen Hoheitstitel.* Tübingen: Mohr (Siebeck).

KECK, Fridolin
1976   *Die öffentliche Abschiedsrede Jesu in Lk 20,45–21,36: Eine redaktions- und motivgeschichtliche Untersuchung.* FB 25. Stuttgart: Katholisches Bibelwerk.

KEE, Howard Clark
1963   "Becoming a Child in the Gospel of Thomas." *JBL* 82:307–14.
1977   *Jesus in History: An Approach to the Study of the Gospels.* 2d ed. New York: Harcourt Brace Jovanovich.

KELBER, Werner H.
1979   "Mark and Oral Tradition." *Semeia* 16:7–55.
1983   *The Oral and the Written Gospel: The Hermeneutics of Speaking and Writing in the Synoptic Tradition, Mark, Paul, and Q.* Philadelphia: Fortress.

KITCHEN, Kenneth A.
1979   "The Basic Literary Forms and Formulations of Ancient Instructional Writings in Egypt and Western Asia." Pp. 235–82 in *Studien zu altägyptischen Lebenslehren*, ed. Erik Hornung and Othmar Keel. OBO 28. Göttingen: Vandenhoeck & Ruprecht.

KLIJN, A. F. J.
1962   "The 'Single One' in the Gospel of Thomas." *JBL* 81:271–78.

KLOPPENBORG, John S.
1978   "Wisdom Christology in Q." *LTP* 34:129–47.
1984   "Tradition and Redaction in the Synoptic Sayings Source." *CBQ* 46:34–62.
1986   "The Formation of Q and Antique Instructional Genres." *JBL* 105:443–62.
1987   *The Formation of Q: Trajectories in Ancient Wisdom Collections.* Studies in Antiquity and Christianity. Philadelphia: Fortress.
1988   *Q Parallels: Synopsis, Critical Notes, & Concordance.* Foundations and Facets: New Testament. Sonoma, Calif.: Polebridge.

1990a   "City and Wasteland: Narrative World and the Beginning of the
             Sayings Gospel (Q)." Pp. 145–60 in *How Gospels Begin*, ed. Dennis
             E. Smith. Semeia 52. Atlanta: Scholars Press.
1990b   " 'Easter Faith' and the Sayings Gospel Q." Pp. 71–99 in *The
             Apocryphal Jesus and Christian Origins*, ed. Ron Cameron. Semeia 49.
             Atlanta: Scholars Press.
1990c   "Nomos and Ethos in Q." Pp. 35–48 in *Gospel Origins and Christian
             Beginnings: In Honor of James M. Robinson*, ed. James E. Goehring,
             Jack T. Sanders, Charles W. Hedrick, and Hans Dieter Betz.
             Sonoma, Calif.: Polebridge.
1991   "Literary Convention, Self-Evidence, and the Social History of the
             Q People." Pp. 77–102 in *Early Christianity, Q and Jesus* ed. John S.
             Kloppenborg, with Leif E. Vaage. Semeia 55. Atlanta: Scholars
             Press.

KNIGGE, Heinz-Dieter
1968   "The Meaning of Mark: The Exegesis of the Second Gospel." *Int*
             22:53–70.

KNOX, W. L.
1957   *The Sources of the Synoptic Gospels. II St. Luke and St. Matthew.*
             Cambridge: Cambridge Univ. Press.

KOCH, Klaus
1969   *The Growth of the Biblical Tradition: The Form-Critical Method*, trans.
             S. M. Cupitt. New York: Charles Scribner's Sons [1964].

KOESTER, Helmut
1957   *Synoptische Überlieferung bei den apostolischen Vätern.* TU 65. Berlin:
             Akademie.
1965   "ΓΝΩΜΑΙ ΔΙΑΦΟΡΟΙ: The Origin and Nature of Diversification
             in the History of Early Christianity." *HTR* 58:279–318.
1968   "One Jesus and Four Primitive Gospels." *HTR* 61:203–47.
1971a   "GNOMAI DIAPHOROI: The Origin and Nature of Diversifica-
             tion in the History of Early Christianity." Pp. 114–57 in James M.
             Robinson, and Helmut Koester, *Trajectories through Early Christianity.*
             Philadelphia: Fortress.
1971b   "One Jesus and Four Primitive Gospels." Pp. 158–204 in James M.
             Robinson, and Helmut Koester, *Trajectories through Early Christianity.*
             Philadelphia: Fortress.
1971c   "The Structure and Criteria of Early Christian Beliefs." Pp. 205–31
             in James M. Robinson, and Helmut Koester, *Trajectories through Early
             Christianity.* Philadelphia: Fortress.
1980   "Apocryphal and Canonical Gospels." *HTR* 73:105–30.
1982   *Introduction to the New Testament.* Vol. 2. *History and Literature of Early
             Christianity.* Philadelphia: Fortress.

KOSCH, Daniel
1989   *Die eschatologische Tora des Menschensohnes: Untersuchungen zur
             Rezeption der Stellung Jesu zur Tora in Q.* NTOA 12. Freiburg:
             Universitätsverlag; Göttingen: Vandenhoeck & Ruprecht.

KRAUSE, Martin, and Pahor C. Labib, ed.
1962   *Die drei Versionen des Apokryphon des Johannes im Koptischen Museum*

zu Alt-Kairo. Deutsches Archäologisches Institut. Abteilung Kairo Abhandlungen. Koptische Reihe 1. Wiesbaden: Harrassowitz.

KÜCHLER, Max
1979   Frühjüdische Weisheitstraditionen: Zum Fortgang weisheitlichen Denkens im Bereich des frühjüdischen Jahweglaubens. OBO 26. Göttingen: Vandenhoeck & Ruprecht; Freiburg: Universitätsverlag.

KUHN, H.-W.
1970   "Der irdische Jesus bei Paulus als traditionsgeschichtliche und theologisches Problem." ZTK 67:295–320.
1980   "Nachfolge nach Ostern." Pp. 105–32 in Kirche: Festschrift für Günther Bornkamm zum 75. Geburtstag, ed. Georg Strecker and Dieter Lührmann. Tübingen: Mohr (Siebeck).

KUHN, Karl Georg
1965   " Ἰσραήλ, Ἰουδαῖος, Ἑβραῖος in Jewish Literature after the OT." TDNT 3:359–69.

KÜMMEL, Werner Georg
1964   "Die Naherwartung in der Verkündigung Jesu." Pp. 31–46 in Zeit und Geschichte: Dankesgabe an Rudolf Bultmann, ed. Erich Dinkler. Tübingen: Mohr (Siebeck).
1973   The Theology of the New Testament According to Its Major Witnesses, Jesus, Paul, John, trans. John E. Steely. Nashville: Abingdon [1969].
1975   Introduction to the New Testament. Rev. ed. Trans. Howard C. Kee. Nashville: Abingdon [1973].

KÜNZI, Martin
1977   Das Naherwartungslogion Markus 9, 1 par: Geschichte seiner Auslegung. BGBE 21. Tübingen: Mohr (Siebeck).

LAKE, Kirsopp, ed. and trans.
1912–13   The Apostolic Fathers. LCL. London: Heinemann; Cambridge, Mass.: Harvard Univ. Press.

LAMBDIN, Thomas O., trans.
1977   "The Gospel of Thomas." Pp. 117–30 in The Nag Hammadi Library in English, ed. James M. Robinson. San Francisco: Harper & Row.

LANG, Bernhard
1972   Die weisheitliche Lehrrede: Eine Untersuchung von Sprüche. SBS 54. Stuttgart: Katholisches Bibelwerk.

LAUFEN, Rudolf
1980   Die Doppelüberlieferungen der Logienquelle und des Markusevangeliums. BBB 54. Königstein: Hanstein.

LICHTHEIM, Miriam
1979   "Observations on Papyrus Insinger." Pp. 283–305 in Studien zu altägyptischen Lebenslehren, ed. Erik Hornung and Othmar Keel. OBO 28. Göttingen: Vandenhoeck & Ruprecht.
1983   Late Egyptian Wisdom Literature in the International Context: A Study of Demotic Instructions. OBO 52. Freiburg: Universitätsverlag; Göttingen: Vandenhoeck & Ruprecht.

LIEBERMAN, Saul
1962   Hellenism in Jewish Palestine: Studies in the Literary Transmission, Beliefs and Manners of Palestine in the I Century B.C.E.—IV Century C.E. 2d

improved ed. Texts and Studies of the Jewish Theological Seminary of America 18. New York: Jewish Theological Seminary of America.

LINNEMANN, Eta
1960   "Überlegungen zur Parabel vom grossen Abendmahl Lc 14,15–24/Mt 22,1–14." *ZNW* 51:246–55.

LÖVESTAM, E.
1968   *Spiritus blasphemia: Eine Studie zu Mk 3:28.* Lund: Gleerup.

LUCK, Ulrich
1968   *Die Vollkommenheitsforderung der Bergpredigt: Ein aktuelles Kapitel der Theologie des Matthäus.* Theologische Existenz heute, n.s., 150. Munich: Kaiser.

LÜHRMANN, Dieter
1969   *Die Redaktion der Logienquelle.* WMANT 33. Neukirchen-Vluyn: Neukirchener Verlag.

1985   *Synopse der Q-Überlieferung.* Unpublished version distributed to the SBL Q Seminar.

LUZ, Ulrich
1973   "Die wiederentdeckte Logienquelle." *EvT* 33:527–33.

1975   "Das Jesusbild der vormarkinischen Tradition." Pp. 347–74 in *Jesus Christus in Historie und Theologie: Festschrift für Hans Conzelmann,* ed. Georg Strecker. Tübingen: Mohr (Siebeck).

MAASS, Fritz
1937   *Formgeschichte der Mischna, mit besonderer Berücksichtung des Traktats Abot.* Neue Deutsche Forschungen 165. Berlin: Junker und Dunnhaupt.

McARTHUR, Harvey K.
1959–60   "The Dependence of the Gospel of Thomas on the Synoptics." *ExpTim* 71:286–87.

1960   "The Gospel According to Thomas." Pp. 43–77 in *New Testament Sidelights: Essays in Honor of Alexander Converse Purdy,* ed. Harvey K. McArthur. Hartford: Hartford Seminary Foundation.

McDONALD, James I. H.
1979   *Kerygma and Didache: The Articulation and Structure of the Earliest Christian Message.* SNTSMS 37. Cambridge and New York: Cambridge Univ. Press.

MACK, Burton L.
1989   "Elaboration of the Chreia in the Hellenistic School." Pp. 31–67 in *Patterns of Persuasion in the Gospels,* ed. Burton L. Mack and Vernon K. Robbins. Foundations & Facets: Literary Facets. Sonoma, Calif.: Polebridge.

1990   *Rhetoric and the New Testament.* Guides to Biblical Scholarship. Minneapolis: Fortress.

MACK, Burton L., and Vernon K. Robbins
1989   *Patterns of Persuasion in the Gospels.* Foundations & Facets: Literary Facets. Sonoma, Calif.: Polebridge.

McKANE, William
1970   *Proverbs, A New Approach.* OTL. Philadelphia: Westminster.

M'NEILE, A. H.
1915   *The Gospel According to St. Matthew: The Greek Text with Introduction, Notes, and Indices.* London: Macmillan.
MADDOX, Robert
1968–69   "The Function of the Son of Man According to the Synoptic Gospels." *NTS* 15:44–74.
1972   "Methodenfragen in der Menschensohnforschung." *EvT* 32:143–60.
MANSON, T. W.
1935   *The Teaching of Jesus; Studies of Its Form and Content.* 2d ed. Cambridge: Cambridge Univ. Press.
1949   *The Sayings of Jesus.* London: SCM.
1951–52   "The Old Testament in the Teaching of Jesus." *BJRL* 34:312–32.
MARCH, W. Eugene
1974   "Prophecy." Pp. 141–77 in *Old Testament Form Criticism*, ed. John H. Hayes. Trinity University Monograph Series in Religion 2. San Antonio: Trinity Univ. Press.
MARCUS, Ralph
1950–51   "On Biblical Hypostases of Wisdom." *HUCA* 23:157–71.
MARSHALL, I. Howard
1965–66   "The Synoptic Son of Man Sayings in Recent Discussion." *NTS* 12:327–51.
1970   "The Synoptic Son of Man in Contemporary Debate." *EvQ* 42: 67–87.
1978   *The Gospel of Luke: A Commentary on the Greek Text.* NIGTC. Exeter: Paternoster; Grand Rapids: Eerdmans.
MARXSEN, Willi
1969   *Mark the Evangelist: Studies on the Redaction History of the Gospel*, trans. Roy A. Harrisville. Nashville: Abingdon [1956].
MÄRZ, Claus-Peter
1991   *". . . lasst eure Lampen brennen!" Studien zur Q-Vorlage von Lk 12,35— 14,24.* ETS 20. Leipzig: St. Benno.
MERKLEIN, Helmut
1981   *Die Gottesherrschaft als Handlungsprinzip: Untersuchung zur Ethik Jesu.* 2d ed. FB 34. Würzburg: Echter.
METZGER, Bruce M.
1964   *The Text of the New Testament: Its Transmission, Corruption, and Restoration.* New York: Oxford Univ. Press.
MEYER, Paul Donald
1967   "The Community of Q." Ph.D. diss., University of Iowa.
1970   "The Gentile Mission in Q." *JBL* 89:405–17.
MEYER, Rudolf
1970   *Der Prophet aus Galiläa: Studie zum Jesusbild der drei ersten Evangelien.* Darmstadt: Wissenschaftliche Buchgesellschaft.
MINEAR, Paul S.
1972   *The Commands of Christ.* Nashville and New York: Abingdon.
MONTEFIORE, Hugh
1962   "A Comparison of the Parables of the Gospel According to Thomas and of the Synoptic Gospels." Pp. 40–78 in Hugh Montefiore and H. E. W. Turner, *Thomas and the Evangelists.* SBT 1/35. London: SCM.

MORGENTHALER, Robert
1971   *Statistische Synopse.* Zurich and Stuttgart: Gotthelf.

MÜLLER, Ulrich B.
1975   *Prophetie und Predigt im Neuen Testament: Formgeschichtliche Unter-*
suchungen zur urchristlichen Prophetie. SNT 10. Gütersloh: Gerd
Mohn.

MUSSIES, G.
1974–76   "Greek in Palestine and the Diaspora." Pp. 1040–64 in *The Jewish*
People in the First Century: Historical Geography, Political History, Social,
Cultural and Religious Life and Institutions, ed. Shemuel Safrai and
Menachem Stern. CRINT, Section 1. 2 vols. Assen: Van Gorcum;
Philadelphia: Fortress.

MUSSNER, Franz
1959   "Der nicht erkannte Kairos (Mt 11,16–19 = Luke 7,31–35)." *Bib*
40:599–612.

NADEAU, Raymond E., ed. and trans.
1952   "The Progymnasmata of Aphthonius." *Speech Monographs* 19:264–85.

NEIRYNCK, Frans
1976   "Q." *IDBSup* 715–16.
1982   "Recent Developments in the Study of Q." Pp. 29–75 in *Logia: Les*
Paroles de Jésus—The Sayings of Jesus: Mémorial Joseph Coppens, ed. Joël
Delobel. BETL 59. Leuven: Uitgeverij Peeters and Leuven Univ.
Press.
1988   *Q-Synopsis: The Double Tradition Passages in Greek.* Studiorum Novi
Testamenti auxilia 13. Leuven: Leuven Univ. Press.

NEIRYNCK, Frans, and Frans Van Segbroeck
1980   "Studies on Q since 1972." *ETL* 56:409–13.

NEUGEBAUER, F.
1962   "Geistessprüche und Jesuslogien." *ZNW* 53:218–28.

NOACK, Bent
1948   *SATANAS und SOTERIA: Untersuchungen zur neutestamentlichen*
Dämonologie. Copenhagen: Gad.

NORTH, Robert
1962   "Chenoboskion and Q." *CBQ* 24:154–70.

NOTH, Martin
1967   *Überlieferungsgeschichtliche Studien: Die sammelnden und bearbeitenden*
Geschichtswerke im Alten Testament. Königsberger gelehrte Gesell-
schaft, Geisteswissenschaftliche Klasse 18. Jahrgang, Heft 2. 3d ed.
Tübingen: Niemeyer.
1981   *The Deuteronomic History.* JSNTSup 15. Sheffield: JSOT [1967].

NOUGAYROL, J., and E. Laroche, ed.
1968   "Shube-Awilum." Pp. 273–90 in *Ugaritica V,* ed. Claude F. A.
Schaeffer. Mission de Ras Shamra 16. Paris: Geuthner.

OTT, Wilhelm
1965   *Gebet und Heil: Die Bedeutung der Gebetsparänese in der lukanischen*
Theologie. SANT 12. Munich: Kösel.

PERRIN, Norman
1967   *Rediscovering the Teaching of Jesus.* New York: Harper & Row.

PERVO, Richard I.
1987   *Profit with Delight: The Literary Genre of the Acts of the Apostles.* Phila-
          delphia: Fortress.

PESCH, Rudolf, and Rudolf Schnackenburg, ed.
1975   *Jesus und der Menschensohn: Für Anton Vögtle.* Freiburg: Herder.

PIPER, Ronald A.
1982   "Matthew 7,7–11 Par. Lk 11,9–13: Evidence of Design and Argu-
          ment in the Collection of Jesus' Sayings." Pp. 411–18 in *Logia: Les
          Paroles de Jésus—The Sayings of Jesus: Mémorial Joseph Coppens,* ed. Joël
          Delobel. BETL 59. Leuven: Uitgeverij Peeters and Leuven Univ.
          Press.

1989   *Wisdom in the Q-tradition: The Aphoristic Teaching of Jesus.* SNTSMS
          61. Cambridge and New York: Cambridge Univ. Press.

PLETT, Heinrich F.
1975   *Textwissenschaft und Textanalyse: Semiotik, Linguistik, Rhetorik.*
          Grundlagen der Sprachdidaktik, Uni-Taschenbücher 328. Heidel-
          berg: Quelle & Meyer.

POLAG, Athanasius
1966   "Der Umfang der Logienquelle." Dr. Theol. diss., University of
          Trier.

1968   "Zu den Stufen der Christologie in Q." *SE* 4 (TU 102):72–74.

1977   *Die Christologie der Logienquelle.* WMANT 45. Neukirchen-Vluyn:
          Neukirchener Verlag.

1979   *Fragmenta Q: Textheft zur Logienquelle.* Neukirchen-Vluyn: Neukir-
          chener Verlag.

PRITCHARD, James B., ed.
1969   *Ancient Near Eastern Texts Relating to the Old Testament.* 3d ed. with
          supplement. Princeton: Princeton Univ. Press.

PUECH, H.-C.
1957   "Une collection de paroles de Jésus récemment retrouvée:
          L'Évangile selon Thomas." *CRAIBL* (1957):146–67.

QUISPEL, Gilles
1957   "The Gospel of Thomas and the New Testament." *VC* 11:189–207.
1958–59   "Some Remarks on the Gospel of Thomas." *NTS* 5:276–90.
1981   "The Gospel of Thomas Revisited." Pp. 218–66 in *Colloque interna-
          tional sur les textes de Nag Hammadi,* ed. Bernard Barc. Bibliothèque
          copte de Nag Hammadi, Section «Etudes» 1. Quebec: Les Presses de
          l'université Laval.

RAD, Gerhard von
1972   *Wisdom in Israel,* trans. James D. Martin. London: SCM [1970].

REED, Jonathan
1992   "The Social Map of Q." Paper presented at the 1992 annual meet-
          ing of the Society of Biblical Literature, San Francisco.

RINGGREN, Helmer
1947   *Word and Wisdom: Studies in the Hypostatization of Divine Qualities and
          Functions in the Near East.* Lund: Ohlssons.

ROBBINS, Vernon K.
1991   "The Social Location of the Implied Author of Luke-Acts." Pp.
          305–32 in *The Social World of Luke-Acts: Models for Interpretation,* ed.
          Jerome H. Neyrey. Peabody, Mass.: Hendrickson.

ROBBINS, Vernon K., ed.
1989   *Ancient Quotes and Anecdotes: From Crib to Crypt.* Foundations & Facets: Reference Series. Sonoma, Calif.: Polebridge.

ROBERTS, Colin H., and T. C. Skeat
1983   *The Birth of the Codex.* London: Published for the British Academy by Oxford Univ. Press.

ROBINSON, James M.
1957   "A Formal Analysis of Col. 1,15–20." *JBL* 76:270–87.
1960   *Kerygma und historischer Jesus.* Zurich: Zwingli.
1962   "Basic Shifts in German Theology." *Int* 16:76–97.
1964   "ΛΟΓΟΙ ΣΟΦΩΝ: Zur Gattung der Spruchquelle Q." Pp. 77–96 in *Zeit und Geschichte: Dankesgabe an Rudolf Bultmann*, ed. Erich Dinkler. Tübingen: Mohr (Siebeck).
1965   "The Problem of History in Mark, Revisited." *USQR* 20:131–47.
1966   "A Critical Inquiry into the Scriptural Bases of Confessional Hermeneutics." *JES* 3:48–49.
1967   "A Critical Inquiry into the Scriptural Bases of Confessional Hermeneutics." *Encounter* 28:28–29.
1968   "The Coptic Gnostic Library Today." *NTS* 14:356–401.
1971a   "Kerygma and History in the New Testament." Pp. 20–70 in James M. Robinson and Helmut Koester, *Trajectories through Early Christianity.* Philadelphia: Fortress.
1971b   "LOGOI SOPHON: On the Gattung of Q." Pp. 71–113 in James M. Robinson and Helmut Koester, *Trajectories through Early Christianity.* Philadelphia: Fortress [1964].
1975   "Jesus as Sophos and Sophia." Pp. 1–16 in *Aspects of Wisdom in Judaism and Early Christianity*, ed. R. L. Wilken. Notre Dame: University of Notre Dame Press.

ROBINSON, James M., and Helmut Koester
1971   *Trajectories through Early Christianity.* Philadelphia: Fortress.

ROTH, Wolfgang
1980   "On the Gnomic-Discursive Wisdom of Jesus Ben-Sirach." Pp. 59–79 in *Gnomic Wisdom*, ed. John Dominic Crossan. Semeia 17. Chico, Calif.: Society of Biblical Literature.

SABBE, M.
1982   "Can Mt 11,25–27 and Lc 10,22 Be Called a Johannine Logion?" Pp. 363–71 in *Logia: Les Paroles de Jésus—The Sayings of Jesus: Mémorial Joseph Coppens*, ed. Joël Delobel. BETL 59. Leuven: Uitgeverij Peeters and Leuven Univ. Press.

SATAKE, Akiru
1978   "Zwei Typen von Menschenbildern in den Gleichnissen Jesu." *AJBI* 4:45–84.

SATO, Migaku
1988   *Q und Prophetie: Studien zur Gattungs- und Traditionsgeschichte der Quelle Q.* WUNT 2/29. Tübingen: Mohr (Siebeck).

SAUNDERS, Ernest W.
1963   "A Trio of Thomas Logia." *BR* 8:43–59.

SCHELKLE, Karl Hermann
1971-78　　Theology of the New Testament, trans. William A. Jurgens. 4 vols. Collegeville, Minn.: Liturgical [1968-1976].

SCHENK, Wolfgang
1979　　"Der Einfluss der Logienquelle auf das Markusevangelium." ZNW 70:141-65.
1981　　Synopse zur Redenquelle der Evangelien: Q-Synopse und Rekonstruktion in deutscher Übersetzung. Düsseldorf: Patmos.

SCHENKE, Hans-Martin
1978　　"Die Tendenz der Weisheit zur Gnosis." Pp. 351-72 in Gnosis: Festschrift für Hans Jonas, ed. Barbara Aland. Göttingen: Vandenhoeck & Ruprecht.

SCHILLEBEECKX, Edward
1979　　Jesus: An Experiment in Christology, trans. Hubert Hoskins. New York: Seabury [1975].

SCHMID, Hans Heinrich
1966　　Wesen und Geschichte der Weisheit: Eine Untersuchung zur altorientalischen und israelitischen Weisheit. BZAW 101. Berlin: Töpelmann.

SCHMID, Josef
1930　　Matthäus und Lukas: Eine Untersuchung des Verhältnisses ihrer Evangelien. BibS(F) 23/2-4. Freiburg: Herder.

SCHMIDT, Daryl
1977　　"The LXX Gattung 'Prophetic Correlative.'" JBL 96:517-22.

SCHMIDT, Karl Ludwig
1923　　"Die Stellung der Evangelien in der allegmeinen Literaturgeschichte." Pp. 50-134 in ΕΥΧΑΡΙΣΤΗΡΙΟΝ: Festschrift Hermann Gunkel, ed. Hans Schmidt. FRLANT 36. Göttingen: Vandenhoeck & Ruprecht.

SCHNACKENBURG, Rudolf
1970　　"Der Eschatologische Abschnitt Lk 17,20-37." Pp. 213-34 in Mélanges bibliques en hommage au R. P. Beda Rigaux, ed. Albert Descamps and André de Halleux. Gembloux: Duculot.

SCHNEIDER, Gerhard
1975　　"'Der Menschensohn' in der lukanischen Christologie." Pp. 267-82 in Jesus und der Menschensohn: Für Anton Vögtle, ed. Rudolf Pesch and Rudolf Schnackenburg. Freiburg: Herder.

SCHOTTROFF, Luise, and Wolfgang Stegemann
1986　　Jesus and the Hope of the Poor, trans. Matthew J. O'Connell. Maryknoll, N.Y.: Orbis [1978].

SCHRAGE, Wolfgang
1964a　　"Evangelienzitate in den Oxyrhynchus-Logien und im koptischen Thomas-Evangelium." Pp. 251-68 in Apophoreta: Festschrift für Ernst Haenchen zu seinem siebzigsten Geburtstag, ed. Walther Eltester and F. H. Kettler. BZNW 30. Berlin: Töpelmann.
1964b　　Das Verhältnis des Thomas-Evangeliums zur synoptischen Tradition und zu den koptischen Evangelienübersetzungen: zugleich ein Betrag zur gnostischen Synoptikerdeutung. BZNW 29. Berlin: Töpelmann.

SCHULZ, Siegfried

1964   "Die Bedeutung des Markus für die Theologiegeschichte des Ur-christentums." *SE* 2 (TU 87):135–45.

1972   *Q: Die Spruchquelle der Evangelisten.* Zurich: Theologischer Verlag.

1973   "Die Gottesherrschaft ist nahe herbeigekommen (Mt 10.7/Lk 10,9): Der kerygmatische Entwurf der Q-Gemeinde Syrien." Pp. 57–67 in *Das Wort und die Wörter: Festschrift Gerhard Friedrich*, ed. Horst Balz. Stuttgart: Kohlhammer.

SCHÜRMANN, Heinz

1957   *Jesu Abschiedsrede Lk 22,21–38. Teil 3 einer quellenkritischen Untersuchung des lukanischen Abendmahlberichtes (Lk 22,7–38).* NTAbh 20/5. Münster: Aschendorff.

1968a   "Die Sprache des Christus: Sprachliche Beobachtungen zu den synoptischen Herren-worten." Pp. 83–108 in *Traditionsgeschichtliche Untersuchungen zu den synoptischen Evangelien: Beiträge.* Kommentare und Beiträge zum Alten und Neuen Testament. Düsseldorf: Patmos.

1968b   *Traditionsgeschichtliche Untersuchungen zu den synoptischen Evangelien: Beiträge.* Kommentare und Beiträge zum Alten und Neuen Testament. Düsseldorf: Patmos.

1969   *Das Lukasevangelium.* HTKNT 3/1. Freiburg: Herder.

1974   *Jesu ureigener Tod.* Freiburg: Herder.

1975   "Beobachtungen zum Menschensohn-Titel in der Redequelle." Pp. 124–47 in *Jesus und der Menschensohn: Für Anton Vögtle*, ed. Rudolf Pesch and Rudolf Schnackenburg. Freiburg: Herder & Herder.

1982   "Das Zeugnis der Redenquelle für die Basileia-Verkündigung Jesu." Pp. 121–200 in *Logia: Les Paroles de Jésus—The Sayings of Jesus: Mémorial Joseph Coppens*, ed. Joël Delobel. BETL 59. Leuven: Uitgeverij Peeters and Leuven Univ. Press.

1983   *Gottes Reich, Jesu Geschick: Jesu ureigener Tod im Licht seiner Basileia-Verkündigung.* Freiburg and Basel: Herder.

1986   "Die Redekomposition wider 'dieses Geschlecht' und seine Führung in der Redenquelle (vgl. Mt 23,1–39 par Lk 11,37–54): Bestand—Akoluthie—Kompositionsformen." *Studien zum Neuen Testament und seiner Umwelt* Series A, 11:33–81.

1991   "Zur Kompositionsgeschichte der Redenquelle: Beobachtungen an der lukanischen Q-Vorlage." Pp. 326–42 in *Der Treue Gottes trauen: Beiträge zum Werk des Lukas: Für Gerhard Schneider*, ed. Claus Bussmann and Walter Radl. Freiburg, Basel, and Wien: Herder.

SCHWEIZER, Eduard

1963   "Der Menschensohn: Zur eschatologischen Erwartung Jesu." Pp. 56–84 in *Neotestamentica: Deutsche und englische Aufsätze, 1951–1963.* Zurich: Zwingli.

1973   *Das Evangelium nach Matthäus.* NTD 2. Göttingen: Vandenhoeck & Ruprecht.

1975   *The Good News According to Matthew*, trans. David E. Green. Atlanta: John Knox [1973].

SEVENSTER, Jan Nicolaas

1968   *Do You Know Greek? How Much Greek Could the First Jewish Christians Have Known?* NovTSup 19. Leiden: Brill.

SHULER, Philip L.
1982   *A Genre for the Gospels: The Biographical Character of Matthew.* Phila-
            delphia: Fortress.

SMITH, Duane E.
1975   "Wisdom Genres in RS 22.439." Pp. 215–47 in *Ras Shamra Parallels
            II*, ed. Loren R. Fisher. AnOr 50. Rome: Pontificium Institutum
            Biblicum.

SPIVEY, R. A.
1962   "The Origin and Milieu of the Gospel According to Thomas."
            Ph.D. diss., Yale University.

STANTON, Graham N.
1973   "On the Christology of Q." Pp. 25–40 in *Christ and Spirit in the
            New Testament: In Honour of C. F. D. Moule*, ed. Barnabas Lindars and
            Stephen S. Smalley. Cambridge: Cambridge Univ. Press.
1977   "5 Ezra and Matthean Christianity in the Second Century." *JTS*
            28:67–83.

STECK, Odil H.
1967   *Israel und das gewaltsame Geschick der Propheten.* WMANT 23.
            Neukirchen-Vluyn: Neukirchener Verlag.

STOLDT, Hans-Herbert
1980   *History and Criticism of the Marcan Hypothesis*, trans. Donald L.
            Niewyk. Macon, Ga.: Mercer Univ. Press; Edinburgh: T. & T. Clark
            [1977].

STRACK, Hermann L., and Paul Billerbeck
1922–61   *Kommentar zum Neuen Testament aus Talmud und Midrasch.* 6 vols.
            Munich: Beck.

STRECKER, Georg
1966   *Der Weg der Gerechtigkeit: Untersuchung zur Theologie des Matthäus.*
            FRLANT 82. 2d ed. Göttingen: Vandenhoeck & Ruprecht.

STREETER, B. H.
1911   "On the Original Order of Q." Pp. 141–64 in *Oxford Studies in the
            Synoptic Problem*, ed. William Sanday. Oxford: Clarendon.
1924   *The Four Gospels: A Study of Origins, Treating of the Manuscript Tradi-
            tion, Sources, Authorship, and Dates.* London: Macmillan.

SUGGS, M. Jack
1970   *Wisdom Christology, and Law in Matthew's Gospel.* Cambridge, Mass.:
            Harvard Univ. Press.

TALBERT, Charles H.
1975   *Literary Patterns, Theological Themes, and the Genre of Luke-Acts.*
            SBLMS 20. Missoula, Mont.: Society of Biblical Literature.
1977   *What Is a Gospel? The Genre of the Canonical Gospels.* Philadelphia:
            Fortress.

TALBERT, Charles H., and Edgar V. McKnight
1972   "Can the Griesbach Hypothesis Be Falsified?" *JBL* 91:338–68.

TAYLOR, Charles, ed.
1897   *Sayings of the Jewish Fathers, Comprising Pirqe Aboth in Hebrew and En-
            glish, with Notes and Excursuses.* 2d ed. Cambridge: Cambridge Univ.
            Press.

TAYLOR, R. O. P.
1946   *The Groundwork of the Gospels.* Oxford: Blackwell.

TAYLOR, Vincent
1953   "The Order of Q." *JTS* 4:27–31.
1959   "The Original Order of Q." Pp. 246–69 in *New Testament Essays: Studies in Memory of T. W. Manson,* ed. A. J. B. Higgins. Manchester: Manchester Univ. Press.

TEEPLE, Howard Merle
1965   "The Origin of the Son of Man." *JBL* 84:213–50.

THEISOHN, Johannes
1975   *Der auserwählte Richter: Untersuchungen zum traditionsgeschichtlichem Ort der Menschensohngestalt der Bilderreden des Äthiopischen Henoch.* SUNT 12. Göttingen: Vandenhoeck & Ruprecht.

THEISSEN, Gerd
1978   *Sociology of Early Palestinian Christianity,* trans. John Bowden. Philadelphia: Fortress [1977].

THRALL, William Flint, and Addison Hibbard
1962   *A Handbook to Literature.* Revised and enlarged by C. Hugh Holman. New York: Odyssey.

THYEN, Hartwig
1970   *Studien zur Sundenvergebung im Neuen Testament und seinen alttestamentlichen und jüdischen Voraussetzungen.* FRLANT 96. Göttingen: Vandenhoeck & Ruprecht.

TILL, Walter C.
1959   "New Sayings of Jesus in the Recently Discovered Coptic 'Gospel of Thomas.'" *BJRL* 41:446–58.

TÖDT, Heinz Eduard
1959   *Der Menschensohn in der synoptischen Überlieferung.* Gütersloh: Gerd Mohn.
1965   *The Son of Man in the Synoptic Tradition,* trans. D. M. Barton. London: SCM [1959].

TRILLING, Wolfgang
1960   "Zur Überlieferung des Gleichnisses vom Hochzeitsmahl Mt 22, 1–14." *BZ* n.s. 4:251–65.
1964   *Das Wahre Israel: Studien zur Theologie des Matthäusevangeliums.* SANT 10. 3d ed. Munich: Kösel.

TURNER, Eric G.
1977   *The Typology of the Early Codex.* Haney Foundation Series Publication 18. Philadelphia: University of Pennsylvania Press.

TURNER, Henry E. W.
1962   "The Theology of the Gospel of Thomas." Pp. 79–116 in Henry E. W. Turner and Hugh Montefiore, *Thomas and the Evangelists.* SBT 1/35. London: SCM.

TURNER, Nigel
1968–69   "Q in Recent Thought." *ExpTim* 80:324–28.

VAAGE, Leif E.
1991   "The Son of Man Sayings in Q: Stratigraphical Location and Significance." Pp. 103–29 in *Early Christianity, Q and Jesus,* ed. John S. Kloppenborg, with Leif E. Vaage. Semeia 55. Atlanta: Scholars Press.

VASSILIADIS, Petros
1975   "Prolegomena to a Discussion on the Relationship between Mark and the Q-Document." *Deltion Biblikon Meleton* 3:31–46.
1978   "The Nature and Extent of the Q Document." *NovT* 20:49–73.
VIELHAUER, Philipp
1965a   "Gottesreich und Menschensohn in der Verkündigung Jesu." Pp. 55–91 in *Aufsätze zum Neuen Testament*. TBü 31. Munich: Kaiser.
1965b   "Jesus und der Menschensohn." Pp. 92–140 in *Aufsätze zum Neuen Testament*. TBü 31. Munich: Kaiser.
1975   *Geschichte der urchristlichen Literatur*. Berlin: de Gruyter.
VÖGTLE, Anton
1962   "Menschensohn." *LTK* 7:297–300.
1971a   "Exegetische Erwägungen über das Wissen und Selbstbewusstsein Jesu." Pp. 296–344 in *Das Evangelium und die Evangelien: Beiträge zur Evangelienforschung*. Düsseldorf: Patmos.
1971b   "Die hermeneutische Relevanz des geschichtlichen Charakters der Christusoffenbarung." Pp. 16–30 in *Das Evangelium und die Evangelien: Beiträge zur Evangelienforschung*. Düsseldorf: Patmos.
1971c   "Der Spruch vom Jonaszeichen." Pp. 103–36 in *Das Evangelium und die Evangelien: Beiträge zur Evangelienforschung*. Düsseldorf: Patmos.
1971d   "Wunder und Wort in urchristlicher Glaubenswerbung (Mt 11,2–5/Lk 7,18–23)." Pp. 219–42 in *Das Evangelium und die Evangelien: Beiträge zur Evangelienforschung*. Düsseldorf: Patmos.
1973   "Wie kam es zur Artikulierung des Osterglaubens." *BibLeb* 14:231–44.
1974   "Wie kam es zur Artikulierung des Osterglaubens." *BibLeb* 15:16–37, 102–20, 174–93.
1983   "Jesus von Nazareth." Pp. 3–24 in *Ökumenische Kirchengeschichte*. 2d ed., ed. Bernd Moeller, Raymund Kottje, and Remigius Baumer. Mainz: Matthias-Gruewald.
WANKE, Joachim
1980   "Kommentarworte: Älteste Kommentierung von Herrenworten." *BZ* n.s. 24:208–333.
1981   "Bezugs- und Kommentarworte in den synoptischen Evangelien." ETS 44. Leipzig: Benno.
WEISS, Bernhard
1908   *Die Quellen der synoptischen Überlieferung*. TU 32. Leipzig: Hinrichs.
WEISS, Johannes
1892   *Die Predigt Jesu Vom Reiche Gottes*. Göttingen: Vandenhoeck & Ruprecht.
WELLHAUSEN, Julius
1904a   *Das Evangelium Lucae*. Berlin: Reimer.
1904b   *Das Evangelium Matthaei übersetzt und erklärt*. Berlin: Reimer.
1905   *Einleitung in die drei ersten Evangelien*. Berlin: Reimer.
1911   *Einleitung in die drei ersten Evangelien*. 2d ed. Berlin: Reimer.
WERNLE, Paul
1899   *Die synoptische Frage*. Leipzig, Freiburg, and Tübingen: Mohr (Siebeck).

WESTERMANN, Claus
1967   *Basic Forms of Prophetic Speech*, trans. Hugh Clayton White. Fore-
            word by Gene M. Tucker. Philadelphia: Westminster [1960].
WHITE, H. G. Evelyn
1920   *The Sayings of Jesus from Oxyrhynchus, Edited with Introduction, Critical
            Apparatus and Commentary.* Cambridge: Cambridge Univ. Press.
WILCKENS, Ulrich
1965–66   "Jesusüberlieferung und Christuskerygma: Zwei Wege urchristlicher
            Überlieferungsgeschichte." *Theologia Viatorum* 10:310–39.
1971   "Σοφία. C. Judaism, D. Gnosticism, E. The New Testament."
            TDNT 7:496–528.
WILD, Robert A.
1985   "The Encounter between Pharisaic and Christian Judaism: Some
            Early Gospel Evidence." *NovT* 27:105–24.
WILLIAMS, James G.
1981   *Those Who Ponder Proverbs: Aphoristic Thinking and Biblical Literature.*
            Bible and Literature series 2. Sheffield: Almond.
WILSON, Robert McL.
1958–59   "The Coptic 'Gospel of Thomas.'" *NTS* 5:273–76.
1960a   *Studies in the Gospel of Thomas.* London: Mowbray.
1960b   "Thomas and the Growth of the Gospels." *HTR* 53:231–50.
1960–61   "Thomas and the Synoptic Gospels." *ExpTim* 72:36–39.
1982   "Nag Hammadi and the New Testament." *NTS* 28:289–302.
WINK, Walter
1968   *John the Baptist in the Gospel Tradition.* SNTSMS 7. Cambridge:
            Cambridge Univ. Press.
WOLFF, Hans Walter
1982   "The Kerygma of the Deuteronomic Historical Work." Pp. 83–100
            in Walter Brueggemann and Hans Walter Wolff, *The Vitality of Old
            Testament Traditions.* 2d ed. Atlanta: John Knox.
WORDEN, Ronald D.
1975   "Redaction Criticism of Q: A Survey." *JBL* 94:532–46.
WREDE, William
1901   *Das Messiasgeheimnis in den Evangelien.* Göttingen: Vandenhoeck und
            Ruprecht.
1971   *The Messianic Secret*, trans. J. C. G. Greig. Greenwood, S.C.: Attic
            [1901].
WREGE, Hans-Theo
1968   *Die Überlieferungsgeschichte der Bergpredigt.* WUNT 9. Tübingen:
            Mohr (Siebeck).
ZELLER, Dieter
1975   "Der Zusammenhang der Eschatologie in der Logienquelle." Pp.
            67–77 in *Gegenwart und Kommendes Reich*, ed. P. Fiedler and Dieter
            Zeller. Stuttgart: Katholisches Bibelwerk.
1977a   "Prophetisches Wissen um die Zukunft in synoptischen Jesuswor-
            ten." *TP* 52:258–71.
1977b   *Die weisheitlichen Mahnsprüche bei den Synoptikern.* FB 17. Würzburg:
            Echter.
1980   "Die Versuchungen Jesu in der Logienquelle." *TTZ* 89:61–73.

1982   "Redaktionsprozesse und wechselnder 'Sitz im Leben' beim
              Q-Material." Pp. 395–409 in *Logia: Les Paroles de Jésus—The Sayings
              of Jesus: Mémorial Joseph Coppens*, ed. Joël Delobel. BETL 59.
              Leuven: Uitgeverij Peeters and Leuven Univ. Press.
1984   *Kommentar zur Logienquelle.* Stuttgarter kleiner Kommentar, Neues
              Testament 21. Stuttgart: Katholisches Bibelwerk.
1991   "Θησαυρός." *EDNT* 2:149–51.
ZIMMERLI, Walther
1976   "Concerning the Structure of Old Testament Wisdom." Pp. 175–
              207 in *Studies in Ancient Israelite Wisdom*, ed. James L. Crenshaw.
              New York: Ktav.
ZIMMERLI, Walther, and Helmer Ringgren
1962   *Sprüche/Prediger. Das Hohe Lied/Klagelieder. Das Buch Esther.* ATD 16.
              Göttingen: Vandenhoeck & Ruprecht.
ZMIJEWSKI, Josef
1972   *Die Eschatologiereden des Lukas-Evangeliums: Eine traditions- und redak-
              tionsgeschichtliche Untersuchung zu Lk 21,5–36 und Lk 17,20–37.*
              BBB 40. Bonn: Hanstein.

Index of Names

Index of Ancient Sources

JEWISH SCRIPTURES

PSEUDEPIGRAPHA

QUMRAN LITERATURE

RABBINIC LITERATURE

SAYINGS GOSPEL Q

NEW TESTAMENT

OTHER EARLY CHRISTIAN WRITINGS

GRAECO-ROMAN LITERATURE